# Bilingual Brokers

# Bilingual Brokers

RACE, LITERATURE, AND LANGUAGE
AS HUMAN CAPITAL

Jeehyun Lim

FORDHAM UNIVERSITY PRESS    *New York*    2017

THIS BOOK IS MADE POSSIBLE BY A COLLABORATIVE GRANT
FROM THE ANDREW W. MELLON FOUNDATION.

Copyright © 2017 Fordham University Press

Fordham University Press has no responsibility for the persistence or accuracy of URLs
for external or third-party Internet websites referred to in this publication and does not
guarantee that any content on such websites is, or will remain, accurate or appropriate.

Fordham University Press also publishes its books in a variety of electronic formats. Some
content that appears in print may not be available in electronic books.

Visit us online at www.fordhampress.com.

Library of Congress Cataloging-in-Publication Data available
online at http://catalog.loc.gov.

Printed in the United States of America

19 18 17    5 4 3 2 1

First edition

*for my mother, Young-hye Sung*

# CONTENTS

Bilingual Brokers

# Introduction

*Bilingual Personhood and the Cultural Politics
of Asian American and Latino Literature*

"What do you call someone who speaks three languages? A trilingual. What do you call someone who speaks two languages? A bilingual. What do you call someone who speaks one language? An American." This common joke actually contains several observations about what the sociologist Pierre Bourdieu might call the linguistic habitus of the United States. First, the punch line of the joke assumes that the dominant culture in the United States is monolingual. Less obvious but also embedded in the joke is the definition of an American. This joke, for example, would not apply to a Spanish-speaking Latino in New York City or a Cantonese-speaking Chinese American in San Francisco. At the same time that it pokes fun at the seeming lack of interest among Americans in learning languages, the joke in the same breath excludes bilingual Americans from normative Americanness. From an academic standpoint, what the longtime scholar of bilingualism François Grosjean says about the changes to the linguistic habitus of the United States helps one to further reflect on the contingent humor of the joke. In one of his recent studies on bilingualism, the psycholinguist compares the lingual culture of contemporary United States to that of the 1970s when he was working on his seminal study of the bilingual experience, *Life with Two Languages*.[1] After analyzing the 1976 Survey of Income and Education, Grosjean recalls that he "concluded that the United States was a heavily monolingual country when compared with other countries of the world," with only about 6 percent of the population "speaking both English and a minority language on a regular basis."[2] In the 2010 publication, however, he

1

revises this conclusion after tracking the US census data since 1976 on people who speak a language other than English at home: 11 percent of the population in 1980, 14 percent in 1990, and almost 18 percent in 2000.[3] Cross-referencing these numbers with the self-reports on English fluency that are also a part of the census data, Grosjean concludes that depending on whether one includes those with limited English fluency in the category of bilinguals or not, the bilingual population in the United States in 2000 ranges from 13.71 percent to almost 17 percent.[4] While the numbers are still small compared to European countries, Grosjean suggests that his initial assessment of the United States as a monolingual country may not be so valid any more.

If one still hears a ring of truth in the joke despite Grosjean's recent findings about the changes to US lingual culture, this probably speaks to how new the recognition of bilingualism as a socially significant phenomenon is in the United States. In the same study, Grosjean also details which non-English languages have the largest numbers of speakers. Unsurprisingly, Spanish tops the list. But Grosjean also notes that "several Asian languages (Chinese, Tagalog, Korean, Vietnamese)" are on the list of the top ten non-English languages.[5] This, he further adds, is a change from the mid-twentieth century. These Asian languages have replaced languages such as Yiddish and the Scandinavian languages on the list of the top ten.[6] While it is impossible to map a direct, one-to-one correspondence between this change and the changes in demographics due to the liberalization of immigration, anyone who is familiar with the effects of the 1965 Hart-Celler Act would notice the connections between the rise of immigration from Asia and Latin America and the shifting linguistic habitus of the United States discussed by Grosjean.[7]

The premise of this study is that the growth of Asian American and Latino communities since 1965 is the driving force behind the steady shift in US linguistic habitus away from monolingualism. In light of this shift, I turn to writings by Asian Americans and Latinos to trace how the social changes accompanying the new bilingualism affect cultural representations of language difference and how, vice versa, cultural representations engage with the social lives of language minorities. Throughout the study, I seek to construct a dialogic relationship between the social significance of bilingualism and its cultural ramifications. The focus of this study, then, is not just to trace the role that Asian American and Latino writers play in conceptualizing and illustrating the cultural consequences to the changes in America's linguistic habitus but, more importantly, to examine literature as the site where insights on the social construction of bilingual personhood—how bilingual persons are produced and reproduced within a set of social habits, relations, and practices of language—can be gleaned and from which the cultural ramifications of this personhood can be noted and discussed.

A similar assumption of monolingualism that informs the joke in the beginning of this introduction has also informed much of the study of US literature. In the past twenty years or so, however, that assumption has been challenged by studies that variously call for a recognition of and engagement with the multilingual origins of US literature or draw attention to the aesthetic qualities of bilingualism.[8] Most notable, arguably, has been the persistent efforts of scholars in Latino studies to demonstrate the essential place of Spanish in the creative life of US writers and in Latino communities, especially against the vilification of Spanish in expressions of anti-Latino racism and xenophobia.[9] Ironic as it may seem, the English Only movement of the 1990s has been a watershed moment in the affirmation and cultivation of language difference as a legitimate and productive area of study in US literary scholarship.[10] In terms of laws and policies, the populist movement resulted in the repeal of bilingual laws and policies, such as the passage of Proposition 227 that banned bilingual education in California. Yet in terms of academic interest in multilingualism and language difference, the populist movement also alarmed many academics with its anti-intellectualism and rallied them to speak up against the drive toward monolingualism and for the benefits of multilingualism. This is not surprising when one considers that multilingualism, when taken as the ability to be fluent in several languages, has long been a sign of cosmopolitanism for intellectuals and, hence, something to be cultivated and valued. From the perspective of the twenty-first century when English Only is no longer making news headlines and populism has targets other than language, the mass anxieties about language seems largely a sign of a bygone era, and it remains to be seen if the surge of academic interest in multilingualism will make a lasting difference in US literary and cultural criticism. On the one hand, I share with the recent works of literary and cultural criticism the sympathies for bilingualism and the critical task of affirming language difference. On the other hand, as a latecomer to the academic response generated by English Only, *Bilingual Brokers* has an avowed interest in examining when, why, and how bilingualism becomes symbolic value. This investment, I hope, imbues this study with a self-reflectiveness about the constraints of valorizing bilingualism in academia, which is already favorably inclined toward multilingualism because its encounters with language difference are usually of the kind where the symbolic value of such difference is taken for granted. My hope is that a focused look at the contingencies of value for bilingualism will contribute to making the recent critical interest in bi/multilingualism in US academe into not just another repetition of the academic mantra that familiarity and facility with more than one language is valuable but into a more sustained look at the social and cultural meanings of language difference.

## THE TWO FACES OF BILINGUALISM

The cultural politics of bilingualism that manifested itself nationally during the time of the English Only movement is a culmination of a larger set of concerns about American identity amid the growth of minority voices and presence. In *Bilingual Brokers* I am interested in how language difference becomes crucial for negotiating American identity in Asian American and Latino writings, especially as it intersects with racial difference. Language difference becomes something of an index by which the selective social incorporation of racialized difference can be recognized as bilinguals who can present their linguistic capabilities as assets are valorized as human capital, while bilinguals whose language difference is considered a liability are castigated as undesirable aliens. This seemingly contradictory coexistence of two very different assessments of bilingualism actually is at the heart of the complex dynamic of racialization after the end of legal racism.

Two contrasting attitudes on the value of bilingualism among Spanish-speaking Puerto Rican Americans that were discussed during the height of English Only in the 1990s encapsulate the duality of bilingualism I mention above. On the one hand, "un hombre que hablo dos idiomas vale por dos (a man who speaks two languages is worth two men)."[11] On the other hand, "un niño que vive dos idiomas no llega a ser nunca un hombre doble; se queda siempre en medio hombre (a child who speaks two languages never grows up to be a double man; he always remains a half man)."[12] The former statement belongs to a Puerto Rican American who supports bilingual education. The latter is a statement by the Puerto Rican intellectual Epifanio Fernández-Vanga that dates back to the 1930s but the sentiment, as Frances Negrón-Muntaner shows, still lives on in the Puerto Rican diaspora.[13] These two very different evaluations of bilingualism are reiterated in Asian American and Latino literature to express a structure of feeling borne out of a complex nexus of race, language, and minority subjectivity, a nexus that I suggest is crucial to understanding post–World War II racialization.

The writer and critic Gustavo Pérez-Firmat's coupling of the *bilingüe* ("someone who speaks two languages") and the *nilingüe* ("someone who doesn't speak either") also reveals the two-sidedness of bilingualism wherein an aspiration for excellence is tied to a fear of linguistic annihilation. In Miami Spanish, Pérez-Firmat says, one cannot have *bilingüe* without the *nilingüe*.[14] While Miami Spanish reserves the latter term for undesirable bilingualism, for a long time the very term "bilingualism" encompassed both poles of *bilingüe* and *nilingüe* in common usage, as linguist Einar Haugen sharply points out. In a 1972 essay, Haugen writes that "for many people 'bilingual' is a euphemism for 'linguistically handicapped.' It is a nice way of referring to children whose parents have handicapped them in the race for success by teaching them their mother tongue, which happens not to be the dominant language in the country they now inhabit."[15] The popular definition of bilingualism that Haugen mentions equates bilingual with *nilingüe*. The exposure to two languages itself is a sign of negative difference, and those who are from a household where a language other than English is spoken are immediately suspected of deficiency. The activist interest in and advocacy of bilingualism from the 1960s up until the English Only movement—which can be seen in the debates about bilingual education and public services for non- or limited-English populations, such as bilingual ballots, bilingual interpreters in court and bilingual (or non-English) signage—was largely about challenging the stigma of bilingualism and supporting it as a social-justice project. While such activism and advocacy played an important role in seeking equal opportunities for language minorities and changing popular misconceptions about bilingualism, the language and logic of activism and advocacy also remained locked in the duality of bilingualism as either good or bad. The bilingual personhood in the Asian American and Latino writings I examine shows a supple and nuanced portrait of the good and bad of bilingualism that goes beyond the reductionist impulses of a bipolar view, even as it references it as a world view. It bears the weight of the popular stigma of bilingualism while striving for and experimenting with other expressions that move beyond the popular stigma. The structure of feeling expressed through bilingual personhood in these writings presents the *nilingüe* and the *bilingüe*, the "half man" and the man that is "worth two men," as coexisting alongside each other to reveal a continuum of racialization marked by selective incorporation of racialized difference. Instead of falling on the side of either half the value or double the value, this structure of feeling focuses on and evolves around the conditions and processes of such value assessment.

Focusing on bilingual personhood as the site through which racial difference is negotiated and managed is to both acknowledge the complexities of using race as an analytic of inclusion (or exclusion) and argue for its continued significance in an era where antiracism has become the norm of liberal governmentality. Sociologist Eileen O'Brien's thesis that Asian Americans and Latinos form a "racial middle" between the two poles of black and white in the post–civil rights era is one succinct example of complicating the racial binary that characterized race relations in the United States prior to World War II.[16] Schematic as it may seem, the sociological heuristic of race allows one to conceptualize social relations as not taking place in a vacuum but within the matrix of racial relations that constitute and are constituted by sociological observations. Interestingly, the two theses of "whitening" and "browning" mentioned in O'Brien's study as sociological predictions of how the demographic changes attendant on post-1965 immigration will affect race relations rely on color metaphors to articulate racial difference.[17] The whitening thesis posits that Asian Americans and Latinos will adopt the norms and values of white people. The browning thesis has both a neoconservative argument, which O'Brien calls the "doomsday version" and which bemoans the dissipation of purported Anglo-American values in the face of Latino immigration, and a progressive argument that sees the growth of the nonwhite population as a propellant for more democratic distribution of power among different races.[18] Helpful in mapping trajectories of large-scale social change per race, the sociological prism of color also raise questions about the relationship between color and race, or, to put it more precisely, it brings into high relief the conundrum of a bodily (if not biological) presence in the semantic translation of racial difference into words like "white," "brown," "black," and "yellow," even as the content of this difference is viewed through behaviors, attitudes, and values that bespeak cultural difference at large.

For Asian Americans and Latinos, language difference is ensconced in both implications of racial difference as something that is generationally transmitted—most noticeable in the legal terminology of race as an "immutable trait" in equal-protection laws, a trait that one is born with and cannot change at will—and something that is culturally performed in everyday life. It is on the one hand a sign of heritage (i.e., who your parents are) and private (or familial) upbringing that relates to your home language environment. On the other hand, it is a sign of affiliation by choice (i.e., what language one speaks on a daily basis) and public schooling that is closely related to the dominant linguistic culture. Scholars who see a deterministic and exclusionist tendency in discussions of racial difference (and for some in any discussion of race in toto) emphasize the latter understanding of language difference and downplay the former. Language, that is to say, is taken as a sign of free affiliation and association; therefore, examining language difference is a way of supporting difference (or diversity) without suggestions of determinism or proclivities toward exclusion.[19] Yet to view language solely as an expression of choice and individual freedom is to ignore the social and cultural conditions for the development of affiliations, affinities, and the self in any language. Instead of adopting the view of language as either solely heritage or solely individual choice, as either immutable or mutable, I am interested in how fluidly language difference moves between what seem to be incompatible conceptual domains in postwar racial politics. Where language difference suggests a difference that is given to a person rather than something one willingly chooses, the intersections between racial and language difference can most clearly be seen. The representations of bilingual personhood I trace here are about these ambivalent, multivalent, and on the whole messy expressions of difference where language difference variously translates into, evades, and overdetermines racial difference. The flexibility of bilingual personhood lends itself to an examination of both embodied and disembodied permutations of racial difference, which, in turn, allows a close look at how language difference becomes a mode of managing racial difference that is suited to new ideas of human capital that emerge on the scene of postwar capitalist developments.[20]

## LANGUAGE AND CAPITAL, LANGUAGE AS CAPITAL

Throughout *Bilingual Brokers*, I trace the ways in which language is viewed as capital in the debates on bilingualism in the areas of education, law, and policy as well as in Asian American and Latino literature. I mainly engage with two kinds of symbolic capital: cultural capital and human capital. Cultural capital is a term and concept that is familiar to the field of literary and cultural criticism, whereas human capital is still a term that is scarcely used in humanities scholarship despite its increasing usage in disciplines beyond economics. Examining language as capital in bilingual personhood as it appears in social debates and in literature requires an attention to the interconnections between these two kinds of symbolic capital that have different disciplinary implications yet that converge in narrating the assimilation of Asian Americans and Latinos into the US polity and culture. Tracing the figuration of language as capital in bilingual personhood actually shows that the concepts of cultural and human capital, though they have come to be used in different disciplines with little to no overlap, are much more intertwined than is generally understood, especially in their investment in the individual as the core unit of imagining the norms and principles of social exchange in liberalism.

A brief explanation on the critical vocabulary of symbolic capital I employ in *Bilingual Brokers* may illustrate what I mean by the deep imbrication of cultural and human capital in liberalism. My analysis of language as capital is guided primarily by the sociologist Pierre Bourdieu's insights on symbolic capital, which I supplement with the ideas and arguments on symbolic capital from linguists like Joshua Fishman and economists like Gary Becker. Bourdieu's notion of cultural capital, delivered variously in such works as *Distinction*, *The Field of Cultural Production*, and *Language and Symbolic Power*, has been widely used by literary critics to analyze the production, distribution, and circulation of symbolic value and of the role of educational institutions in mediating cultural value.[21] In tracing language as capital through the fields of publishing, institutional valorization of certain kinds and forms of languages over others, and the commodification of language in the marketplace, I rely on Bourdieu's insights on identifying symbolic power and structures of domination that elide conventional Marxist analyses of class struggle. From this perspective, my use of language as cultural capital does not diverge significantly from standard applications of the concept in literary and cultural criticism.

More fundamental to my reliance on Bourdieu's notion of cultural capital in *Bilingual Brokers*, however, are the questions of inequality in education and the production and transmission of symbolic value that Bourdieu claims were germane to his developing the concept of cultural capital in the first place. This is where I locate the convergence between the two kinds of symbolic capital, cultural and human, in this study, and where I see my analytic of language as capital diverging somewhat from the dominant critical uses of language as symbolic capital. In a short essay entitled "The Forms of Capital" Bourdieu states that "the notion of cultural capital initially presented itself to me, in the course of research, as a theoretical hypothesis which made it possible to explain the unequal scholastic achievement of children originating from the different social classes."[22] The germination of my interest in the postwar debates on bilingualism in the United States as the place where racial difference was negotiated through language is likewise based on my observations of how racial inequality was diagnosed and solutions proposed in relation to bilingual children in public schools in the United States, the majority of whom were Latino at the time when the issue was first nationally discussed. The attention to the educational institution as the site of (re)producing inequality, despite the expectation that in a democratic meritocracy education is actually the engine of socioeconomic mobility based on individual talent and effort, is the starting point for my engagement with symbolic domination and structures of inequality within the terms of liberalism in *Bilingual Brokers*.

From this point of view Bourdieu's discussion of how he sees his concept of cultural capital in relation to the economist Gary Becker's notion of human capital is worth heeding since human capital, unlike cultural capital, is a term numerous critics in the humanities frown upon.[23] This aversion both seems to stem from the term's linking of two words that humanities scholars do not want to think of in association with each other—"human" and "capital"—and from concerns over adopting an economically reductionist view of the world where everything, including humans, is translated into economic value. It may come across as a surprise to such scholars, then, that Bourdieu himself does not see a substantial difference between cultural and human capital in terms of the conceptual interest in the role of education to create economic value out of noneconomic factors. This is not to say that Bourdieu sees the two terms as commensurate. He first sees a distinction in how researchers understand the purview of each term. According to him, sociologists employing the concept of cultural capital adopt a more holistic view of what affects education, whereas economists "tak[e] account only of *monetary* investments and profits, or those directly convertible into money, such as the costs of schooling and the cash equivalent of time devoted to study."[24] Secondly, he suggests that economists are not interested in education as reproduction. In other words, "because they neglect to relate scholastic investment strategies to the whole set of educational strategies and to the system of reproduction strategies, they inevitably, by a necessary paradox, let slip the best hidden and socially most determinant educational investment, namely, the domestic transmission of cultural capital."[25] The blind spots in the economism of human capital Bourdieu points out are well worth taking into account for those interested in cultural capital because this attentiveness is what allows the concept of cultural capital to be used in examinations of systemic inequality and in analyses of differences in outcome that are often justified when one focuses solely on liberalism as formal equality. Yet it is also important to note that cultural capital shares with human capital an interest in materializing a system of conversion of value through which one can trace the making of wealth, influence, and power.

My active engagement with the concept of human capital in discussing how language becomes a form of racialized capital in representations of bilingual personhood is based on the consonances I see between the idea of human capital and the idea of the possessive individual that is constitutive of liberal personhood.[26] Bourdieu's discussion of cultural capital in what he calls "the embodied state" I think best reveals these consonances.[27] "Most of the properties of cultural capital," Bourdieu suggests, "can be deduced from the fact that, in its fundamental state, it is linked to the body and presupposes embodiment. The accumulation of cultural capital in the embodied state, i.e., in the form of what is called culture, cultivation, *Bildung*, presupposes a process of em-bodiment, incorporation, which, insofar as it implies a labor of inculcation and assimilation, costs time, time which must be invested personally by the investor."[28] The body as the anchor for cultural capital that Bourdieu illuminates here is evocative of John Locke's famous thesis that "every Man has a *Property* in his own *Person*."[29] Both Bourdieu's concept of cultural capital in the embodied state and Locke's idea of property in the person require one to revise one's view of economic value as mostly concerned with commodities or with tangible goods to confront the idea of person-hood, as it is assumed in liberalism, as a bearer of economic value.

A word on how Bourdieu's notion of cultural capital in the embod-ied state relates to Marx's notion of labor power may be necessary here since the Marxist discussion of "estranged labor," or the alien-ation of labor, is a widely acknowledged way of accounting for the human relationship to economic value.[30] To put it very simply, the worker, or the "free laborer" as Michel Feher says, sells his labor power to the capitalist in exchange for wages.[31] While this Marxist paradigm offers a way of approaching the question of the generation of economic value from work as well as a way of explaining the ulti-mate alienation of this value from the worker, I differentiate between cultural capital in the embodied state (or human capital) and labor power and rely on the former as opposed to the latter in this study. The primary reason is that Marx's discussion of the worker's estrange-ment from his own labor is premised on labor's realization in a prod-uct while my critical interests are in the liberal investment of value in the idea of the person regardless of whether this value is objectified or not. According to Marx, "the product of labor is labor which has been embodied in an object, which has become material," and the alienation of labor is preceded by such materialization of labor in a product, or the objectification of labor.[32] This creates quite a bit of challenge when reading Marx's notion of labor power alongside the Lockean idea of "*Property* in his own *Person*," as Étienne Balibar perceptively points out in his incisive discussion of what notion of self may subtend Marx's discussion of labor power.[33]

Outside the factory as the primary site of capitalist production in post-Fordist capitalism, it is often unclear where to draw the line between the laborer and his labor power, between what is alienable and what not. In these situations, Bourdieu's idea of cultural capital in the embodied state becomes most helpful as it is based on the dis-solution of a clear distinction between the person and the part of him that is convertible to material gain. As Bourdieu states:

> Because it [cultural capital] is linked in numerous ways to the person in his biological singularity and is subject to a hereditary transmis-sion which is always heavily disguised, or even invisible, it defies the old, deep-rooted distinction the Greek jurists made between inherited properties (*ta patroa*) and acquired properties (*epikteta*), i.e., those which an individual adds to his heritage. It thus manages to combine the prestige of innate property with the merits of acquisition. Because the social conditions of its transmission and acquisition are more

disguised than those of economic capital, it is predisposed to function
as symbolic capital, i.e., to be unrecognized as capital and recognized
as legitimate competence, as authority exerting an effect of (mis)rec-
ognition, e.g., in the matrimonial market and in all the markets in
which economic capital is not fully recognized, whether in matters of
culture, with the great art collections or great cultural foundations,
or in social welfare, with the economy of generosity and the gift.[34]

Strikingly, the biological and the nonbiological meld together in
the formation of cultural capital in the embodied state as "inherited properties (*ta patroa*)" which can range from physical traits to
cognitive capacity or mental propensities, combine with "acquired
properties (*epikteta*)." In this definition, the part of a person that is
potentially convertible to material gain is not limited to labor power
but potentially encompasses such elements as physical beauty or mental aptitude (or the even more ambiguous term of "character") that
are assessed through dominant sociological standards at the time of
conversion. In discussions of property, I think one sees a similar blur-
ring of the line between "things" and "rights." As political theorist
Crawford Macpherson suggests, while one often regards property as
things, "philosophers, jurists, and political and social theorists have
always treated property as a right, not a thing: a right in the sense of
an enforceable claim to some use or benefit of something."[35] When
one looks at property as a right, then it becomes hard to think about
property in isolation from the property holder, or, in other words, the
bearer of rights.

The idea of the possessive individual that undergirds liberal personhood locates the capacity for economic value at its core concept
of personhood. Nobody points out this element of liberal personhood
as well as the legal theorist Cheryl Harris, whose 1993 argument on
"whiteness as property" shows how the racial regime in the United
States created economic value in social and legal determinations of
whiteness and the creation of boundaries around whiteness.[36] From
the perspective of the groups that have variously undergone, and
undergo, racialization, the idea of the possessive individual is like a
double-edged sword in that while historically it has been used to dis-
possess people of color, arguments for inclusion have also often been
made in terms of inclusion in the order of possessive individualism.
Tracing language as capital in literary representations of bilingual personhood through the lens of human capital, then, is not so much to
concede to the terms of economism that the term suggests but to bring

attention to one operation of the logic of valuation that bridges political and economic liberalism. The second half of the twentieth century that saw a waning of the stigma of bilingualism as a handicap and a waxing of the benefits of bilingualism in popular conversations is also the time when such terms as "the knowledge worker" or "credential society" or the "professional-managerial class" emerged to illustrate changes to the ideas of work and of the worker that accompanied the evolution of capitalism.[37] The slow rise of what Maurizio Lazzarato, among others, calls immaterial labor as a widespread form of labor in the last few decades of the twentieth century goes hand in hand with cultural changes in the view of bilingualism as an asset and not a liability.[38] In the chapters to follow I hope to show how language, when read with an eye to its function as capital, maps how Asian American and Latino experiences are organized by the conditions of what I call flexible incorporation.

Late in the writing of this book, I came across another strand of thought regarding human capital in recent discussions of neoliberalism in political philosophy. While the bulk of the research on bilingual personhood in the social debates concerning bilingualism from the 1960s to the 1990s was already done when I encountered this body of scholarship, and while the frame of my discussion largely rests on critiques of liberalism from scholars working with issues of representation, inclusion, and injury in Asian American studies, Latino studies, and critical race theory, this new body of scholarship on neoliberalism informed my views on human capital and my use of the term. Going beyond studies of neoliberalism that mainly discuss it through economic policies and state practices of deregulation, theorists such as Maurizio Lazzarato, Michel Feher, and Wendy Brown have extended the critical discussion of neoliberalism to the realm of the production of subjectivity, enabling an understanding of the reach and influence of economic neoliberalism in spheres beyond economics like politics and culture.[39] While each individual theorist's usage of the term differs slightly, human capital in these discussions of neoliberalism in political philosophy is used to refer to the economic subject of neoliberalism, loosely evolving from, and sometimes coterminous with, the "entrepreneur of the self" in liberalism.[40]

In Wendy Brown's discussion of the evolution of *homo oeconomicus*, which she traces with and through Foucault's work on biopolitics, a key characteristic of neoliberalism is that "neoliberal rationality disseminates the *model of the market* to all domains and activities—even where money is not at issue—and configures human beings exhaustively as market actors, always, only and everywhere as *homo oeconomicus*."[41] From this angle, a neoliberal subject is the subject "as human capital," "at once in charge of itself, responsible for itself, yet an instrumentalizable and potentially dispensable element of the whole," and citizens are responsibilized into seeing themselves as "self-investor[s]" and "self-provider[s]," with no one to blame for their failures to build and manage their human capital.[42] The bilingual personhood I illuminate throughout this book, oscillating between the two poles of bilingualism as disadvantage and as advantage, as liability and as asset, is constituted by a process of subjectivation similar to what Brown sees in the neoliberal subject.

To see a correspondence between the neoliberal subject limned by such theorists as Lazzarato, Feher, and Brown and the bilingual personhood in Asian American and Latino writings is not to anachronistically apply the idea of the neoliberal subject as abstraction to a discourse on bilingualism and race that developed in a specific time and place preceding the emergence of critical interest in neoliberalism. Rather, it is to call for a recognition of and a reckoning with the continuities between liberalism and neoliberalism through a scrutiny of how the racialization of Asian Americans and Latinos has been managed in liberalism's march toward neoliberalism in the second half of the twentieth century. What correspondence exists between the neoliberal subject of contemporary Left theorizing and the bilingual personhood in Asian American and Latino social history and literature, as I see it, is a reminder of the genealogy of the neoliberal *homo oeconomicus* in the possessive individual of liberalism.

Turning to bilingual personhood in Asian American and Latino literature is to examine the conditions of liberalism's fissures and schisms as they appear around the question of the reduction of the person to *homo oeconomicus*, even before the era of neoliberalism, often referred to by historians as the last thirty years. I would like to illustrate this through the valences of the term "necessity" that arise in different contexts in Wendy Brown's recent work on neoliberalism and in the literary critic Sau-ling Wong's *Reading Asian American Literature*, now a classic in Asian American literary criticism. In her warning about the erosion of freedom effected by neoliberalism and in her passionate defense of "bare democracy," Brown recounts well-rehearsed political theories of freedom.[43] In these theories of freedom, humans cannot fully be free when they are plagued daily by issues of survival, such as finding enough to eat or finding a place to sleep. Such life, as Brown summarizes, is characterized as a "limited form of human existence that Aristotle and later Hannah Arendt designated as 'mere life' and that Marx called life 'confined by necessity.'"[44] Against such a minimal notion of freedom are the "'good life' (Aristotle)" and "'the true realm of freedom' (Marx)" as "the cultivation and expression of distinctly human capacities for ethical and political freedom, creativity, unbounded reflection, or invention."[45]

To students of Asian American literature, this discussion of freedom resonates with the dichotomy of necessity and extravagance that Sau-ling Wong offers as the antipodean tropes of Asian American literature. Wong's terms of necessity and extravagance are adopted from and inspired by Maxine Hong Kingston's *The Woman Warrior*, especially the chapter "No-Name Woman," which shows the young narrator caught in the grip of her immigrant mother's story of an aunt in China who committed suicide.[46] In the mother's story, the aunt, whose husband has left for the Gold Mountain and has been gone for many years, becomes pregnant from a secret affair. On the night of her childbirth, the aunt's house is raided by a village mob in search of village justice, and the aunt throws herself and the newborn into the family well after the raid. In her narrative, Kingston uses the terms extravagance and necessity to connect as well as contrast the aunt's act of defiance and the mother's attitude in narrating this defiance. In the context of a small, rural village where village morals and laws strictly forbid sex outside the reproductive unit of the family, "adultery is extravagance."[47] Upon hearing the story, the young narrator prods the mother for more elaboration of the bare-bones story she delivers—terrifying in its lack of details, in the dismissal of discursive contextualization and engagement—to no avail. She knows asking is futile as her mother "will add nothing unless powered by Necessity, a riverbank that guides her life."[48] A tightly regulated life that is based on rules set by the material needs of life cannot account for actions that militate against the philosophy of subsistence. By juxtaposing the mother's adherence to necessity and the narrative principle of austerity, its formal counterpart, to the aunt's extravagance and the narrative potential this presents to the imaginative narrator, Kingston suggests that narrative techniques are intimately connected to ways of life and the philosophical outlooks on the world they give rise to. In Wong's study, necessity and extravagance characterize the push and pull between the plight of being caught in conditions of minimal freedom and the desire for and imaginative leaps toward something more in Asian American literature. Bringing to bear on Wong's tropes Brown's discussion of the political theories of freedom, then, allows one to see literature as a place where reflections on social, political, and literary freedom abound and a creative effort to strive toward the ideal of substantial freedom, or freedom in a maximum sense, take place.

In the sense that the bilingual subject's social and cultural formation takes place in an environment where an economic understanding of the value of racialized lives dominates, bilingual personhood in Asian American and Latino literature can be said to prefigure some of the concerns of neoliberal subjectivity. Even as the postwar incorporation of Asian Americans and Latinos became an alibi for the narrative of liberal progress, this incorporation was premised on Asian Americans and Latinos showing proof of assimilation into the norms and values of possessive individualism. My use of the term human capital as an analytic for the incorporation of Asian Americans and Latinos is intended to illuminate the overwhelming economization of racial assimilation that profoundly impacted the lives of these people, the signs of which pervade the representations of bilingual personhood in Asian American and Latino literature. What theorists like Wendy Brown are saying is happening in contemporary neoliberal America regarding the transformation of democratic subjects into human capital actually may have already been the conditions of subjectivation for Asian Americans and Latinos.

## BILINGUAL BROKERING AND REPRESENTATIONS OF LANGUAGE DIFFERENCE

If the bilingual personhood of this study converges at some points with the neoliberal subject of contemporary theories, the notion of bilingual brokering, which I use expansively to refer to acts of mediation between different language communities, also evokes sociological and historical discussions of bilinguals as ethnic entrepreneurs. Bilingual brokering, in the context of Asian American and Latino histories, is a term that immediately brings to mind the ethnic interpreters who used their language skills to connect the immigrant newcomers who did not speak English to English-speaking persons and institutions. The historian Mae Ngai's micro-history of the Tape family in exclusion-era California as the prototype of the Chinese

American middle class is an apt example of bilinguals as brokers in a sociological sense.[49] In her meticulous and skillful reconstruction of the lives of the Tape family—known to students of Asian American history through *Tape v. Hurley* (1885), the lawsuit filed by Joseph and Mamie Tape to send their children to San Francisco's public schools, which only admitted white children—Ngai insightfully points out the Tapes' dual imperative of protesting their exclusion from white institutions and profiting from the isolation and segregation of the Chinese as such condition structurally enabled their position as brokers.

I would like to make it clear that I am by no means equating or analogizing the social position of the Tapes to that of the bilingual characters in Asian American and Latino writings or the writers I examine in this study. While the broker class of ethnic entrepreneurs like the Tapes comes up in some of the texts I examine in this study, my use of brokering is neither limited to a particular class or profession of people nor to thinking of profit merely in economic terms. Admittedly, there is a displeasing connotation to the term broker as it relates to translation, something that can be seen in the trope of the translator as traitor.[50] Understandably, in both Asian American and Latino literature, the figure of the translator has at times come under fierce criticism especially by writers and critics of cultural nationalist orientation. Despite this baggage, I use the term broker to discuss the mediatory work performed by bilingualism because it forces one to confront the conditions within which any act of mediation takes place as seminal to interpreting such acts. That is, if bilingualism is to lend itself to a hermeneutic of any kind, the conditions of seeing and evaluating what is mediated, why, and how need to be central to this hermeneutic. In Ngai's discussion of the Tapes, the meaning of brokering only becomes clear when one situates it within the particular conditions of a regime of racialization (i.e., Chinese exclusion). Likewise I am interested in elucidating how bilingual brokering functions as a hermeneutic when one reads the numerous acts of mediation in Asian American and Latino writings through the lens of language as racialized capital.

My focus, hence, is on the implications of ambivalence, convergence, and divergence in the structural position of the bilingual broker that blurs the line between protest and profit as I examine the mediations that occur across and between different language communities in the literary representations of bilingual personhood. From this perspective, Ngai's reflections on the significance of the Tapes

for American history are due careful consideration. Her insight on
the dynamic of exclusion and inclusion, in particular, has theoretical ramifications for examining the narrative of liberal progress in
the postwar era, which is based on the idea of a break from the past.
In this influential narrative of progress, the second half of the twentieth century is characterized as a continuous march toward greater
inclusion and the expansion of rights for marginalized groups. Racial
and imperial violence are largely viewed as historical relics or anoma-
lous residues of the past and incongruous with the present and the
future. According to this narrative, the exclusion era in which the
Tapes lived is a historical mistake and what should be remembered is
the exclusion of the Tape children from public schools—documented
in *Tape v. Hurley*—rather than some of the trappings of the American Dream the Tapes acquired, which is what Ngai deftly excavates
in her book. Ngai rejects the plot of this narrative that moves seam-
lessly from exclusion to inclusion when she claims that "the brokers'
story suggests that exclusion and inclusion are not necessarily succes-
sive, but sometimes are concurrent and dynamically intertwined—if
seemingly opposite—vectors of the immigrant experience."[51] The critic's task, then, is to parse the dynamic intertwining of inclusion and
exclusion, to examine the contingencies of this dynamic, and to assess
its significance at any given time. Ngai's complication of the dynamic
of inclusion and exclusion, so fundamental to the ideological work
of the narrative of liberal progress, not only contests the idea that
racial inclusion is once and for all achieved in the postwar era but
also makes room for a more nuanced understanding of the structural
position of the broker in the capitalist economy.[52] Attending to the
acts of mediation that accompany the expression of language difference, acts that I call bilingual brokering, allows me to examine the
imbrication of Asian American and Latino formations in capitalist
developments. This imbrication, as I illustrate throughout this study,
is not just about the commodification of ethnicity, or even about "the
ethnic-as-commodity," but about the uneven applications and realiza-
tions of liberal personhood across racial and ethnic groups.[53]

Another objective I have in using the term broker, for all its sociological descriptiveness and implications, is to distinguish my approach
to language and its significance in Asian American and Latino writings from what has arguably been the most prominent approach
to examining language difference in literary criticism: vernacular
criticism. A brief engagement with African American vernacular

criticism, representative examples of which include Houston Baker's discussion of the blues aesthetic and Henry Louis Gates's theory of black Signifyin(g), will help clarify some assumptions in my take on the significance of language and bilingualism for Asian American and Latino literature. Published a few years apart in the mid-to-late 1980s, *Blues, Ideology, and Afro-American Literature* and *The Signifying Monkey* have had far-ranging repercussions in consolidating an idea of the African American literary tradition that is based on a distinctive African American literary language.[54] Despite their different methodological orientations—Baker's study alludes to a Marxist orientation whereas Gates's study is explicitly deconstructionist—both studies contributed to linking African American history, popular culture, and literature, simultaneously pointing to African American literature as the repository of the essence of the African American experience and articulating a formal continuity in African American letters through time. The black vernacular is the medium that connects these disparate realms of human life in their works, a sign of African American resilience, and the source of African American creativity. Their approach is one that both venerates the black vernacular and mines its cultural force and influence to carve out a distinctive space for African American literature and to challenge some of the epistemic limitations in professional criticism that have blinded critics from properly appreciating African American literature. Here is a passage from Baker's *Blues, Ideology, and Afro-American Literature* that superbly illustrates this:

> There is no such thing as an "objective" history. . . . Rather than as a *real* substrate on which literary critical analyses can be grounded, the critic should view history as a discourse conditioned by discoverable laws of formation. Further, any traditional historical discourse should be analyzed to determine precisely where its boundaries of exclusion lie. . . . Excluded from such history, of course, is the very possibility that sophisticated verbal art is an always already present feature of the Afro-American landscape. Traditional American literary history . . . has repeatedly bracketed this always already present feature of Afro-America under the category of "non-art."[55]

There is a lot to unpack in the above passage. But for the purpose of this study, I would like to draw attention to Baker's critical self-reflectiveness that allows him to see his critical actions as contesting the historical formation of cultural capital that has excluded African American literature. In order to rectify this exclusion, Baker marshals what he terms "the blues matrix" as the hermeneutic basis for a new recognition of African American literary aesthetic.[56] It is important to keep in mind that although vernacular criticism reached its height with critics like Baker and Gates, it is built upon a long, illustrious, and vexed tradition of orality in African American literature, perceptively captured in studies like Gayl Jones's *Liberating Voices*. In other words, the significance of the blues needed to have already been established for Baker to articulate a "blues matrix" as a hermeneutic for African American literature. In addition to the problem of racial authenticity that undergirds Baker's and Gates's deployment of the vernacular, aptly pointed out by critics like Daniel Kim, the widespread recognition of the influence of an oral, expressive culture as a prerequisite condition for vernacular criticism creates a critical problem for applying the method to Asian American or Latino literature.[57] In short, a focus on the vernacular may not adequately speak to the literary expression of the lived experiences of language for Asian American and Latino writings.

This is not to say that vernacular expressions, or speech as it reflects the experiences of Asian American and Latino communities, have no place in writings by Asian Americans and Latinos. More so in Latino literary and cultural criticism than in Asian American literary and cultural criticism, the everyday experience of a non-English language has been given considerable attention.[58] Yet in these discussions, seldom are distinctions between a non-English language, such as Spanish, and the vernacular (such as *caló* or other nonstandard forms of Spanish) considered important. More often than not, the fine distinctions within a non-English language are folded into the distinction between English and the other language. From this perspective I would venture to say that the vernacular in Asian American and Latino criticism cannot be made legible to an English-speaking audience the way that the African American vernacular can be. Henry Louis Gates indirectly says as much when he defines "the relationship that black 'Signification' bears to the English 'signification'" as "a relation of difference inscribed within a relation of identity."[59] It is this difference-within-identity between the African American vernacular and (white) English that makes it possible for Baker's and Gates's vernacular criticism to be widely understood. If the African American vernacular is English-with-a-difference, African American literature, by extension, is American literature-with-a-difference, its integral relationship to American literature made all the more clear through the positing of this difference. My discussion of language difference in Asian American and Latino literature presupposes that this relationship of the African American vernacular to English is not available to Asian American and Latino vernaculars.

More importantly, I do not view this difference as just a matter of language difference but also of racial difference. The particular racialization of Asian Americans and Latinos vis-à-vis African Americans affects how their language difference is comprehended. In her nuanced approach to the condition of minority subjectivity in late twentieth-century US literature and culture, Crystal Parikh suggests that what "discursively *de*links Asians and Latina/os from African Americans in liberal discourses about ethnic assimilation in the late twentieth century" is the "specific racialization of Asians and Latina/os as *national* aliens."[60] The racialization of Asian Americans and Latinos as national aliens not only affects their precarious social belonging but also Asian American and Latino literature's relationship to American literature. This, of course, is not to say that works by Asian American and Latino writers invariably bear an "accent." The vexed relationship to national language and literature I see in works by Asian American and Latino writers is not so much a matter of individual virtuosity over what is generally called the language arts but a matter of the cultural effect of Asian American and Latino racialization on what Yasemin Yildiz calls the "monolingual paradigm" of national literature.[61] In discussing the emergence of the monolingual paradigm as the governing paradigm for national literatures in the eighteenth century, Yildiz shows that a particular, post-Enlightenment conception of language as "a clearly demarcated entity that has a name, is countable, and is the property of the group that speaks it, while also revealing that group's idiosyncrasies" undergirds this paradigm.[62] The German intellectual Friedrich Schleiermacher's idea of the mother tongue, according to Yildiz, is the quintessential metaphor of the monolingual paradigm, positing "a unique, irreplaceable, unchangeable biological origin that situates the individual automatically in a kinship network and by extension in the nation."[63] From the perspective of the monolingual paradigm, the racialization of Asian Americans and Latinos as national aliens places a strain on the assumed organic relationship between the writer and her language as the most immediate effect of racial alienation is that they are ejected from this mythic kinship that mediates an individual's relationship to her language, her neighbors, and ultimately her motherland. The mother tongue that animates the assumption of an organic relationship between a writer and her words remains an aporia for Asian American and Latino writers in the monolingual paradigm of national literature.[64]

Given this literary dilemma, one can think about what the incorporation of Asian American and Latino literature into US literature does to the monolingual paradigm of US literature. On the one hand, English as the dominant language of writing and publishing for Asian American and Latino writers seems to affirm the monolingualism of national literature. On the other hand, the inclusion of Asian American and Latino writers in anthologies, their prominence in prestigious literary awards and fellowships, and the critical acclaim they garner in mainstream magazines and journals also destabilize the organic, biological metaphor of the mother tongue and its attendant ideas of linguistically mediated kinship in the monolingual paradigm. In other words, Asian American and Latino literature in English may be said to engage in a cultural practice of using the symbolic capital of English to undo the naturalized metaphor of the mother tongue. The irony here, of course, is that the assumptions of English as the mother tongue in US literature can only be unmade by the demonstration of literary capital in English. In *Bilingual Brokers*, I regard this irony as the cultural symptom of the flexible incorporation of Asian Americans and Latinos. If literary capital remains concentrated in English in Asian American and Latino literature, the value of language and its social role, especially as they intersect with Asian American and Latino racialization, appear as key concerns in representations of bilingual personhood.

Breaking away from the metaphor of the mother tongue in the paradigm of national literature, however, means that a lot of ideas about language that could have been taken for granted need to be reexamined. If language is not a natural medium of self-expression, or of *Gemeinschaft*, or of an imagined motherland, then what kinds of ideas about language fill in the hole created by questioning the longheld metaphor that assumes a seamless unity between language and the subject of language? In this study I try to show that language as capital steps in to reorganize the relations around the self, society, and the nation in literary representations of bilingual personhood that unsettle the supremacy of the mother tongue in the monolingual paradigm of national literature. As I show throughout, the postwar American capitalist economy creates the conditions under which language becomes a constitutive element of human capital for Asian Americans and Latinos who are racialized as linguistic impostors, if not outsiders.[65] The hermeneutic offered by bilingual brokering creates the space to attend to language as symbolic capital as one of the most significant dimensions of literary and cultural mediation that resonates with the developments of racial capitalism.

## COMPARATIVE RACIALIZATION

In showing the social construction of bilingual personhood through Asian American and Latino literature, I view the categories of Asian American and Latino as neither having stable referents nor having fixed boundaries.[66] Pan-ethnic in their scope, the categories of Asian American and Latino both came into existence after the 1960s and have been the topic of intense scholarly debates ranging from whether these categories are racial or ethnic to whether the use of these terms is complicit with the bureaucratic and corporate management of minorities.[67] These debates in and of themselves constitute an important part of the evolving meaning of "Asian American" and "Latino." The way I use these terms mainly follows Michael Omi and Howard Winant's discussion of racial formation. Based on the thesis that "the state *is* inherently racial," Omi and Winant's racial formation perspective makes room for examining race as not just something that is imposed by the state on minorities or something that is self-imposed by minorities but as a dialectical process between the racial state and those who live in this state.[68] For example, according to them, the racial movements of the 1960s, such as Black Power, do not simply reinforce the state-oriented racial order by adopting the same racial terms but "*rearticulate* the meaning of race, and responses to such efforts."[69] As Omi and Winant suggest, "the rearticulation of preexisting racial ideology is a dual process of *disorganization* of the dominant ideology and of *construction* of an alternative, oppositional framework."[70] From this point of view, Asian American and Latino are identities-in-the-making that reflect and refract the racial order and racial movements of postwar liberalism. Another key insight from Omi and Winant's racial formation perspective I draw on is their view of race as "a matter of both social structure and cultural representation."[71] "Racial projects" they claim, "connect what race means in a particular discursive practice and the ways in which both social structures and everyday experiences are racially organized, based upon

that meaning."[72] This view of race acknowledges the interconnected-
ness among institutions, everyday experiences, and textual and visual
mediation that I think is effective in understanding race as an opera-
tive force in postwar America.

Viewed in light of race as simultaneously structure and representation, it can be said that bilingual personhood in Asian American and
Latino literature is a key element of postwar racial formation that
requires a comparative approach. The series of policies, laws, and
state-led initiatives involving bilingualism in postwar multiculturalism created an empirical basis for relations between Asian Americans and Latinos, relations that neither were entirely calculated nor
entirely random. From the mid-twentieth century, language difference
was the means by which the state identified Latinos. Up until 1980
when the term "Hispanic" appeared, the US census used the category
of "Persons of Spanish Mother Tongue" or a variant of this category
that still used language difference as the main point of identification.[73]
Bilingual education, arguably the bilingual policy that instigated the
most heated debates and that had the biggest cultural impact among
state-led bilingual initiatives, also initially was designed to accommo-
date Spanish-speaking students.[74] With the influx of new immigrants
from Asia after the 1965 immigration reform and with the waves of
Asian refugees that followed US military interventions abroad, however, Asian groups became visible in bilingual education and other
bilingual policies.[75] It should not be a surprise, then, that *Lau v.
Nichols*, the 1974 legal case that is regarded as creating the basis
for considering bilingual education as civil right, involved Chinese-
speaking students in San Francisco.[76] The historical coincidence of
Asian Americans and Latinos in bilingual policies and politics is also
rearticulated, to borrow Omi and Winant's term, as Asian Americans
and Latinos actively engage with these policies and politics within the
climate of multiculturalism. From this perspective, bilingual personhood is at once an invention of and intervention into postwar racial
formation.

In recent years, a number of scholarly works that take a comparative approach to examining race in US literature and culture have
shed light on the productiveness of tracing histories of interracialism
and its cultural effects.[77] In light of this interest, it may be instructive
to revisit what makes comparative racialization into a useful method
of analysis. As Shu-mei Shih points out, there is nothing inherently of
critical noteworthiness in the act of comparison itself. "Comparisons

as the arbitrary juxtaposition of two terms in difference and similarity," as Shih says, will not affect one's understanding of either of the terms being compared.[78] Yet Shih also heeds to what a comparative approach can accomplish when it comes to excavating racial knowledge that has been suppressed or made invisible because it does not serve hegemonic interests or because it does not speak to dominant epistemologies of race. Instead of reifying the terms being compared, "comparison as a recognition and activation of relations," Shih argues, can be effective in scrutinizing what goes unexamined when each term is treated discretely.[79]

One of my critical objectives in engaging in a comparative inquiry is to raise some questions about the dominance of Spanish-English bilingualism in discussions of bilingualism by relating it to the less-examined bilingualisms among Asian Americans. Just as the demonization of Spanish by the English Only movement happened rapidly, the rehabilitation of Spanish after 9/11, I would suggest, is also taking place rapidly. The series of conversations on foreign language instruction among members of the Modern Language Association in the journal *Profession* offer an example of the renewed interest in foreign language instruction in the wake of the war on terror and in light of the new emphasis on national security.[80] What Carlos Alonso says in regard to the status of Spanish in US institutions of higher education is of particular interest to me. Noting the mismatch between the number of students who want to enroll in Spanish language courses—unsurprisingly, Spanish is the most popular foreign language in US institutions of higher education—and the number of Spanish language courses, which are regulated in relation to courses on other foreign languages, Alonso asks whether it makes sense for US institutions of higher education to keep on regulating the number of Spanish language courses for parity's sake. Instead, he argues that "academic institutions in the United States [should] behave as if Spanish possessed second national language status and deal in a forthright and decisive fashion with all the ramifications that such a supposition would entail."[81] While limited to US institutions of higher education, Alonso's argument is still remarkable for its open acknowledgement of the value of Spanish in the strife for the accumulation of human capital. Drawing attention to the value of Spanish in the current scene of foreign language instruction in higher education is not to suggest that prejudices against Spanish or discrimination against speakers of Spanish have completely vanished. It is, rather, an attempt to bring into high relief the political economy of languages that influences the assessment of language as capital.

When one looks back on the debates on bilingual education in the 1960s, Alonso's argument on Spanish as a foreign national language is actually not that surprising or that provocative. As I discuss in more detail in Chapter 1, the politicians, educators, and community leaders who discussed the pros and cons of bilingual education all acknowledged the linguistic and cultural capital of Spanish. The problem was not that Spanish was not a language that could be (potentially) turned into capital but that the Spanish used by students under consideration for bilingual education (in the present) was far removed from any kind of capital. While often understood as such, the politics of bilingualism is not so much about what languages other than English can be represented in the public sphere but more about under what conditions non-English languages, including vernaculars and nonstandard forms, can become publicly acceptable and, even, desirable. A critical desire that motivates my comparative analysis is to shift the focus from an identity-politics model of viewing non-English languages where Spanish, or any other language for that matter, automatically and immediately suggests resistant politics, to the material conditions of linguistic capital.

Addressing bilingual personhood in Asian American and Latino literature as a matter of comparative inquiry is also to suggest that there is knowledge to be gained about the cultural organization and manifestation of racial difference when it is viewed through rubrics of language difference like "Anglophone," "Hispanophone," or "Sinophone." The fact that there is no language that parallels Spanish for Asian Americans is only one of the palpable signs of a lack of commensurability between Asian Americans and Latinos in *Bilingual Brokers*. Such unevenness, however, is exactly what allows for a deeper look into the schisms of pan-ethnic thinking before reformulating the terms of coalitional politics. The multilingualism of Asian American writers brings into high relief the legacy of imperialism in the construction of such rubrics as "Anglophone," "Hispanophone," and "Sinophone" and in the concentration of linguistic and literary capital in certain languages. The ambivalent place of Filipino Americans in the category of Asian American and their linguistic affinity with Latinos as a result of a shared history of Spanish imperialism, for example, troubles both categories of Asian American and Latino. As I show in Chapter 2, the interpellation of Carlos Bulosan as an "Oriental" in Asian exclusion and his later incorporation into Asian

American literature, necessitate a critical scrutiny of how Asian difference is evaluated and deployed. While it is beyond the purview of this study, the question of how South Asian American literature, which has a historical relationship to the rubric of Anglophone due to British colonialism, fits into the language-world(s) of Asian American literature or how the rapidly growing social and educational interest in Arabic due to the strategic importance of the Middle East for the United States in the present will affect Asian American literature are all questions that need to be asked.

While "Sinophone" may be the term that comes closest to such rubrics as "Anglophone" or "Hispanophone," the term has vexed implications for Asian American literature, something that I think Maxine Hong Kingston captures brilliantly in *China Men*. In this book that is widely read as a literary documentation of the struggles of early Chinese male migrant workers in the United States, one of the chapters is written from the perspective of a young Chinese American man, referred to as "the brother," who is drafted to the Vietnam War. Later, in the army, the young man is offered a coveted spot at the Defense Language Institute Foreign Language Center in Monterey, California, the US military's school of foreign language instruction. The ostensible reason for this recruitment is "the brother's record as a communications expert with language aptitude," but he knows that it is really because the military wants to expropriate his Chinese.[82] It does not take long for him to figure out that he would probably be asked to learn "the Pentagon's *Vietnam Phrase Book*."[83] At this point in the chapter, Kingston punctuates her prose with a list of English sentences taken from this imaginary phrase book used to train soldiers in basic Vietnamese. The formal layout of these sentences in the middle of the page imitates the form of a poem, but there is no poetry in such sentences as "Open the door or we will force it," and "Are you afraid? Why?"[84] How would sentences like these translate into Vietnamese? Such question seems to provoke the brother as well, as he thinks about what words are common to Vietnamese and Chinese. "The Vietnamese call their parents Ba and Ma; *phuoc* means 'happiness,' 'contentment,' 'bliss,' the same as Chinese; *lan* is 'orchid,' the same as his mother's name. . . . *Study, university, love*—the important words the same in Chinese and Vietnamese."[85] The recognition of linguistic homology between Vietnamese and Chinese, which for him is a sign of shared humanity in the face of racial violence, ultimately leads the brother to reject the military's offer.

I think a literary precedent to the brother's refusal can be found in Herman Melville's short story, "Bartleby, the Scrivener: A Story of Wall Street." As Miranda Joseph notes, Melville's short story has become a kind of parable for theorists looking "to locate a mode of intervention within the neoliberal discourse of entrepreneurial subjectivity" as Bartleby's passivity or inaction, encapsulated in his repetition of "I would prefer not to," becomes a model of thinking about an outside for or an alternative to the entrepreneurial subjectivity.[86] The brother's refusal is much more contexualized than Bartleby's. In so far as the lack of action becomes a valid way of response when confronted with an option, though, Kingston's brother is an affective corollary of Melville's Bartleby.

For the brother, lack of action is based on and furthers the opportunity for reflection. His recognition of the linguistic affinity between Chinese and Vietnamese simultaneously creates affiliations and disaffiliations that reveal Kingston's vision of Asian America. This recognition is first and foremost a critique of state racial violence. The transnational sense of linguistic and racial kinship he feels becomes a counterpoint to the wartime loyalty imposed on him by the US military. It also presciently anticipates the arrival of Vietnamese America for Asian America. Kingston's brother's act of affiliating Chinese America with the Vietnamese abroad who suffer from US militarism and with future Vietnamese America, then, is simultaneously an act of disaffiliating Chinese America from the racial military state. Another move of disaffiliation, however, is additionally embedded in his reflections on the similarities between Chinese and Vietnamese. The Sinophone affinity the brother highlights also temporarily suppresses the history of Chinese imperialism in Vietnam, the reason behind a common vocabulary between Chinese and Vietnamese in the first place. He has to also disaffiliate Chinese America from the specter of Chinese imperialism to create the basis of a new coalition between Chinese and Vietnamese America. In contrast to the uses the military sees in his bilingualism, he uses it to imagine new possibilities of ethical affiliations that resist global histories of racial violence. Chinese is not an alternative language to English for him since, as a former language of domination, Chinese still wields symbolic power over Vietnamese. While Chinese is not an alternative to English, it still allows the brother to see the inadequacies of English alone to express the full experience of ongoing racialization and to temporarily step outside the assumptions of the national language in the monolingual paradigm. It is in the interstices of the Anglophone and the Sinophone that the seeds of imagination for a new vocabulary of coalitional politics can be found. While the kinds of insights on affiliation and disaffiliation yielded by literature are unlikely to be immediately translated into blueprints for a politics of social change, what Kingston suggests is that a politics of social change cannot exist without ample space for reflection.

The kind of temporary albeit evocative line of Asian American connection the brother's Sinophone imagination constructs in *China Men* is at the center of the cultural work engaged in by *Bilingual Broker*'s examination of the intersections of racial and language difference. The significance of the brother's ruminations on Chinese and Vietnamese, mediated in English in Kingston's text, only becomes comprehensible under the military's utilitarian view of languages. The military's identification of an asset in the bilingual Chinese American community may be a stark example of an antihumanist reduction of the person to human capital against which Kingston presents another form of use for his bilingualism—imagining antiwar, antiracist affiliation between those who experience common racial violence. Tracing language as capital in literary representations of bilingual personhood is to attend to the dialectics of such appropriation and reappropriation.

In Chapter 1, I examine the formation of Asian American writers in the era of Asian exclusion through a comparative analysis of Younghill Kang's and Carlos Bulosan's responses to Orientalism in their works. By shifting the focus of reading these writers from exclusion to Orientalism, I attempt to draw attention to the terms of cultural inclusion that existed during legal exclusion and to the performance of social and cultural belonging under such circumstances. As legal exclusion created the racial category of Asian in the United States, migrant Asian writers faced the challenge of creating modern Asian subjects in literary English. I suggest that as cultural brokers between Orientalist images of their countries of origin and the modern lives of Asian migrants in the United States, Kang and Bulosan tested the boundaries of English to represent migrant experiences lived in languages other than English. As a heterogeneous cultural epistemology, Orientalism placed different constraints on Kang, who contended with the Orientalist valorization of the Far East, and Bulosan, who resorted to the Filipino intellectual tradition of the *ilustrado* in the face of Orientalist prejudices of primitivism. Writing before the emergence of a cultural politics of bilingualism that involved state-led efforts at educational and policy reforms, Kang and Bulosan prefigure some of the questions on the evaluation of bilingualism and racial difference that would appear acutely in the works of postwar Asian American and Latino writers.

In Chapter 2, I turn to the debates on public bilingualism to examine the rhetorical and social construction of bilingual personhood as part of the American Dream. With the waning of institutional legal exclusion in the postwar years, literary and cultural bilingual brokering would seldom encounter racial difference in terms of legal exclusion. Yet instead of disappearing from significance, racial difference continued to influence bilingual brokering as bilingual personhood became a key site for reexamining the American dream. The debates on bilingual education and bilingualism as civil right in the 1960s and '70s centered on what language befitted an American citizen concordant with the vision of the American Dream. The argument against public bilingualism viewed English as the colorblind language of the American Dream whereas the argument for public bilingualism presented the idea that the American Dream could be in many languages. While these two poles of opposition and advocacy are well-rehearsed positions in the social debates on bilingualism, both positions presuppose possessive individualism in the construction of bilingual personhood, which limits the parameters of discussing public bilingualism. Through the three stages of racial liberalism, cultural pluralism, and multiculturalism, I examine the different logics of the relations between linguistic personhood and the American Dream to trace the centrality of the idea of the possessive individual in the postwar affirmation of bilingual personhood.

In Chapter 3, I examine Américo Paredes's *George Washington Gómez* and Maxine Hong Kingston's *The Woman Warrior* as multicultural literary models of growing up in two languages. By reading Paredes's novel side by side with Kingston's widely discussed text, I hope to illuminate the contradictions of literary multiculturalism around representations of the bilingual child. These contradictions, I suggest, can best be seen in the multiple valences of bilingualism for ethnic formation that Paredes and Kingston portray. Paredes's active engagement with the regional specificity of the United States-Mexico border and the history of border conflicts imbue *George Washington Gómez* with a keen awareness of the relations of power behind the valorization or the stigmatization of bilingualism. In the course of the novel, the bilingual child Guálinto goes through the affects of racial shame and pride regarding his Mexican heritage to surprisingly end up a proverbial race traitor as an adult, utilizing his bilingualism in the service of the US government as a spy. The much-discussed controversy around *The Woman Warrior* restages in the real world the fictional controversy over Guálinto's betrayal in *George Washington Gómez* as Asian American cultural nationalists accused Kingston of "selling out" by misrepresenting Chinese American experiences. By reading Kingston's seminal text through Paredes's insights on the bilingual child, I revisit this controversy as ultimately symptomatic of the competing visions of bilingualism as cultural and human capital in multiculturalism. Together, the two texts reveal a syncretic composition of bilingual personhood in which various anxieties of language's value as property are worked out in relation to an ethnic subject's formation as a key component of literary multiculturalism.

In Chapter 4, I place the writings of the contemporary writers Richard Rodriguez and Chang-rae Lee in the social and legal context of what I call "language covering," borrowing from legal scholar Kenji Yoshino's concept of covering, to examine the relationship between language and race in neoliberal America. As literary accounts of post–civil rights assimilation, Richard Rodriguez's memoirs and Chang-rae Lee's debut novel, *Native Speaker*, reflect the social concerns on multilingualism and civic disunity that permeated the last two decades of the twentieth century and locate the immigrant's loss of the mother tongue in this context. Yet Rodriguez's and Lee's narratives are distinct from what could be called a prototypical narrative of language assimilation in US literature in that their representations of what psycholinguist François Grosjean calls dormant bilingualism appear in the shadows of racial tropes. I first examine the use of the rhetorical figure of analogy employed by bilingual plaintiffs—the claim that language is "like race"—in the legal briefs contesting English-only workplace rules, and then trace a similar relation between language and race in Rodriguez's and Lee's representations of language and race. While the analogy between language and race mostly fails in the courtrooms, I argue that it is a productive rhetorical move for investigating the contingencies of bilingualism in post–civil rights America for Rodriguez and Lee. Through their exploration of the intersections of language and race, Rodriguez and Lee show that language is prone to be influenced by the same capitalist logic that commodifies race.

The complex web of relations among language, race, and capital in their writings brings into high relief how illusory such terms as freedom and choice are in neoliberal America for racialized subjects.

In Chapter 5, I examine the writings of Julia Alvarez and Ha Jin as examples of literary bilingual brokering in the age of global English. Unlike Younghill Kang and Carlos Bulosan, Alvarez and Ha Jin are not faced with the kind of institutional racism that constrains the writer's self-presentation to a limited range of racially determined styles of difference and that sets up the stakes of literary acceptance in relation to national inclusion. The alleviation of the conditions of legal exclusion and discrimination, however, does not mean that the millennial bilingual writers of color are free of literary constraints related to the management of racial difference. To the contrary, I argue in this chapter that the coexistence of World Literature in English and US multicultural literature in these bilingual writers' works places their representations of political oppression and human rights abuse abroad within the pedagogy of neoliberal multiculturalism at home that is geared toward an individualistic understanding of freedom and rights. Even as Alvarez and Ha Jin seek to claim belonging in the homeland of language outside the narrow confines of national literature, that choice itself is circumscribed by the cultural politics of writing in English at a time of global English hegemony.

In the epilogue I turn to David Henry Hwang's recent play, *Chinglish*, which raises important questions about bilingual brokering in the twenty-first century. In the story of a white American businessman's attempts to broker a deal in China, Hwang prioritizes the ethics of intercultural exchange and the play of languages over bilingualism as skill. On the one hand, Hwang seems to overturn the social construction of bilingual personhood along the terms of possessive individualism by championing interlingual lapses, irregularities, and mistakes. Ironically, though, this attempt to free the linguistic subject from the constraints of language as capital is delivered through a careful rendition of English-Mandarin bilingualism, which is made possible through institutional support from both sides of the Pacific. These conditions of possibility for Hwang's bilingual play—an important landmark in American literature for the challenge it poses to stereotypes of Asian English—serve as a gentle reminder that while bilingual personhood may recede from cultural significance as a site of examining the relationship between racial subjectivity and capital, bilingualism in cultural politics is still enmeshed in the flows of capital.

CHAPTER ONE

# Cultural Brokers in Interwar Orientalism

In this chapter I examine two writers, Younghill Kang and Carlos Bulosan, who lived and wrote during the era of Asian exclusion
(1882–1952).[1] As a regime of immigration set up by laws and policies,
Asian exclusion not only imposed a racial group identity on individuals socially and legally but also made it the determining factor of
American citizenship. By prioritizing racial identity above everything
else in determining national character and culture, Asian exclusion
also homogenized the "barred Asiatic zone" in the public imaginary
and "constitut[ed] 'Asian' as a peculiarly American racial category."[2]
The numerous bids for whiteness in the legal briefs filed by Asians
of a range of national origins during the exclusion era exemplify the
disappearance of Asian particularities in the demonstration of exemplary whiteness.[3] Not surprisingly, Asian exclusion has received much
critical attention by scholars working on race and immigration, especially in Asian American studies.[4] More importantly for my discussion, Asian exclusion has also functioned as what Fredric Jameson
would call a "*semantic* precondition" for Asian American literary
and cultural criticism, a foundational event that sets the parameters
for interpretation.[5] Even in cases where it is not explicitly referenced,
the historical experiences of exclusion underwrite the definition and
significance of Asian American identity deployed in critical exegesis
of literary texts. One example of this is Elaine Kim's interpretation
of Kang and Bulosan as progenitors of Asian American literature on
the basis that they "illustrate the transition from writers who view
themselves as guests or visitors to those who want to find a place for

themselves in American society."[6] If the US laws claimed them unfit for citizenship due to their racial identity, Kim's argument locates the essence of Americanness not in the law but in cultural spirit, in Kang's and Bulosan's defiant claims on social membership in the face of exclusion.[7]

While an important revision of what constitutes an American (writer), Kim's argument also relies on the very legal distinction between visitors and residents that she critiques when she distinguishes Kang and Bulosan from Asian writers who preceded them. The figure of ownership she evokes here, while being figurative and limited to the cultural domain, still carries the suggestion of a liberal order of possessive individualism. The investment in an Asian *Americanness*, in other words, potentially becomes a "possessive investment," as George Lipsitz terms it, even if the investment is not in whiteness.[8] What political scientist Ange-Marie Hancock shows as the "but for" approach to equality (or "the equality as sameness logic")—"We are just like you [normative Americans], but for [this difference that should be immaterial to social and legal equality]"—could be viewed as one line of development in arguments for inclusion by marginalized groups that presume the idea of possessive individualism.[9] I would like to make it clear that I am not suggesting that Kang and Bulosan, or any other writer subject to racial laws such as Asian exclusion, should not argue for inclusion or criticize the racial laws that fall short of democratic ideals. Rather I see this as one example of how the idea of the possessive individual functions as a double-edged sword for people of color and how protest and profit entwine in social struggles within the liberal economy.

In this chapter I shift the context of reading Kang and Bulosan from exclusion to Orientalism with the aim of revising the narrative of American belonging from whether one claims to be American or not to what the cultural performance of citizenship entails. I am interested in what we can learn about the historical period of Asian exclusion and the liberal mode of inclusion by turning to Orientalism as the cultural condition of performing acceptable Asian identities at the time of Asian exclusion. In particular, I am interested in how Orientalism, as Edward Said's conceptualization of Western ideas of the East that reflect Western desires of the Other more than Eastern realities, becomes a cultural epistemology for Kang and Bulosan as they negotiate belonging in a largely hostile world. If bringing Younghill Kang and Carlos Bulosan together through Orientalism seems like a curious move, this is not because Bulosan was not affected by Orientalism but because the Orientalist tropes used in representations of the Philippines were not the same as those more common tropes associated with East Asia, or more specifically Japan and China. By no means was Orientalism an even terrain for Kang and Bulosan. The differential application and influence of Orientalism on these writers, however, should not preclude one from thinking about how the legal regime of Asian exclusion relates to the cultural imagination of Orientalism. In a recent cultural history of Filipino *ilustrados*, Megan Thomas cautions against viewing Orientalism as homogeneous or cohesive as she shows how it was deployed and appropriated by both Spanish colonial administrators and Filipino *ilustrados*, "used for liberatory projects as well as repressive ones."[10] While I do not suggest that Orientalism was liberatory or empowering for Kang and Bulosan, I do suggest that they appropriated the cultural epistemology of Orientalism to explore the compatibility between being a modern Asian and being a writer of American literature. If "Asian" was constituted as "a peculiarly American racial category" through Asian exclusion, the formation of "Asian American," through writers like Kang and Bulosan, involves negotiations of the peculiar coming together of different strands of Orientalism.

Within the exigencies of Asian exclusion, Kang and Bulosan had to negotiate the triad of a racialized foreignness, English as the universal language of literary modernity, and the specter of the other language. In *America Is in the Heart* (1943), Bulosan writes that he turned to his contemporary Kang for "some kind of order to guide [him] in the confusion that reigned over [his] life."[11] Noticing that Kang, "a Korean who had immigrated to the United States as a boy" could "wor[k] his way up until he had become a professor at an American University," Bulosan wonders why this trope of the American Dream cannot also apply to him. Kang, he notes, "had come from a family of scholars and had gone to an American university—but was he not an Oriental like myself? Was there an Oriental without education who had become a writer in America?"[12] Bulosan notices and embraces the interpellation as an "Oriental," yet this recognition is immediately undercut by another recognition of his difference from Kang, that of educational background. This textual moment of negotiating difference and sameness is exemplary of Kang's and Bulosan's navigation of the cultural epistemology of Orientalism, which is about an incessant exploration of how Orientalism creates differences and sameness in the tropes of the East and how the cultural capital of Asian identity is produced within the currents of such differentiation. Kang and Bulosan may have been both "Orientals," but they were not affected in the same ways by Orientalism. While Bulosan articulates his difference from Kang through educational background, I focus on the different models of cultural brokering that were available to these writers based on the different places these writers' countries of origin and native languages occupied in Orientalism. Kang's and Bulosan's most profound reflections on Orientalism revolve around their questions of what languages can represent modernity and what levels and kinds of mediation are involved in making the "Orient" compatible with modernity. Kang satirizes interwar Orientalism's valorization of an undifferentiated Asia that is aestheticized through Sinophilia, even as he takes advantage of this Orientalist tendency in his career as a writer. On the other hand, Bulosan forges a writer's path by fashioning himself after the Filipino tradition of the *ilustrado*, contending with the primitivist skepticism that Orientalism casts on the Philippines. Both Kang's and Bulosan's works palpably convey the precarious social position of being a juridical nonsubject in the exclusion era. Bilingual personhood, for these juridical nonsubjects, was an ambiguous confirmation of property in the person at best. At the same time, being outside the realm of the juridical also allowed Kang and Bulosan to explore in depth the cultural performance of citizenship through the desires and fantasies around language difference, an exploration that was international in imaginative scope and probing in its critique of the uneven applications of modernity to nonwhite subjects.

## THE ORIENTALIST ORIENTAL YANKEE

As Bulosan notes in *America Is in the Heart*, it was not common for a writer of Asian descent to achieve literary fame in the United States in the 1930s. Younghill Kang, in this sense, was something of an exception. Born in Korea in 1903, Kang came to the United States in 1921. He passed through several universities, but the most important time for his literary career may have been his years as a composition instructor at New York University where he met Thomas Wolfe, who became a friend and a patron of sort. Wolfe introduced Kang to his own editor at Charles Scribner's Sons, Maxwell Perkins, well known for shepherding the manuscripts of such luminaries as F. Scott

Fitzgerald and Ernest Hemingway.[13] Kang's first autobiographical fiction, *The Grass Roof* (1931), which chronicles the boyhood of Chungpa Han in Japanese-occupied Korea, was well received and earned Kang invitations to lectures as an Asian expert and most likely contributed to his winning a Guggenheim fellowship. After his second autobiographical fiction, *East Goes West: The Making of an Oriental Yankee* (1937), Kang's literary career was interrupted by the war. He is said to have worked as a Japanese language instructor for the US military during the Pacific War. After the partition of the Korean peninsula, Kang traveled to Korea as part of the United States Army Military Government in Korea and took part in postpartition politics until his strident opposition to the first South Korean president elect, Syngman Rhee, alienated him from both the South Korean government and the US military. Back in the United States, he worked on translating Korean poetry into English and composed a historical play set in Korea. Kang virtually disappeared from the literary scene after his involvement in the wars and with the military.[14]

The one line from the self-profile he wrote for *Twentieth Century Authors* describes well how Kang saw himself during those politically turbulent times when he was rendered stateless by both Japanese imperialism and US racism. "To be a Korean in this world," he says, "is to be unorthodox."[15] While being Korean may have been something that preoccupied Kang, his literary maneuver in *East Goes West* resorts to the category of Asian, or Oriental, over that of Korean. Such move is at odds with his first publication, *The Grass Roof*, which refrains from evoking any idea of Asian cultural coherence. In fact, the indictment of Japanese imperialism in the book makes it impossible not to see the intraregional dissonances and conflicts. Yet he makes the tropes of Orientalism the subject of his second book by seemingly presenting East and West as separate entities with discrete boundaries. As Elaine Kim notes, the reception of *East Goes West* was not as good as *The Grass Roof* despite the fact that Kang himself viewed it as showing himself as a more seasoned writer than the first.[16] Kim offers two reasons for this. One is that the first book was something of a novelty, that it "told a good deal about a country about which very little was known here."[17] The other is that American reviewers were not fond of Kang's criticism of racism and prejudices against people of color. A third reason, I think, can be located in Kang's self-awareness of interwar Orientalism, which seems to have grown after the publication of the first novel and is a noticeable motif in the second.

The reception of his first novel most likely alerted Kang to the character of interwar Orientalism. The reviews of *The Grass Roof* placed the book within a discursive frame of books on foreign affairs and were strongly inflected by a curiosity over the novelty of a Korean perspective delivered in English.[18] They highlighted the freshness of Kang's perspective and compared Korea's colonial situation to that of Ireland's, analogizing the unfamiliar to the familiar. After the publication of the book, Kang was invited to lecture on a wide-range of Asia-related topics, spanning religion, politics, arts and culture.[19] The authority and expertise that were conferred on Kang through such invitations speak less to Kang's extensive knowledge of Asia and are more telling of how he was viewed as a native informant during a time of growing desire to know the exotic East when knowledge of the East was scant. At the same time that it brought him minor public fame, being called on as an expert on Asia also may have further deferred his American authorship. Literary historian Mark McGurl's comparison of Thomas Wolfe and Kang shows well that Kang was not able to claim the status of an American author the way Wolfe could. He comments that while Wolfe could "entertain the possibility of 'speaking for everyone,' absorbing the national body into his own Bardic self like a Whitman from hell," "Kang could only aspire to (and lobby Congress for) legitimate 'American' authorship."[20] While Wolfe indulges in "self-expressive creative writing" with abandon, Kang, in contrast, engages in a negation of this self-expressiveness by making his main character in *The Grass Roof* "a *translator* of English literature into Korean."[21] The longstanding idea that the copy, or the translation, is inferior to the original subtends McGurl's comparison of Wolfe and Kang.

Compared to his first publication, Kang delivers a much more nuanced portrait of the circumscribed role of the translator for the Asian intellectual émigré and its duality in *East Goes West*. On the one hand, the Asian translator serves the role of a cultural ambassador, proudly representing key cultural characteristics to an unknowing (if curious) audience.[22] On the other side of the glamor of cultural elitism implied in the trope of the translator as cultural ambassador is the more sinister trope of the translator as native informant, engaging in the ethically dubious act of passing on information on a native community without taking responsibility for how the information will be used. Kang employs typology as a heuristic to explore the central role of translation in the articulation of an Asian intellectual's identity, moving through the types of the Asian cosmopolitan and the anticolonial nationalist to arrive at the Orientalist Oriental Yankee, a final destination of sorts. In *East Goes West*, Chungpa Han, the young Korean émigré and main character, traverses North America in the 1920s and '30s, witnessing the force of industrialization, picking up odd jobs here and there, running into other Asian expatriates, and observing the lifestyles and cultural customs of white and black Americans. Throughout, Kang pays sustained attention to what identity and identifications are available to Asians in America. First Chungpa gathers into social types the various Asian expatriates he meets before he himself has to think about what type of Asian he will become. Chungpa's apperceptive self-examination regarding the option of becoming an Orientalist registers as both a paralysis of social imagination and a critique of the prescriptive influence of Orientalism.

Kang surveys a number of social types of Asian intellectuals in the novel as foils to the Orientalist Oriental Yankee. A much more positive and hopeful rendering of the Asian émigré intellectual, the Asian cosmopolitan is the utopian type against which the dystopic type of the Orientalist Oriental Yankee is measured. The character of To Wan Kim, Chungpa's friend and mentor who introduces him to New York's elite Orientalists, exemplifies the Asian cosmopolitan.[23] Han immediately recognizes Kim as a learned man when he first meets him, and true to this perception, Kim has traveled to all four corners of the world—"He had lived long in Europe, he had visited in the Near East, even in Africa"—and exudes a cosmopolitan flair in his choice of friends and cultural taste.[24] At the same time that Kim functions in the narrative as Chungpa's foil, he is also more than that. Based on the title of his novel-in-progress that Kang recorded on his Guggenheim application, "The Death of an Exile," which evidently echoes Kim's fate in *East Goes West*, it is possible to speculate that Kang initially may have had Kim in mind as the protagonist of his narrative on the Asian émigré's experiences in the United States.[25] As a replaced protagonist, Kim is also the alter ego of Chungpa in the narrative, his more worldly self.

For all his worldliness, or maybe because of his worldliness, Kim never feels at home in New York. Remarking that "the Oriental exile of Kim's generation is really a new character in history," Chungpa explains Kim's rootlessness by viewing the Asian cosmopolitan as an emergent social type that is ahead of the times.[26] Raymond Williams's triad of the residual, the dominant, and the emergent as the terms of analyzing "the internal dynamic relations" of epochal transition is helpful here because the Asian cosmopolitan can be a viable future option for an émigré intellectual like Chungpa if the social type corresponds to the emergent in Williams.[27] According to Williams, the concept of the emergent needs to be distinguished from what is merely "novel" and what is easily "incorporated" into the dominant.[28] In brief, "since what the dominant has effectively seized is indeed the ruling definition of the social," a truly emergent process is that which holds out the promise of redefining the social instead of being a temporary outlier or being absorbed into the existing social order.[29] From this perspective, the Asian cosmopolitan fails as an emergent formation because the radically new character of this social type leads not to new sociality but reduced sociality, or an extreme version of the "minimum sociality" that Yoon Sun Lee notes is a characteristic of Asian American realism.[30] The leap of faith that this social type calls for in historical imagination is so radical that it is almost as if the Asian cosmopolitan inherently undermines his own existence. "His break with his own kind is so profound," Chungpa marvels, "by reason of the abnormal expansion of his knowledge and experience; he is at the same time so outside the alien worlds he travels in, so isolated and apart, he gives a new interpretation of the solitariness of the human soul."[31]

The impossibility of translating Kim's name captures the extremity of the Asian cosmopolitan's isolation. Whereas in Korean his name, "To Wan (島園)," or "Garden Isle," implies an "island" of mystical serenity and peace, something that Chungpa immediately notices, Kim becomes more or less an "I-land" as a "Korean ghost" in New York.[32] The untranslatability of Kim's name into English illustrates the degree of his "break with his kind" and accentuates the "abnormal expansion of knowledge and experience" that challenges dominant understandings of being and doing. However, Kim's name suggests more than the separation between Korean and English, two languages of very different language "families."[33] While the loss of meaning in translating Kim's name from Korean to English seemingly points to a common issue in cultural translation, the meaning of the name, To Wan, in Korean is already a translation of Chinese characters used in the name. To Wan, in other words, is only a phonetic approximation of the Chinese characters as they are pronounced in Korean. Viewed this way, the transparency of meaning that was assumed in the Korean name also becomes uncertain. The opacity of To Wan's name originates not so much from the inherent characteristics of Korean, Chinese, or English but from the complex and unevenly excavated histories of arduous crossings and mixings that precede the emergence of the social type of the Asian cosmopolitan in the United States.

Anticolonial nationalism, a global phenomenon that gave rise to numerous alliances among people of color worldwide and that was a dominant political platform for non-Western countries in the pre–World War II era, informs the second social type of the Asian émigré that Kang offers in *East Goes West*. The Chinese expatriate intellectuals, such as Hsu Tsimou, exemplify the anticolonial nationalist. The debate on "Pei-hua"—more commonly transliterated as baihua (白话) in the Mandarin phonetic transcription system of pinyin, and that literally means "common speech"—occurs only briefly in the novel.[34] Yet it reveals Kang's reflections on Asian compatibility with modernization like nowhere else in the novel. The debate on Pei-hua in *East Goes West* is a snippet of the conversations on language reform in China in the late nineteenth and early twentieth centuries, which reflected the Chinese realization of the need to reexamine its culture in light of Western encroachment and modernity. The primary concern of Chinese language reform in the early twentieth century, led by reformers such as Wu Rulun, was the advocacy of a national language, or guoyu (国语).[35] "Hu-Shih's new movement of Pei-hua or literature in the spoken language," which Hsu supports ardently in the novel, is a literary movement that recapitulates some of the tenets of the national-language movement in the realm of literature.[36] By extolling the spoken language over the classical literary language, or wenyan (文言), Hsu defies traditional expectations of linguistic and literary capital and valorizes common people as agents of national literature and culture. Hsu identifies the Pei-hua movement as an emergent social and cultural formation and decides to return to his country of origin after completing his education in the West to contribute to the modernization of the Chinese language through literature in the vernacular.

While he clearly acknowledges the political importance of the anticolonial nationalist, Kang does not present Hsu as a model for Asians in the United States.[37] I think this reflects Kang's ambivalent relationship to anticolonial nationalism, which can be seen in the way he draws attention to the contradictions in the anticolonial nationalist's

strivings for a democratic literary culture. Hsu's turn to the idea of
Chinese national literature evokes postcolonial derivativity as Kang
depicts him as being inspired by the notion of national literature in
Europe, particularly by Dante's idea of Italian literature, and calls
him "a child of the Western nineteenth century."[38] At the same time
that he suggests an origin-and-copy relationship between European
nationalist literary movements and the Pei-hua movement, Kang is less
concerned with the unilateral direction of the intellectual exchanges
than with the anticolonial nationalist's elitism. In fact, a strange mix
of Chinese ethnocentrism and anxiety about modernization underwrites the Pei-hua movement in the novel, as Hu-Shih, the leader of
the Pei-hua movement, is said to have initially settled on baihua as an
appropriate medium for translating "the vulgarities of Western novels
and plays" that cannot be expressed in "the formal stilted elegance
of a purely classical and literary writing."[39] From this perspective, the
Pei-hua movement's turn to the language of the common people, then,
is guided as much by the sense that classical written Chinese is too
good for the masses and for Western-import mass culture as by the
desire to seek a new language to express modernity.

The fact that the anticolonial nationalists' elitism is enabled by
their involvement in capitalist modes of creating wealth that only
a few, select Asians can take advantage of also creates a contradiction between the anticolonial nationalist's populist aspiration and
his rarefied economic status. Hsu's elitist Euro-American education
has been paid for by his father's wealth, made through global commerce. Kang hints at the suppressed relationship between the formation of Asian anticolonial nationalism and Asian participation in the
development of global capitalism through the example of Hsu. In
this regard, Kang's skepticism toward Hsu's ethnic nationalism may
well forebode later critiques of the postcolonial national bourgeoisie's
collusion with imperial power to exploit the most vulnerable populations of the newly independent states. Frantz Fanon's critique of
"the national bourgeoisie" as an "intermediary" between the "met-
ropolitan bourgeoisie," or the bourgeoisie of the former empire, and
the people of the postcolonial nation is instructive here.[40] Fanon sees
this group's interests as "not to transform the nation but prosaically
serve as a conveyor belt for capitalism, forced to camouflage itself
behind the mask of neocolonialism."[41] In guarding its own interests,
the national bourgeoisie ends up becoming an agent for the West.
Such Fanonian insight on the degenerative possibility of anticolonial

nationalism seems to be behind Kang's hesitance to present the social type of the anticolonial nationalist as a model of Asians in the United States.

If Kang turns a skeptical eye to anticolonial nationalism as a viable mode of Asian existence, he is keenly aware of how the status of the postcolonial intellectual can be appropriated to one's social advantage among circles of white American liberals. At one moment in the novel, through a duel of words between an outspoken South Asian intellectual and Chungpa at a party thrown by an upper-class white American woman, Kang intimates that even postcolonial injuries can be transformed into signs of distinction depending on how the postcolonial intellectual plays to white liberal sympathies. The host of the party, Miss Churchill, is a philanthropist, whose involvement in the Friends' Society in Philadelphia allows her to support charity work all across the globe from "relief work in Belgium" to aiding "famine sufferers in China and Armenia" and even to lend a helping hand to Asians in the United States, "rais[ing] scholarship funds for Japanese scholars in America in order to console them for the exclusion laws."[42] Kang emphasizes that Miss Churchill's dinner party is "international," since it was given in honor of "some English actors" and included himself and another person of color, "the Hindu student Senzar."[43] Senzar, however, refuses to participate in endorsing the liberalism and goodwill of his host and instead enters into a long tirade about the inferiority of US education to English education, the brutality of English imperialism in India, and future Indian revenge against the English. In what seems to be a mixed motivation of appearing chivalrous and culling the host's favor, Chungpa chastises Senzar for his postcolonial resentment and lack of social decorum, using the Korean experience of Japanese colonialism as his weapon. "You Hindus are better off under the English than we are under the Japanese," he claims in a self-serving comparison.[44]

In this strange scene of dueling colonial injuries, the postcolonial resentment of the anticolonial nationalist is presented as being irrational and, more importantly, against social decorum. Rather than read this as indicative of the writer's lack of sympathy for outspoken postcolonial intellectuals, I read this scene as Kang's illustration of how the generation of social capital for Chungpa hinges on his showing proof of racial difference that is acceptable to and accommodating of white American liberalism. By the point in the novel when he admits that he was "almost decorated for merit by the exhausted

Westerners" after his debate with Senzar, it is hard to miss Chungpa's opportunism.[45] His reward for the fiery defense of social conventions is a secure place in the circle of the white American woman's patronage as Chungpa becomes "a regular guest now, for dinner and the evening, every Wednesday."[46] The way Senzar's castigation becomes the occasion for Chungpa's inclusion suggests that an Asian intellectual's inclusion in influential social networks, which produces and transacts in symbolic capital, is based on a manipulation of racial difference on white American liberal terms. Karen Kuo's point that Chungpa can only be included as "an Asian ward of white paternalistic benevolence," that he can only achieve contingent inclusion, also attests to the dependence of the Asian intellectual on white liberalism that Kang suggests.[47]

Kang's most scathing satire of the terms of an Asian émigré intellectual's existence in the United States, however, comes up in the social type of the Orientalist Oriental Yankee. This social type is first brought up when Kim suggests that Chungpa become a professional scholar of the East, as he predicts a "future for Oriental scholarship in the West."[48] What seems like friendly career advice is soon revealed as an indirect commentary on Western imperialism and the political economy of art and culture. According to Kim, the West has to be the locus of the study of the East because Asian material artifacts of value have become "private collections" owned by Westerners or Western institutions.[49] Now that Chungpa is in the United States where the material objects of Eastern history and culture are, he should look into the study of the East to "enter into the economic life of Americans."[50] It is questionable, Kim continues, whether the Oriental scholar can be aware of the role he plays since adopting this role requires a complete transformation of attitude and perspective. Chungpa, in other words, would have to be "like a Western man approaching Asia."[51] Kim asserts that this may be Chungpa's only option. "As a transplanted scholar," he says, "this is the only road I could point to, for your happy surviving."[52]

The idea of the Orientalist Oriental Yankee that Kim presents to Chungpa echoes the sociologist Robert E. Park's 1914 metaphor of the racial uniform, which employed the figure of the uniform to show how the biological notion of race constricts certain groups, such as Asian Americans and African Americans, from assimilation. At a time when the meaning of race was often reduced to skin color and racism was based on such notion of race, Park's metaphor of the racial uniform suggests that race was more ornamental than essential, something that can be taken off without affecting the person underneath. In her compelling analysis of Park's metaphor of the racial uniform, Cynthia Tolentino shows the metaphor as illustrative of a shift in the dominant episteme's understanding of race from a biologically based notion to something rooted in culture.[53] In that he recommends a career path for Chungpa that is based on his knowledge of a culture rather than his skin color, Kim seems to adopt this idea of the racial uniform when he suggests to Chungpa that he become a scholar of the East. If Chungpa turns himself into "a Western man approaching Asia," the only thing that would differentiate him from the white Orientalists would be his yellow skin as his racial uniform, which seems to intimate his assimilability to white America.

Yet, ironically, it is exactly because of his racial uniform that Chungpa becomes valuable as an Orientalist to white Orientalists. This becomes clearer when one takes into account the static, ahistorical, and depoliticized notion of culture that becomes the new basis for race in Robert Park's idea of the racial uniform. According to Tolentino, Park's culturalization of race has limited utility in alleviating racism because "in emphasizing the concept of culture, the figure of the 'racial uniform' also effaces the historical origins of the production of difference by rendering them as fixed categories."[54] Viewed through the example of the Orientalist Oriental scholar in *East Goes West*, one might venture that the notion of culture that has come to replace biology in Park's definition of race is still based on racialized ideas of culture. That is, the Asian culture that Chungpa would embody as an Oriental for the white Orientalists is predetermined in Orientalist terms as fixed, apolitical, and timeless, which is why Chungpa would have to be "like a Western man approaching Asia." Instead of being liberated from racism the metaphor of the "racial uniform" shows that culture is the new racial uniform for Chungpa that he has to wear over his yellow body.

Henry Yu's study of Orientalist practices in the development of the Chicago School of Sociology shows that the Orientalist epistemology Kim mentions undergirded sociology's disciplinary knowledge production on racial difference. Yu illustrates in detail how the production of white cosmopolitan knowledge was predicated on the service of Asian American native informants, made up of both students and scholars. The Chicago sociologists of the 1920s and '30s, Yu asserts, were heirs to the white American missionaries in the East.

In both cases of the missionaries and the sociologists, Yu suggests that the self-stylization of white cosmopolitanism and an Orientalist epistemology were mutually constitutive. "At the same time that [elite whites] searched for and produced knowledge about the Orient," Yu says, "they also produced themselves as cosmopolitan travelers, expert purveyors of the exotic."[55] Just as the missionaries had willing converts who became bearers of the gospel, the developing academic discipline of sociology was also aided by the instrumental use of Asians in the United States who had knowledge of Asian languages and ties to the community. What authority or expertise the "thinking Orientals" gained, however, was dependent on white institutions and their agendas of knowledge production. The cultural brokering of these "thinking Orientals," henceforth, cannot be thought of apart from the discrepancy in power between the white institutions and their Asian native informants.

In *East Goes West*, Kang employs a striking metaphor of the bilingual brain to portray how Asian racial difference is valorized through Orientalism's fetish of Asian culture. When Chungpa is met with the tragic news of Kim's suicide, he mourns the loss of his friend by mourning the loss of his bilingual brain:

> He [Kim] was wasted. All his work had been burned in that Bleecker Street fireplace, nothing was left. But the greatest loss to me, Kim's friend, was himself, his brain which bore in its fine involutions our ancient characters deeply and simply incised, familiar to me. And over their classic economy, their primitive chaste elegance, was scrawled the West's handwriting, in incoherent labyrinth, and seamy Hamlet design. To me—to me almost alone—a priceless and awful parchment was in him destroyed. Could it not have been deciphered, conveyed to the world?[56]

While it might make Chungpa's eulogy of his friend unconventional, the metaphor of the bilingual brain presents Kim's life—and by extension Chungpa's own life—as emblematic of the Asian intellectual's fate in modernization. As a doubly scripted document, with one language written over by another, the bilingual brain is a transitional symbol from race as biology to race as culture. As a biological organ, the bilingual brain indexes biologically based race thinking's tendency to equate a person with a bodily trait. As a scripted document, however, it shows that the value of Asian racial difference lies in its perceived cultural value.

Chungpa's metaphor of the bilingual brain is also notable for its lack of specificity regarding the languages involved. While it is likely that the languages that comprise Kim's bilingualism are classical Chinese and English, Chungpa focuses on the aesthetic of the letters rather than naming the languages. The Eastern language—"our ancient characters"—shows a "classic economy," characterized by a "primitive chaste elegance," whereas the Western one is in the particular typeface called Hamlet, which apparently offsets the labyrinthine writing. On the one hand, the interest Chungpa shows in the visual presentation of the languages evokes the Orientalist interest in calligraphy. On the other hand, it also brings into high relief language as a system of representation, a topic that comes up in the novel in another context when Kim expounds on what languages are compatible with modernity. "You and I know," he proclaims to Chungpa at one point, "that such writing [classical Chinese]—unlike the worthier phonetic systems—retards the progress of man."[57] Kang partly attributes the cause of Kim's tragic suicide to his inability to switch his linguistic sense of being and affiliation despite knowing that he needs to do so to live in the modern world. While he advises Chungpa to do so, Kim himself could not be an Orientalist Oriental Yankee, lingering between the Sinophone and Anglophone orders rather than transitioning from the one to the other. Yet even the Sinophone order is not something that Kim can naturally claim as he needs to suppress the imperial influence of China on Korea over centuries in order to identify Chinese as his own language and present his identity as a Sinophone Asian. When he seemingly embraces the fate of classical Chinese as his own, Kim naturalizes himself as a subject thoroughly interpellated by Chinese cultural imperialism and engages in an Orientalist logic of undifferentiated and timeless Asia.

Kang leaves it to the reader's imagination as to whether Chungpa will follow Kim's advice and fashion himself as an Orientalist Oriental Yankee. But in the case of his doing so, the roles that his languages will assume are predictable enough. His Asian languages will be used to collect raw data on the East while the organization of the data and its distribution will be carried out in English. An unspoken hierarchy of languages underscores the cultural work assigned to the Orientalist Oriental Yankee, a hierarchy that reflects the different power relations between the Orientals and the Yankees. Neither being an Oriental nor being a Yankee is regarded as natural in *East Goes West*. Rather, Kang poses each as a particular social construction reflective of the times. What would enable the combination of the two into a hyphenated identity for Chungpa is the Korean émigré intellectual's adoption of Orientalism as a way of being and doing. Bilingual brokering in this case is not about translating between two languages but about translating the bilingual brain's capabilities into discrete, socially recognizable units and acts of mediation. For Carlos Bulosan, another bilingual broker who navigated the cultural epistemology of Orientalism, these units and acts of mediation were quite different from Kang.

## THE WORKING-CLASS ILUSTRADO

Bulosan reflects that his lack of formal education compared to Kang may have disadvantaged him in starting his publishing career. Yet his involvement in the cause of Filipino migrant labor and his interest in representing the voices of the dispossessed Filipinos have earned him a firm place both in Asian American studies and in studies of the popular front in American culture.[58] Ironically, what Bulosan viewed as a lack during his time—not having had a formal education—is no longer a hindrance to his place in the canon of American literature. Arguably, Bulosan's identity as a working-class writer has played a role in the interest shown him by critics and scholars in Asian American studies and of the popular front. For Asian American studies, Bulosan is a writer who both represents the lives of Asian migrant laborers and whose life is rooted in that of the Filipino diasporic community in the United States. For studies of the culture of the American Left, the inclusion of Bulosan serves to pluralize the tradition and culture of the popular front.

While class and race have been important keywords in reading the two writers in relation to each other, I focus here on how Bulosan's language background put him in a position where he had to contend with Orientalist prejudices against primitivism. Unlike Kang who resorts to typology in the search for an Asian American identity, Bulosan finds a viable model of this identity in the intellectual tradition of the Filipino elites. By modeling his literary self after the *ilustrados*, Bulosan suggests a historical continuity between the Orientalism of Spanish colonialism and that of US imperialism. Yet even as he borrows from the *ilustrado* tradition and valorizes the power of critique that came with their absorption of Enlightenment values, Bulosan also revises the elitism of this identity by staying close to the experiences of Filipino migrant laborers.

Historically, the term *ilustrado* refers to young Filipino men from affluent families who were educated in Europe—mainly

Spain—during the period of Spanish colonialism. While they were typically of the ruling class, the *ilustrados* were distinguished from "either principalia or elite" through a critical faculty associated with the Enlightenment idea of reason.[59] "The etymology of the word," says Caroline Hau, "plays on the metaphor of light' in the 'enlightenment,' holding up knowledge (via education) against the 'darkness' of ignorance, error, and obscurantism."[60] According to Hau, this aspect of the *ilustrado* makes him not just someone who is "defined sociologically by mere acquisition of wealth, education, or power" but someone whose very political identity lies in a *"critical* stance."[61] Bulosan's attachment to the *ilustrado* tradition and the Enlightenment idea of knowledge as the foundation for social and political change can be seen not only in his repeated evocation of José Rizal as a model in *America Is in the Heart* and in his other writings but also in his frequent use of the trope of enlightenment. Carlos, in *America Is in the Heart*, explicitly evokes this trope when he reflects on his transformation through self-directed book learning: "The darkness that had covered my present life was lifting. I was emerging into sunlight, and I was to know, a decade afterward in America, that this light was not too strong for eyes that had known only darkness and gloom."[62]

Examining Bulosan's inheritance of the ideal of *ilustración* is also to think about his relationship to English through the *ilustrados'* relationship to Spanish. In *East Goes West*, the type of the anticolonial nationalist that Kang explores is based on a model of language-based nationalism. The Chinese intellectual Hsu in Kang's novel is attracted to the idea of a literary movement that would express the sentiments of nationalism using a language that is close the lives of the people being represented. The model of anticolonialism Bulosan draws on has a very different politics of language. According to Caroline Hau and Benedict Anderson, "the efforts of both official and antistate nationalism to create self-consciously language-based political and cultural frameworks for articulating nationness" emerged in the 1960s and '70s in the Philippines.[63] Added to this, the fact that Tagalog became an official language decades after World War II makes it anachronistic to demand a language-based nationalism from Bulosan.[64] In his study of Filipino and Filipino American literature, Martin J. Ponce cautions against what he calls the "impositionist view of English" that fails to adequately account for the creative ways in which Filipino writers have used English.[65] Bulosan's own view on language seems to accord with the critics' views above. He viewed the Philippines as a multilingual country, with English, Spanish, and Tagalog as the languages of literary publishing.[66]

This does not mean, however, that Bulosan was free from the historical baggage of colonial language politics. Megan Thomas suggests that the method of Orientalism employed in Spanish colonial rule over the Philippines was chosen based on the linguistic culture of the Philippines. Whereas philology was used as a method of knowledge production in those parts of the Orient that employed Sanskrit or other ancient languages that were the object of Western fascination, racial anthropology became the method of Orientalism to turn the raw material of Philippines into units of knowledge because the Philippines was considered a "textless" society.[67] The civilizationist hierarchy that held societies based on orality to be inferior to those that were textually based also roughly corresponded to a racial hierarchy that placed the Filipinos below Europeans. In this colonial context, Filipino *ilustrados*, Thomas shows, utilized intellectual traditions of the Spanish colonizers to construct a pre-Hispanic history of the Philippines that would prove its place in civilization. According to Thomas, they resorted to both Orientalist philology and the new science of racial and cultural anthropology and used extant textual material, oral languages, and material culture to create a common origin for multilingualism in the Philippines.[68] From this perspective, the *ilustrado* intellectual tradition is partly constituted by the struggle over the linguistic and cultural capital of representation.

In Bulosan's writings, the recurring themes of literacy and mediation of knowledge and information may be where the language predicament of the *ilustrado* tradition can be seen. The acquisition of literacy for those removed from the circuits of symbolic capital is a hard struggle, and once one enters the realm of enlightened knowledge, she has to figure out the proper role of mediation she will perform with the hard-earned symbolic capital. From this perspective, my definition of literacy follows John Guillory's definition in *Cultural Capital*. In developing a materialist critique of canon formation, Guillory defines literacy "not simply as the capacity to read but as the *systemic regulation of reading and writing.*"[69] From this point of view, Guillory suggests, one can reexamine the assumptions that underwrite the critiques of the canon in English for not including writers of certain social identities. Whereas such critiques of the canon view exclusion as "exclusion from representation," Guillory suggests that what may be more important to think about is exclusion "from access to the *means of cultural production*."[70] Such definition of literacy is useful in thinking about Bulosan as not just a writer who represents the voices of the oppressed Filipinos but a writer who actively engages with the question of a democratic literary culture where participation in the economy of literary production and consumption is not limited to select groups.

As an alternative approach to literacy, Bulosan turns to the lived experiences of Filipino migrant labor as the basis for a critical literacy. While *America Is in the Heart*, his most well-known autobiographical fiction, is replete with the motif of literacy, Bulosan's short stories illustrate his search for an alternative path to literacy most vividly. Oscar Campomanes and Todd Gernes examine the epistolary form and the motif of letter writing in Bulosan as the place where the writer's metafictional accounts of writing and his reflections on mediating reality through the "aestheticized language of the oppressed" can be seen.[71] In "The Story of a Letter," the short story that Campomanes and Gernes examine as an early draft of *America Is in the Heart*, literacy is something that is acquired not in school but within the trans-Pacific circuits of migrant labor. The narrator's father receives a letter in English from his son, Berto, who joined the stream of migrant Filipino laborers headed to the United States. The illiterate father tries to find a translator for Berto's letter in the village but his attempts turn out to be unsuccessful as the older colonial language of Spanish is still viewed as the language of learning in his village. Ultimately, Berto's letter is sent back to the United States, and it becomes the narrator's task to translate his brother's letter for his father. The narrator, like his brother before him, has left the Philippines and has learned English while hospitalized in the United States with a sickness. Yet this arduous process of translation fails to satisfy the father's desire to read Berto's letter. The narrator later finds out when his own letter and translation are returned to him that his father had already passed. The revelation of the content of Berto's letter at the end is anticlimactic: "America is a great country. Tall buildings. Wide good land. The people walking. But I feel sad. I am writing you this hour of my sentimental."[72] Did the father miss much by not having been able to read Berto's letter? The revelation of the content of Berto's letter inevitably raises this question, but Bulosan intimates that this is an impossible question to answer. The lesson of enlightenment in the short story, however, lies not in the content of the letter but how the story of the letter as a whole exposes the exclusion of Filipino peasants from textually based communication and the illusion of the American Dream as an opportunity of socioeconomic mobility for poor Filipinos.

Another short story, "Be American," which E. San Juan Jr., suggests is Bulosan's "most representative work," reimagines the medium of epistolary exchange.[73] The narrator of this short story observes a new immigrant, Consorcio, who arrives in San Francisco as "an illiterate peasant from the vast plains of Luzon," brimming with enthusiasm for the American Dream, gradually learn the reality of limited opportunities and social marginalization for Filipino migrants and transform into an activist of Filipino workers' rights.[74] Such transformation is enabled by his learning "the unwritten law of the nomad," which is how Filipino laborers devise ways of exchanging news and gifts that are not based on the assumption of literacy.[75] Instead of writing letters, the migrant laborers send boxes of produce from wherever they happen to work at the time. "When I received a box of grapes from a friend," says the narrator, "I knew he was working in Stockton. But when it was a crate of lettuce, he was working in Santa Maria or Salinas, depending on the freight mark again."[76] The material products of labor replace words in the system of meaning that governs communication among the Filipino nomads. In addition, communal enjoyment is prioritized over privacy in these exchanges as someone who is not the intended recipient of the mail can still open it and partake in its contents. Consorcio's initiation into the semiotics of Filipino migrant labor marks his transformation from a naïve immigrant who believes that "he make good American citizen" by decking his room with "a cheap edition of the classics, books on science, law and mathematics . . . even . . . some brochures on political and governmental matters" to someone who starts to publish fiery tracts in English "defending the workers and upholding the right and liberties of all Americans, native or foreign born."[77] This Consorcio, who can represent himself and others in public, the narrator calls a "real American."[78] Whereas Kang's prose is marked by a verbosity, an excess of words that draws attention to the relationship between leisure and writing, the leanness of Bulosan's prose style points to the opposite situation where writing is produced despite the lack of leisure.

Even when he ventured alternative ideas of literacy that spoke to the lived experiences of the Filipino migrant laborers, as someone who took up the mantle of the *ilustrado*, Bulosan was keenly aware of the fact that writing and publishing for him entailed a distance between himself and the lives he represented. In other words, Bulosan was well aware of the symbolic capital he had over the Filipino subjects he represented. If Kang continuously alludes to his position as a cultural broker through the figure of the Oriental Yankee in *East Goes West*, Bulosan explicitly acknowledges himself as someone who brokers Filipino folk culture and modern American readers in the essay, "How My Stories Were Written." The essay opens with questions Bulosan received from his readers upon the publication of his first story. "Letters came asking me how I became a writer," Bulosan writes, "pointedly emphasizing the fact that I have a very limited formal education, and why was I writing proficiently in a language which is not my own."[79] In response to such questions that challenge his authority as a writer in the English language, Bulosan constructs a fable of his authorial identity by presenting himself as a translator of a folk sage who, in turn, appears as the repository of Third World culture. Bulosan says as much when he introduces Apo Lacay as "the vast storehouse of rich material with which my childhood world endowed me so generously that I can go on indefinitely writing folkwise stories based on the hard core of reality."[80] In addition to providing the younger generation of Filipinos with a sense of their historical past, which they can use to assess their present, the folk sage also offers a sense of spirituality that stems from knowing one's place in the world. "If the retelling of your stories will give me a little wisdom of the heart," Bulosan confesses, "then I shall have some home again."[81]

While he also reads "How My Stories Were Written" as "a scenario of legitimation, an originary myth," E. San Juan Jr., desists from noting any conflict of interest in Bulosan's self-presentation as a broker of folk knowledge.[82] This is in keeping with his larger argument of Bulosan as a "'Third World' writer" who cannot be interpreted according to what San Juan suggests are the terms of reading Western literature.[83] "Bulosan is different from his EuroAmerican counterpart," San Juan Jr. argues, "because his success in wresting control of the means of representation, the power of textualizing reality, is not a private affair; it cannot be divorced from his people's struggle to enfranchise and represent themselves as a dominated nationality. Bulosan the writer stakes the authorizing voice of the subaltern communities he speaks of, with, and for."[84] From this perspective, the invention of Apo Lacay, the folk sage, who also appears in Bulosan's posthumous

novel of the Huk Rebellion, *The Cry and the Dedication*, is a necessary device "so that the author is conceived of primarily as a transmit-
ter or conveyor of the collective wisdom and history of a people."[85]

Unlike San Juan Jr., I see Bulosan as attuned to the distance
between the writer and the folk sage in the essay, the distance that
necessitates the role of the cultural broker. This is first apparent in
the different symbolic roles assigned to the folk sage and the writer in
the essay. The folk sage is symbolic of an idyllic past ravished by the
avarice of colonialism and modernization; Bulosan, the broker, represents the dialectic of innocence and experience. Despite possessing
all the raw materials for the stories, the folk sage cannot communicate them to an audience that is larger than his fellow villagers. That
task is left to the broker whose facility with the "revitalizing power
of narrative" can mediate the innocent world of the folk sage and the
experienced world outside. Plus, the folk sage does not seem to fully
understand the value of his stories, as can be seen in his constant
undermining of their value: "These are merely the tales of an old and
forgotten man who has lived beyond his time. There are others who
can tell you more fascinating stories of what is happening today."[86]
Because the folk sage lacks the language that is suited to his stories,
it is incumbent on Bulosan to serve as a broker between the folk sage
and modern-day English-speaking readers.

Viewed this way, the similarity between Bulosan the writer cum
broker and the Spanish colonial-era *ilustrados* becomes obvious. Just
as the *ilustrados* used the tools of the colonizers, including "narratives of Orientalism and anthropological sciences" for anticolonial
nationalism, so Bulosan adopts the role of the cultural anthropologist
to preserve Filipino folk culture and to relate its value to non-Filipino
readers.[87] However, what is at stake in Bulosan's discursive appropriation of cultural anthropology is not the objectification of the folk
sage because Bulosan's legitimacy as a writer rests on the reader's
belief of communion between the folk sage and him. Rather, what
belies Bulosan's power of representation in this essay is the question
of ownership over the symbolic capital of folk knowledge. Arguably,
discussing property rights to folklore is inherently tricky business
as folklore is seldom attributed to individual creators and acquires
meaning and significance through oral circulation among members
of a community. Bulosan certainly gestures to the idea of communal ownership over folk knowledge in the essay when the writer and
the folk sage discuss the ownership of the folk stories. When the

bilingual and bicultural narrator, both fluent in the traditional way of life and also experienced in modern life, offers to "retell" the folk sage's stories, the folk sage is struck with gratitude.[88] To this naïve and undemanding folk sage, the narrator's implicit offer of communal ownership is a generous one beyond belief. "You mean it will be your book as well as mine," the folk sage asks in bewilderment. "Your words as well as my words, there in that faraway land, my tales going around to the people? My tales will not be forgotten at last?"[89] In this exchange the distance and distinction between "you" and "I" dissolve into communal ownership. For voluntarily relinquishing any claim to sole ownership over his folk knowledge, the folk sage gets to see the continued life and global transmission of tales that are on the verge of disappearance.

The symbolic economy of folk knowledge that Bulosan creates in the essay relies on the participants' recognition of folklore as valuable knowledge and their good faith that a wide distribution of this knowledge benefits community members. However, it is hard not to notice that such a symbolic economy of folk knowledge is ensconced in the modern capitalist institution of print publishing. Is it still possible to adhere to ideas of communal ownership over narratives of value when the representation of vernacular culture takes place through a field of cultural production, which is based on the notion of intellectual property and to which members of a cultural community have uneven access?

While Bulosan does not answer this question in "How My Stories Were Written," he repeatedly mentions his participation in a modern field of cultural production. His essay, "The Writer as Worker," centrally features a homology between the symbolic economy and the economy of material goods as Bulosan explicitly calls his writings commodities and compares the writer's stories to a laborer's products. Bulosan's homology may seem to go against Fredric Jameson's critique of homology between different structural levels and categories, most explicitly directed at Lucien Goldmann's brand of a sociology of literature, wherein almost a mechanical parallelism is postulated between such different areas such as "social reification, stylistic invention, and narrative or diegetic categories."[90] Jameson, as one may recall, cautions against "assimilat[ing] the 'production' of texts (or in Althusser's version of this homology, the 'production' of new and more scientific concepts) to the production of goods by factory workers."[91] Yet what is an ill-advised homology for a cultural critic turns out to be an effective creative tool for Bulosan in reflecting on how he, as a former worker, has become a writer, against the odds of being an "Oriental" and not having a formal education. The important question to ask regarding Bulosan's homology, then, is not whether it is right or wrong but how it registers the writer's encounter and interactions with a symbolic economy based on his experiences as a worker of color, how, in other words, this homology becomes a crucial rhetorical tool of expression for him.

In the essay, "I Am Not a Laughing Man," Bulosan engages in a gentle self-mockery to show his participation in an economy of symbolic capital that most of the Filipino subjects he represents are excluded from. The essay's ostensible goal is for Bulosan to correct his readers' misreading of him. The essay opens with Bulosan's admission that he is "mad" at how his readers are misreading his work.[92] Whereas he wrote his book *The Laughter of My Father* in a mode of tragedy and intended to communicate the affect of anger, Bulosan's readers attribute to it a "comic spirit," likely a result of viewing the book through an anthropological lens. This tale of mistaken reception, however, soon becomes one of the writer's discovery of writing and publishing as a commercial enterprise: "Five days later I received a telegram that the *Saturday Evening Post* bought my article for nearly a thousand dollars. Then I was really mad. Why didn't somebody tell me that it was easy to make money in America?"[93] Bulosan's discovery of a publishing market is accompanied by the accumulation of different kinds of anger, starting with the anger over the unfair working conditions of Filipino laborers, which then morphs into the confused anger at the willingness of the American publishing industry to consume his stories of Filipino pain and suffering. The loop of misreading proves to be a productive and lucrative one as the writer derives the impetus for writing by penning responses to the misreadings and also profits from the sales of these responses. At this point, the admission that he is "mad" seems more ironic than literal. Bulosan suggests that the writer has no control over the literary market or his reception as even the attempt to rectify his mistaken critical reception has a payoff. The manuscript he writes "to tell the world I am not a laughing man," the "600-page autobiography" he completed in "28 days" is immediately accepted for publication by a New York publisher: "What a life!" Bulosan proclaims, "Here I was, not yet thirty, and already a 600-page autobiography."[94] Through the element of chance Bulosan dismantles his own homology and reinstates the distance and separateness between the capitalist economy of farm work or factory labor and the symbolic economy of cultural capital. At the same time, he leaves the readers with the lingering question of what kind of chance, exactly, is this chance that buoys him and allows him to escape from the fate of manual labor.

The image of competition for symbolic capital that Bulosan includes at the end of the essay, in particular, both complicates Bulosan's suggestion that his literary career is just based on chance and reveals the schism in his self-claimed role as the cultural broker of the Filipino vernacular. The essay ends an image of a duel between Bulosan as an emerging minority writer and established American writers. Saying that he was "sore" at William Saroyan and Thomas Wolfe, Bulosan bases his creative energy on the desire to outdo these writers. "Who do they think they are anyway?" he asks.[95] If these writers were part of his reading list before, when he was an apprentice writer, now his ambition is to outperform them at their craft, a postcolonial resentment of sorts. This image may not be so strange if it were not for the stark contrast it forms with the harmonious relationship with the folk sage Bulosan constructs in "How My Stories Were Written." It is almost as if this is a competition between two countries or two races, and what possible dissension within the team needs to be suppressed for Bulosan to come out as winner in the competition. The uncomfortable question of who is representing whom and how to account for the difference in power between the cultural broker and the culturally brokered refuses to go away even at a moment when Bulosan envisions his rise in the symbolic economy of American letters. Or maybe it is because it is a moment when he is envisioning such that this uncomfortable question rears its head. The social types of the working-class *ilustrado* and the Orientalist Oriental Yankee overlap at this moment as both Bulosan and Kang are embroiled in the politics of Asian racial difference in interwar literary publishing that sanctions some cultural brokering over others based on which strand of Orientalism factors in the reception of these writers' publications.

While Bulosan seems confident in the translatability of Filipino folk tales and in his role as a cultural broker in his essays, his view on cultural brokering is much more ambivalent in *America Is in the Heart*, presumably the "600-page autobiography" he completed in "28 days." A rare passage in which Bulosan uses words from his native Ilocano suggests a radically different approach to communication from the good-faith approach to cultural brokering. In Buelton,

Carlos works for a French immigrant who has become the business owner of a hotel. Despite the fact that he has achieved economic success and also established a family in the United States, the French immigrant pines for home, advising Carlos to go "home to [his] islands before it is too late."[96] The French immigrant's nostalgia is contagious and Carlos is suddenly struck with a bout of nostalgia: "*The sound of home*! Would I also someday yearn for the sound of home? Would I also cry for the sad songs of the peasants in Mangusmana? And before I realized it, I began talking in our dialect: '*Ama! Ina! Manong! Ading! Sicayo*!'"[97] "The sound of home" is associated with an essentialized peasant identity. Contrary to his claim to be "talking in our dialect," Carlos utters a series of Ilocano words that all refer to kinship ties (father, mother, older brother, younger sibling). The discrepancy between the declaration in English and the action in Ilocano here brings into high relief the limited linguistic and cultural reach of his English-speaking readership who cannot comprehend Ilocano, not just the meaning of the words but the language-world of Ilocano. The question of whether readers who cannot understand Ilocano, who cannot notice the difference in "talking in our dialect" and uttering a series of Ilocano kinship words, can understand the depth of Carlos's longing for belonging and closeness is open to question in the text. While the sudden and uncontrollable burst of bilingualism in the narrative occasions the need for Carlos's cultural brokering for the reader, Bulosan leaves the Ilocano words untranslated. There are no English equivalents that can successfully broker the deep longing for home Carlos feels in his state of isolation, and cultural brokering is temporarily suspended in the narrative.

Both Younghill Kang and Carlos Bulosan met with difficulty publishing after World War II. Kang actively participated in US war efforts, both in the Pacific War and in the Korean War, only to be disillusioned at the idea of United States–led democracy in Korea afterward; Bulosan faced a plagiarism allegation, which was settled by the publisher but after which he ceased to publish at the rate he used to. Their late career difficulties are indicative of the challenges they faced as early Asian migrant writers brokering worlds that were rapidly changing, and prefigure some of the challenges of postwar bilingual brokering. When Bulosan published the short story, "The End of War," in the *New Yorker* in 1944, he was accused of plagiarizing Guido D'Agostino's "The Dream of Angelo Zara." D'Agostino's story features an Italian immigrant, Angelo Zara, who has a dream about Benito Mussolini offering him a high-paying job. As Zara tells his friends his dream, each claim it for his own, in the end leaving Zara wondering who owns the dream. Similarly, in "The End of War," Bulosan offers the story of Pascaul Fidel, who dreams about the surrender of Japan and Germany in World War II, and tells his friends about the dream. Each friend subsequently claims the dream as his. In his detailed account of Bulosan's plagiarism case, Augusto Espiritu says that while "Bulosan *applied* D'Agostino's pattern to the West Coast Filipino American experience, perhaps creating a more meaningful story," he "lapsed into 'adapting' a copyrighted work." Espiritu also points out that the practice of "collect[ing] and adapt[ing] legends, myths, and romances" was common among Filipino intellectuals who were keen on constructing a national culture.[98] Viewed from the perspective that collaborative and adaptive practices of writing were common among Filipino intellectuals, Bulosan's being implicated in a plagiarism allegation could be read as how the modern institution of intellectual property was not able to account for Bulosan's approach to cultural brokering. Whereas he might have harbored a communitarian view of languages and literatures for creative use, the parameters of cultural brokering were established in relation to expectations of intellectual property in the interwar publishing industry. His brush with copyright law crystallizes the problematic relationship between cultural brokering and symbolic capital that Bulosan grappled with but never quite resolved in his writings.

Unlike Bulosan who passed in 1954, Kang lived through the height of the Cold War, leaving behind some documentation on the writer's disillusionment with US liberalism. During the Pacific War and the US occupation of Korea, Kang worked for the US military in various capacities to aid US war efforts in Asia, offering his services in translation and language-training and later becoming chief of publications of the United States Army Military Government in Korea.[99] Some twenty years after the US occupation of Korea, Kang's views on US policies and interventions in Asia show sheer disappointment and unadulterated anger, far removed from his earlier enthusiasm for US liberalism. In a brief foreword to a book by Bong-Youn Choy on Korean history published in 1971, Kang delivers what is probably his most scathing critique of the United States, calling the US intervention in Korea "a so-called police action" that only nominally supported "self-determination and democratic processes" and deploring the US use of nuclear bombs in the Pacific War.[100] No longer a cultural broker, Kang engages in what is his probably most trenchant critique of the US liberalism. The angry voice in this foreword perhaps registers a belated realization on Kang's part that his bilingualism had been used as an instrument of the state and that this state is not a guarantor of democracy.

Writing before the emergence of a cultural politics of bilingualism that involved state-led efforts at educational and policy reforms, Kang and Bulosan prefigure some of the questions on the evaluation of bilingualism and racial difference that would appear acutely in the works of postwar Asian American and Latino writers. As "Oriental" writers during the era of Asian exclusion, they faced similar predicaments of exclusion from national culture. At the same time, the different ways in which they were affected by Orientalism also bring into high relief colonial histories that predate Asian exclusion. The imperial rubrics of Sinophone and Hispanophone became the asymmetrical, uneven, and confusing legacies within which Kang and Bulosan had to construct their identities as American writers writing in English. Bilingual brokering, for Kang and Bulosan, took place at the interstices of the institutions of legal exclusion and selective cultural inclusion. With the waning of institutional legal exclusion in the postwar years, literary and cultural bilingual brokering would seldom encounter racial difference in terms of legal exclusion; yet instead of disappearing from significance, racial difference continued to influence bilingual brokering as bilingual personhood became a rallying ground for reexamining the American dream.

CHAPTER TWO

# Bilingual Personhood and the American Dream

In *America Is in the Heart*, Bulosan shows the decline of Carlos's family in the Philippines when the family mishandles their investment in their son Macario's education. On the surface, Carlos seems to endorse American-style education compared to the Spanish one, which "was something that belonged exclusively to the rulers and to some fortunate natives affluent enough to go to Europe."[1] Yet they actually discover that the "free education" introduced by the United States comes at a steep price when their family, like "every family who had a son, pooled its resources" to put Macario, the chosen son, through school.[2] Carlos's father mortgages the family land on egregious terms based on a calculus of investment and profit. While the educational investment requires sacrifice in the present, it will pay off in the end when Macario enters the professional class by becoming a teacher after his schooling and elevates his entire family's socioeconomic status. The family's investment in human capital, however, turns out to be disastrous as Macario fails to meet the family's expectations of becoming a stable member of the professional class and the father becomes a sharecropper after losing his land.

Even before the *Brown v. Board of Education* decision in the mid-twentieth century, education was viewed by many people of color as a crucial means of social and economic uplift. It would not be a stretch to say that the legal briefs on educational inequality during Jim Crow well precede the economist Gary Becker's notion of human capital, which he proposed in 1964 to econometrically assess the value of investment in education. While the most well-known and widely

accepted narrative of educational equality in postwar American liberalism is the progression from segregation to integration, what these
terms mean in relation to a substantial meaning of equality has not
always been clear. In Asian American educational history, for example, the implementation of integration in public schools sometimes
did not get rid of the problem of the lack of support for cultural and
language difference. When *Brown v. Board of Education* made the
integration of public schools a state mandate in California, Chinese
American parents opposed the busing of their children out of Chinatown to schools with white-majority students in a 1971 lawsuit on the
basis that they feared their children would lose their home language
and culture.[3] While the historical path of integration drowned out
these parents' concerns, a similar set of concerns came up again only
a couple of years later in 1973 when Chinese American parents in San
Francisco sued the school district for inadequately supporting their
Chinese-dominant children's language needs in an English-speaking
environment.[4] On the one hand, the Chinese American ambivalence
about English-language public schooling may seem to go against the
ideals of racially integrated classrooms, so crucial to the era of civil
rights struggles.[5] Yet, it also taps into complex questions of what education is expected to offer minorities in a multiracial society with a
vexed history of race.

In this chapter I turn to the debates on public bilingualism to
examine the rhetorical and social construction of bilingual personhood as part of the American Dream. If my discussion of bilingualism
in the previous chapter focused on the colonial histories underwriting language difference's translation into a cultural asset, I anchor
my use of the term bilingualism in this chapter in how it was used
in policy debates. With the debates on bilingual education and bilingualism as civil right in the 1960s and '70s, race was no longer the
sole determining factor of national or civic identity in the juridical
sense as it was the case with Asian exclusion. These debates, rather,
show how cultural factors, such as language, entered the realm of
politics through legislation, litigation, and activism as key compo-
nents of defining American identity and values. On the surface, the
debates became bipolar. The opposition to public bilingualism argued
for English as the one and only national language; the advocacy of
public bilingualism contended that multilingualism did not diminish
the value of English and that it was concordant with the tradition of
American pluralism. At its most polarizing moment, in the 1980s and

'90s, these debates took on the traits of the culture wars, where English Only and English Plus mapped onto the, respectively, conservative and multicultural camps.[6] Instead of rehearsing the well-covered terrain of the bipolarity of these debates, I examine the understanding of language through the lens of possessive individualism as a common thread in the construction of bilingual personhood in this chapter. Doing so requires an attention to the parameters of discussing public bilingualism, which, in turn, shows how embedded the American Dream is in an idea of personhood rooted in possessive individualism. The following tales of two classrooms, seemingly at the opposite ends of the spectrum of attitudes on public bilingualism, illustrate my point.

The first is a fictional classroom in a short story by a Puerto Rican American writer, Nicholasa Mohr. In "The English Lesson," Lali and William, two young Puerto Ricans who move to the Lower East Side of New York City from the island in the 1970s to work at a diner in the Spanish-speaking neighborhood, attend an English-as-a-Second-Language course. The students in this evening class, including Lali and William, attend the class with the hope that fluency in English will aid them in attaining the American Dream. The name of the class, Basic English, suggests Mrs. Hamma's class is carrying on a cultural project of Anglo-Americanism that dates back to 1929 when C. K. Ogden first came up with a carefully selected vocabulary of 850 English words that he deemed essential to basic communication and that he named "Basic English."[7] Ogden's aim in designing Basic English, Yunte Huang notes, was to "give everyone a second, or international language" that was easy to learn.[8] As a descendant of German immigrants herself, Mrs. Hamma views herself as a dutiful gatekeeper cum helper for new immigrants. In Mrs. Hamma's class, English as lingua franca bears the dream of upward mobility as newcomers to America view fluency in English as key to socioeconomic success.

The second classroom, that of Mrs. Dolores Earles, is probably less familiar to many readers than Mrs. Hamma's. In "The Invisible Minority: Report of the NEA-Tucson Survey on the Teaching of Spanish to the Spanish-Speaking," a 1966 booklet that documented the educational hardships faced by Chicanos, Mrs. Earles's first grade class at Nye Elementary School in Laredo, Texas, appears as a model of bilingual instruction.[9] After singing the song, "Teensy Weensy Spider," twice, once in English and once in Spanish, Mrs. Earles asks her class, consisting of both Anglo and Mexican American students, "Wouldn't it be fun

if we could each be two persons? How many of you think you would like
to be two persons?"[10] Apparently, all the first graders in Mrs. Earles's
class think it would be great to be two persons, a feat that Mrs. Earles
teaches them is accomplishable by "speaking two languages."[11]

Mrs. Earles's class forms a sharp contrast to Mrs. Hamma's. Mrs.
Hamma's class is made up of working students, most of whom are
adults, whereas Mrs. Earles's class is composed of children. While
language's function as an instrument of communication is emphasized in Mrs. Hamma's class, viewing language as play is a big part
of learning in Mrs. Earles's class. The pursuit of English overshad-
ows any encouragement of bilingualism in Mrs. Hamma's class, but
in Mrs. Earles's class bilingualism is presented as the path to a desirable life. These two classrooms and the ideas of linguistic personhood
befitting an American citizen they convey were at the heart of the
postwar cultural politics of bilingualism. It is worth emphasizing the
centrality of education to the cultural politics of bilingualism as a site
of subject formation. While they differ on the value of bilingualism,
both classes assume that developing one's capacities—one's preter-
natural property—is what is expected of liberal subjects and the goal
of public education. When one considers that the thesis of the possessive individual—which Macpherson argues is central to the tradition
of liberalism stretching back to Thomas Hobbes and John Locke—
posits that a free individual is someone whose first property lies in
his person and in his capacities, both classes that respectively uphold
English fluency and bilingualism as the ideal linguistic existence for
language minorities may be seen as sharing the investment in possessive individualism as a presupposition.

In the following I examine the different logics of the relations
between linguistic personhood and the American Dream through the
three stages of racial liberalism, cultural pluralism, and multiculturalism. The different relations that link language, personhood, and the
American Dream in the following are not historically discrete in the
sense that they often coexist synchronically despite varying degrees of
influence and reach. While the three stages follow a roughly chrono-
logical arc, I am less interested in historical periodization than locat-
ing the historically situated views of liberal personhood that inform
the cultural views on public bilingualism. Doing so I believe helps one
go beyond the binary positions on public bilingualism in the realm
of policy and brings one closer to the lived truth of bilingualism for
many Asian Americans and Latinos.

## ENGLISH AS THE COLORBLIND LANGUAGE OF THE
## AMERICAN DREAM IN RACIAL LIBERALISM

One of the most vocal, high-profile opponents of public bilingualism during the English Only movement in the 1980s and '90s was Samuel I. Hayakawa, former president of San Francisco State University and later US senator from California. While it has mostly been discussed in the context of late-twentieth-century nativism, Hayakawa's argument for making English the official language of the United States is best understood in light of his earlier, mid-twentieth-century work as a linguist. Hayakawa's discussion of the American Dream and the middleman minority in the 1949 edition of his most well-known book, *Language in Thought and Action*, in particular, powerfully communicates that language occupies a central place in his vision of the American Dream.[12] Initially written for a first-year English course at the University of Wisconsin where Hayakawa taught, *Language in Thought and Action* purports to be a textbook for liberal arts education. It is intended to teach readers how to think and speak critically by understanding the nature of language. Moreover, it suggests that such understanding is crucial for citizen-subjects of a liberal democratic society, which according to Hayakawa should not be organized by race or ethnicity but by other measures of distinction, such as education. The popularity of the book in no small measure has to do with the mid-twentieth century ethos of racial liberalism, which Jodi Melamed characterizes as "a formally antiracist, liberal-capitalist modernity under the management of US global ascendancy."[13] By suggesting that the measure of a citizen's worth would not be such arbitrary factors as the color of one's skin or one's heritage but meritocratic factors such as education, a telling sign of which is how one uses language, Hayakawa participated enthusiastically in racial liberalism with his book.[14]

While the book's argument on race as fiction was embraced by African American leaders during its time, *Language in Thought and Action* has been criticized by contemporary critics for expounding a view of race that divorces it from material realities and conflicts and reduces it to a matter of individual prejudice.[15] In the book, Hayakawa suggests that racism occurs when people fail to recognize that "there is no 'necessary connection' between words and what they stand for."[16] When someone, on hearing "Mr. Miller is a *Jew*," expects Mr. Miller to conform to the stereotype of Jewish people as mercenary, she is demonstrating a primitive logic of thinking that there is a "mystic connection" between the abstract word "Jew" and the particular Mr. Miller.[17] Racism is due to such primitive thinking, or untrained moves of the mind. (Interestingly, Hayakawa recommends learning a foreign language to raise awareness of the arbitrary relationship between signifier and signified!) The inability to distinguish between different levels of abstraction and between words and things, according to Hayakawa, attests to "areas of infantilism" in one's life, and the person who is confined to such errors lives in "a delusional world," where "all 'Jews' are out to cheat you; all 'capitalists' are overfed tyrants, smoking expensive cigars and gnashing their teeth at labor unions."[18] One could easily infer from Hayakawa's explanation that people who believe in stereotypes of minorities are uneducated and immature and that education is the best way to address racism.

Compared to the lessons on language like the above in *Language in Thought and Action*, the section entitled "The Society behind Our Symbols" is something of an aberration. In a rare moment of acknowledging the reality of race and ethnicity as palpable forces of social organization in the United States, Hayakawa delivers an origin story of racism that deviates somewhat from his dominant view of racism as irrational prejudice in this section. Using the example of anti-Semitism as the prototype of racism, he briefly assigns the cause of racism not to prejudice but to economic competition when he suggests that antagonism toward middleman minorities, or those he calls "marginal businessmen," is at the root of racism.[19] While sociological studies of the middleman minority view this group as emerging in societies with rigid and binary hierarchies, Hayakawa's definition is more expansive.[20] He defines the marginal businessman as "one who does not belong in the *established* profitable business of a community. In the United States, he is often a fairly recent immigrant or a member of a minority group."[21]

For Hayakawa, the United States is a land of perpetual middleman minorities, with different newcomer immigrant groups occupying the position before moving into more "established" businesses. As such, the American Dream, for Hayakawa, means that the marginal businessman can move up the socioeconomic ladder. In his own words, "the fact that marginal businessmen need not remain marginal forever is *the* great fact about America."[22] Hayakawa even assimilates African Americans into the model of the marginal businessman with his observation that "at the present time, many Negroes in Chicago have become, and many more are becoming, successful businessmen, starting in marginal enterprises."[23] Such an assimilative move on Hayakawa's part serves the ideological function of imposing a history of immigration onto African Americans while suppressing the history of black enslavement. Instead of reexamining such ideals as "equality" and "freedom" in light of the reality of racial discrimination, Hayakawa instead deduces the meaning of equality and freedom from the premise of socioeconomic uplift. In other words, the success of some people to achieve socioeconomic uplift is taken as a sign that there is "equality of opportunity" or "free enterprise system."[24] Within such a schema, the meaning and significance of liberalism is reduced to economic liberalism as equality or freedom becomes concepts in the service of ensuring the upward mobility of marginal businessmen.[25]

In this lesson that strangely deviates from Hayakawa's tendency to sever semiotics from its social context and links the semiotics of race with a structural and systemic question of racialization, I think one can see inklings of his attachment to English as a colorblind language of individual socioeconomic mobility and national unity, which becomes fully manifest in Hayakawa's later years as an ardent supporter of English Only. With English presumably being the dominant language of business, the middleman minority needs to first and foremost acquire English to take advantage of the socioeconomic mobility structurally available to him. Furthermore, English has to be a colorblind language to guarantee formal equality to those who avail themselves of the language and the opportunities it provides. In ways more than one, Hayakawa's understanding of the American Dream is what the linguist Joshua Fishman holds accountable for making bilingualism into a liability in the first place, as I show later. Hayakawa embraces the tendency of possessive individualism to reduce social relations to "a series of relations between sole proprietors, i.e. a series of market relations."[26] As the social position of the middleman minority is overdetermined by his economic function, there is no social justification or public incentive for the maintenance or cultivation of bilingualism. Bilingualism, in other words, is an entirely private affair.

For all his insistence on English as a colorblind language, however, an anecdote Hayakawa includes in *Language in Thought and Action* strangely belies that view by showing that English is inevitably associated with his racially marked identity because it alone can prove his social belonging. Like all the other sections in the book, "The

Value of Unoriginal Remarks" has the form of a lecture, but unlike the other sections, it is also a personal story. Hayakawa narrates the story of finding himself in a small train station in an unfamiliar city, the only Asian person among white Americans right after the bombing of Pearl Harbor.[27] The anecdote is meant to serve as an illustration of the significance of what Hayakawa calls "the presymbolic uses of language," or "noise."[28] The function of presymbolic language is not to communicate information but to fulfill the social function of decreasing tension among strangers, creating sympathy and affinity, and building a sense of togetherness. In this story, written in the third person, Hayakawa shows how he approached a white American couple with a baby at the train station and successfully made small talk so that the couple ended up not only ceasing to look at him suspiciously but also inviting him home for dinner. On top of successfully influencing the couple in a direction favorable to him, Hayakawa is also able to avoid racial isolation as "the other people in the station, seeing the writer in conversation with people who *didn't* look suspicious, ceased to pay any attention to him and went back to reading their papers and staring at the ceiling."[29]

While the linguistic lesson of the chapter is unmistakably that talk for talk's sake, or small talk, facilitates and improves social relations, the story is startling in the way it draws attention to racial survival through linguistically blending in. His choice of the third person to refer to himself in this lecture brings into high relief the alienation of the person who is racially out of place. "He became aware," Hayakawa writes, "as time went on that other people waiting in the station were staring at him suspiciously and feeling uneasy about his presence."[30] Simultaneously creating distance between Hayakawa the writer and Hayakawa the subject of the story, the third person also creates the impression of Hayakawa being on the outside looking in on the situation, out of his body that is the cause of the problem to start with. Sympathy is the magic affect in this story that dissolves the tension. Starting with the innocuous topic of the weather and moving on to a compliment on the child—both topics that the speaker knows will build fellow feeling between himself and the white American man—Hayakawa finally seizes the chance to prove he is on the American side when the man asks him his opinion on who will win the war, the United States or Japan: "I don't know any more than I read in the papers. (This was true.) But the way I figure it, I don't see how the Japanese, with their lack of coal and steel and oil and their limited industrial capacity, can ever beat a powerfully industrialized nation like the United States."[31] In Hayakawa's self-notation, this answer to the white American's question is "neither original nor well-informed" for it was just a regurgitation of what he read in the newspapers and heard on the radio. "But," Hayakawa goes on to say, "because [radio commentators and editorial writers were saying exactly the same thing], the remark sounded familiar and was on the right side, so that it was easy to agree with."[32] The erasure of Hayakawa's individuality seems almost complete at this point. He is excruciatingly unoriginal.

This exchange proves a turning point in Hayakawa's conversation with the man, as the conversation takes on a more personal tone from there on, with the white American asking after Hayakawa's family—both his parents and his two sisters are in Japan during the time of the war—and sympathizing with his pain of being apart from them. From a suspicious "enemy alien," Hayakawa's status changes to a fellow human being in the eyes of the white American man. While this is one small lecture in the book, it is quite revealing of what Hayakawa values in the acts of learning how to use language. Using language is not about expressing one's authenticity but about erasing one's individuality so that one can assume the position of the universal individual. For someone who is racially marked like Hayakawa, the benefits of such erasure are obvious. He can become an "Everyman," albeit in this case, the morality tale is not about Christianity but about liberal individualism. In a footnote, Hayakawa comments that he was not purposefully using language in this situation, that "he was simply groping, as anyone else might do, for a way to relieve his own loneliness and discomfort in the situation."[33] It is in hindsight that he sees what happened as an example of the "value of unoriginal remarks." The value of social conversation in this instance, however, is more than what Hayakawa makes it out to be for it is not so much improved sociality that he achieves through his linguistic skill here but survival as a racially marked man. Hayakawa may want to show the universalism of language and the human heart. Yet what the story actually brings into high relief is the particularity of Hayakawa's "color."

The genealogy of the argument for English Only in the late twentieth century can be traced back to the logic of racial liberalism in the mid-twentieth century. Samuel Hayakawa's intellectual formation in racial liberalism offers an instructive view on his deep-seated resistance to exploring languages other than English as having any public value or presence. Yet Hayakawa's vision of democracy lacked a thick notion of equality that could extend beyond his view of liberalism as individual economic advancement to make a substantial case for political liberalism. As I discuss below, the debates on public bilingualism, most notably on bilingual education, directly contested the lack of political representation for language minorities even as the most appealing argument on behalf of public bilingualism was based on a rationale of *homo oeconomicus*.

## THE STRIFE FOR BILINGUALISM, HUMAN CAPITAL, AND CULTURAL PLURALISM

The political representation of language minorities that started to be seen in the 1960s indexed a big shift in the vision of the American Dream, especially as it relates to language difference. Bilingual education was attuned to substantial, as opposed to formal, equality and was optimistic about the prospects of striving for substantial equality in education. One can easily tell what kind of break from the past bilingual education marked by recalling Benjamin Franklin's famous invective against the German-speaking population in Pennsylvania. He warned that if the number of Germans who refused to assimilate grew, then "all the advantages we [the English-speaking settlers] have will not, in My Opinion, be able to preserve our language, and even our government will become precarious."[34] Here I focus on how the strife for public bilingualism, as seen through the debates on bilingual education, was based on an idea of language as human capital that intersected well with the ethos of cultural pluralism and the revival of interest in ethnicity in the 1960s.

Bilingual education was passed into law in 1968 as part of the Elementary and Secondary Education Act (ESEA) of 1965, the largest educational reform of twentieth century. The Bilingual Education Act passed the House and the Senate without much resistance after it was proposed and was attached to ESEA as Title VII. The scope of the Act was small. It made it possible to "provide federal funds for 'exemplary pilot or demonstration projects in bilingual and bicultural education in a variety of settings'" based on the assumption that classroom instruction that was solely in English was not sufficient in guaranteeing the equal educational opportunities for non- or limited-English-speaking students.[35] Given the support the bill received in Congress and the limited action entailed in the law, one may wonder what made bilingual education into such a divisive topic in subsequent decades and a target of attack as identity politics.

To understand the legal support for bilingual education, though, one needs to go back a little in time to *Brown v. Board of Education* of 1954 and examine how it ushered in a new way of approaching equality under the law. "Does segregation of children in public schools solely on the basis of race, even though the physical facilities and other 'tangible' factors may be equal, deprive the children of the minority group of equal educational opportunities?" Justice Warren who wrote the opinion of the Supreme Court in the *Brown* decision asked before summarily answering, "we believe that it does."[36] The Supreme Court in the *Brown* decision did not stop at looking at equality simply in formal terms but took into account the symbolic meaning of segregation and its consequences, what the Court called "intangible considerations."[37] This approach to equality as not just formal sameness but as accounting for the harms of institutional racism was evoked in another Supreme Court decision in 1971 when the court ruled in favor of the language minority students in *Lau v. Nichols*, a lawsuit filed by a number of Chinese American students with little to no English proficiency in the Unified San Francisco School District, including Kinney Kinmon Lau, against Alan Nichols, who was then president of the San Francisco Board of Education.[38] In reference to the laws under the Bilingual Education Act, the plaintiffs argued that "laws enacted by both Congress and California State Legislature" required the school to offer them assistance in learning English through bilingual teachers.[39] In language that echoed the *Brown* decision two decades earlier, the *Lau* court decided that "there is no equality of treatment merely by providing students with the same facilities, textbooks, teachers and curriculum; for students who do not understand English are effectively foreclosed from any meaningful education."[40] In following the *Brown* court's interpretation of equality that equality of "tangible factors," such as "physical facilities," is not tantamount to equal educational opportunities and in finding the Unified San Francisco School District "in violation of the equal educational opportunities provision of the Civil Rights Act of 1964," the *Lau* court established a civil rights jurisprudence in regards to bilingualism.[41]

In social and educational histories of bilingualism in the United States, the story of bilingualism's emergence as part of a civil-rights jurisprudence is emphasized. This is understandable given how juridical representation and equality before the law was often at the center of social justice struggles in the second half of the twentieth century. Yet the focus on legal representation can occlude the complex relations among language, advantage or disadvantage, and cultural capital that were at work in the debates on bilingual education. While bolstered by the juridical decisions like the *Lau* decision above, the advocacy for public bilingualism actually involved vexed negotiations of how bilingual personhood relates to the image of the liberal person in the American Dream.

A brief look at the ambivalent meaning of "bilingual" in Congressional Hearings on the Bilingual Education Act (S. 428) shows this well. Many scholars writing on bilingualism in the United States have noted that "bilingual education" in the title of the Bilingual Education Act is something of a misnomer since these are "bills that turn out to mean something like 'help for the linguistically disabled.'"[42] The implication of bilingualism as "a euphemism for 'linguistically handicapped'" is confounding to scholars who do not see bilingualism as a deficiency.[43] Yet the use of the term to designate federally supported educational programs for language minorities aptly reflects the popular definition of bilingualism as a linguistic handicap in the mid-twentieth century, something that the linguist Einar Haugen points out in a 1972 essay on the stigmata of bilingualism.[44] The duality of bilingualism as linguistic handicap in popular usage and as a common linguistic phenomenon in academic usage consistently appears in the Congressional Hearings of 1967.

On the one hand, the popular view of bilingualism as a handicap allowed it to be part of the discussions on educational reform that newly came to understand disadvantage as a social construction reflecting structural inequalities and sought remedies. Historian Adam Nelson shows how "disadvantage," which connoted social circumstances unfavorable to learning in schools, was linked with "disability" in the sense of learning impediments students embodied around this time.[45] Liberal reform in education in the 1960s was very much about identifying the social circumstances of disadvantage and affirmatively addressing the disabilities in students' learning that resulted from disadvantage. And bilingualism fit the bill of both disadvantage and disability at this time. It was used in reference to Spanish speakers in neighborhoods of concentrated poverty, making it possible for legislators to turn to bilingual education as a way of addressing the specific needs of their Spanish-speaking constituency.[46]

Its associations with "untold dangers of retardation, intellectual impoverishment, schizophrenia, anomie, alienation" also made it a likely disability in terms of school performance.[47]

On the other hand, what made bilingual education appealing to many participants of the Congressional Hearings was not bilingualism as a disadvantage or disability but as a resource and human capital, not bilingualism as it was but what it could be. The linguist Joshua Fishman's testimony at the Hearings potently illustrates this hopeful future directive placed on bilingualism. A sociolinguist who had worked extensively on ethnic languages in the United States, Fishman directed the three-year-long Language Resources Project funded by the US Office of Education, which resulted in an 1800-page report published in 1964.[48] While the findings of the project contained many strands of thoughts and analyses, Fishman's recommendations to the Congress emphasized language as a resource and argued that whatever stigma of bilingualism existed was due to poor management:

> The recommendations advanced here are derived from the point of
> view that bilingual language-maintenance [sic] in the United States
> is desirable, in that the non-English language resources of American
> minority groups have already helped meet part of our urgent national
> need for speakers of various non-English languages, and that these
> resources can be reinforced and developed so as to do so; that is, to
> meet this urgent need, to a much greater extent in the future. These
> recommendations are also derived from an awareness that while com-
> petence in two languages can be a decided *asset* to those who have
> this command—indeed, most language learning in and out of schools
> is based on just such an assumption—the bilingualism of hundreds
> of thousands, probably millions, of Americans is viewed as a *liability*
> in their lives, and this for no reason inherent in the nature of bilin-
> gualism per se. It is our treatment of bilinguals and of bilingualism
> that brings this sad state of affairs into being, and, therefore, it is this
> treatment that must be altered. Finally, in the realm of sheer practi-
> cality, it is obvious that our national resources of native non-English
> language competence have long been allowed—even encouraged—to
> languish and disappear at the very time that unprecedented efforts
> and sums were and are being spent to improve and increase the
> teaching of "foreign" languages in the Nation's schools and colleges.
> The recommendations that follow aim to eliminate this wasteful
> ambivalence.[49]

Fishman made a powerful argument on behalf of bilingual education with his resource-management approach to languages. If the nation's attitude to bilingualism to date could be characterized as "wasteful ambivalence," now it was time to switch to an economic mode of managing bilingualism for maximum productivity.[50]

Fishman constructed a narrative for his audience that was based on an emergent recognition of bilingualism as what Pierre Bourdieu calls symbolic capital, as that which is "unrecognized as capital and recognized as legitimate competence, as authority exerting an effect of (mis)recognition."[51] "After many generations of neglect and apathy," Fishman argued, "American speakers of non-English languages have, of late, become objects of more positive attention than has commonly been their lot in most American communities."[52] If language minorities have been considered "objects of curiosity" before, he continued, "they are now frequently viewed as commanding a rare commodity, a skill which has come to be recognized as a valuable asset for the country."[53] Although he never mentions it during his testimony at the Hearings, Fishman's view of bilingualism as commodity aligns well with the view that the value of education can be assessed through the lens of human capital presented by his contemporary, the economist Gary Becker, only a few years earlier in 1964.[54] Whereas education, in the tradition of the Western humanities, has been discussed in terms of the growth and maturation of a person to come to terms with the world around him—the idea of *Bildung*—Becker made it possible to assess the value of education through investments and returns with the notion of human capital. In its implications, it overlaps significantly with Bourdieu's notion of cultural capital, although Bourdieu suggests that human capital is more narrowly focused on capital in the economic sense whereas cultural capital encompasses the economic practices of such social relations that are not reducible to material capital such as "the domestic transmission of cultural capital" from parents to children.[55]

Fishman's idea that bilingualism could be a valuable component of human capital was a marked contrast from the popular view of bilingualism as a disability. It may be instructive here to turn to another linguist's observations on language minorities in the United States to better understand how this drastic change was possible. While his 1977 study, *The American Bilingual Tradition*, is primarily based on the history of European immigration to the United States and focused on European immigrant groups, Heinz Kloss includes some poignant remarks on how language and race function in the United States. Unlike Hayakawa who only focused on assimilation into English as the path toward inclusion and socioeconomic mobility, Kloss suggests that language minorities can build social, cultural, and economic capital through their heritage language. In fact, he states that "foreign-speaking minorities can achieve equal status with the English-speaking majority groups only when they are able to cultivate their own language through separate public or private institutions," emphasizing a form of parallel development between ethnic groups and the Anglo-American majority.[56] According to Kloss, however, this form of parallel development is not available for racial minorities as "the struggle of racial groups has little to do with language differences" and is due to institutional racism and segregated schools in particular.[57] This is why Kloss does not include the "ethnic groups [that] differ from Anglo-Americans by both language and race" in his study of bilingualism in the United States for they constitute "a difficult and tense double polarity."[58] In advancing the idea of bilingualism as a valuable component of human capital, Fishman recognizes the same value of investment in heritage language Kloss saw. Cultivated properly, foreign languages can become symbolic capital parallel to English. By focusing on this aspect of non-English languages and by bracketing the institutional racism that produced bilingualism as a disability in the first place, Fishman was able to argue that bilingualism was a key, overlooked component of human capital.

Fishman's argument on behalf of bilingual education was enthusiastically embraced by many at the Congressional Hearings. Several community leaders and educators, speaking in support of bilingual education, unanimously agreed that "Spanish is going to play an important role in the years to come for our young men and women from all fields, especially in the business world" and that bilingual education can "have a decisive and desirable effect, not only on a significant proportion of our population, but on our relations with all of Latin America."[59] The longtime Chicano civil rights activist Hector García reiterated and concretized Fishman's view of bilingualism as a national resource by suggesting that "Texas and the Southwest United States may well be the training grounds for American diplomacy in Latin America."[60] There was general excitement that bilingual education would be a way to systematically create "culturally sophisticated personnel" that were in demand at a time of growing US influence worldwide.[61] It might not be a stretch to say that the vision of bilingualism as human capital spoke well to the desire for inclusion, or even hyperinclusion, that many minority leaders shared.

The appeal of bilingualism as human capital is not surprising when one looks back on a key rationale on education and racial equality that subtend the *Brown* decision: education increases human capital, and, therefore, differential and racialized production of human capital can be addressed through educational reform.[62] This idea is easily detectable in the *Brown* decision when we look at it a bit more closely. Having defined modern-day education as "the very foundation of good citizenship," Justice Warren, in the majority opinion, emphasizes the role education plays in a person's chances at a culturally rich and economically successful life: "Today [education] is a principal instrument in awakening the child to cultural values, in preparing him for later professional training, and in helping him adjust normally to his environment. In these days, it is doubtful that any child may reasonably be expected to succeed in life if he is denied the opportunity of an education. Such an opportunity, where the state has undertaken to provide, is a right which must be made available to all on equal terms."[63] I quote Justice Warren's statement on the function of education at length because an implicit acknowledgement of education as a means of accumulating human capital underscores the *Brown* ruling on the unconstitutionality of segregation. That is, the *Brown* decision's jurisprudence recognizes the link between the legal task of racial equality and the accumulation of human capital. The fact that being held back in developing one's opportunities at economic success through public education was decided as a violation of one's constitutional right is worth paying attention to since the argument for bilingual education, soon to follow, actively used this aspect of educational right as a right to the development of human capital.

Attending to the imperative of human capital development in the *Brown* decision or the congressional debates on bilingual education—seminal moments in educational equality in the twentieth century—is not to reject or to diminish the importance of the role education has played in the social and economic uplift of people of color in the United States. Rather what I suggest is that the discussion of racial equality in the post–civil rights era requires a reexamination of the terms of liberal inclusion for minorities. A close scrutiny of the Congressional Hearings on the Bilingual Education Act of 1967 shows that revising the American Dream to include bilingualism meant that bilingual personhood itself had to be reconstituted through the terms of possessive individualism.

It deserves mention here that Joshua Fishman's argument for bilingualism and his work on the Language Resources Project were driven not so much by an economistic view of bilingualism but by a deep commitment to a philosophy of cultural pluralism.[64] If Hayakawa's vision of society shown in his discussion of the American Dream in *Language in Thought and Action* was based on an acceptance of a social and economic hierarchy, Fishman's strong pluralism led him to imagine a society where the social positions of the members are determined not so much by their place in a vertical hierarchy but by multiple horizontal affiliations. In that it is based on a nuanced understanding of ethnicity as a complex and dynamic formation with multiple registers of expression, Fishman's cultural pluralism is also qualitatively different from the kind that Hayakawa gestures to in his generic call to the United States as a nation of immigrants. The motto of US English, of which Hayakawa was a representative, was "America—one Nation, indivisible, enriched by many cultures, united by a single tongue."[65] This motto, which Hayakawa repeated in almost every Congressional session on the English Language Amendment, the bill that proposed to make English the official language of the United States, cursorily acknowledges the ethos of cultural pluralism only to reject any policy-based idea of cultural pluralism in favor of the idea of the melting pot.[66] "Melting pot, yes, Tower of Babel, no!" Hayakawa declares elsewhere in purported citation of Saul Bellow.[67]

Fishman resisted the caricatures of "melting pot" or "Tower of Babel" and instead tuned into the varied levels and expressions of ethnic identification in his research on language minorities. For example, noting that students at ethnic schools preferred instruction in "ethnic arts (music, singing, dancing, graphic arts)" to mother tongue instruction, Fishman distinguished between elements of ethnicity that have become largely symbolic and devoid of the implications of everyday life and elements of ethnicity that are "perceived as threatening several highly desirable goals and interactions which depend upon acceptance by American core society."[68] In his estimation, ethnic arts were a weak form of ethnic expression and, therefore, acceptable among assimilated immigrants, whereas language was a strong form of ethnicity, and language maintenance a possible sign of nonassimilation. What Fishman wanted to change were the dominant perception of bilingualism and the social attitudes toward assimilation so that stronger forms of ethnic expression such as language could be viewed as not only acceptable but also desirable. In Fishman's vision of cultural pluralism, the monolingual American Dream, which has facilitated the loss of non-English languages, is an insufficient promise that the United States holds out to immigrants. With too much emphasis on socioeconomic mobility and an inadequate appreciation of the importance of cultural life, the monolingual American Dream impoverishes immigrants' lives through language loss without necessarily guaranteeing socioeconomic success. In his words, it "emasculate[s] . . . functional ethnicity . . . without at the same time providing for structural assimilation in more primary relationships."[69]

Fishman was very well aware that languages did not exist in a social, cultural, and political vacuum. Having researched ethnic language schools extensively and having interviewed numerous teachers of non-English languages, he had a firm grasp of the differential status of non-English languages in the United States. For example, he drew up four categories of non-English languages based on their perceived prestige: untouchable, unenviable, enviable, and holy, with the first two in the lower end of prestige and the latter two at the higher end.[70] He also did not fail to note that the prestigious languages in the United States were colonial languages (i.e., languages of the former colonial powers) and that those faced with the danger of extinction were the indigenous languages.[71] In brief, he was cognizant of a political and symbolic economy behind the ecology of languages regardless of whether he communicated this aspect of his research to his audience at the Congressional Hearings.

The rise of interest in ethnicity in the 1960s, what historians have called the ethnic revival, also dovetailed to some degree with Fishman's views on cultural pluralism.[72] The sentiment that ethnicity was a strong element of social, political, and cultural life was pervasive in the Congressional Hearings in 1967. If ethnicity was a significant factor in the organization of social life, the idea that this could be used to deliver educational goods tailored to the needs of a particular ethnic group seemed appropriate to many at the Hearings. Then US Commissioner of Education, Harold Howe, spoke of "bilingual education techniques" as already being used by schools in the southwest with significant numbers of "non-English-speaking children" to good effect.[73] At a time when the education of Mexican Americans was viewed as in crisis, with high dropout rates among Mexican Americans and low academic achievement, Howe suggested that bilingual education could be a way to enlarge educational opportunities for Mexican Americans. On several occasions before Congress, Howe hinted that bilingual education would serve the agenda of downward redistribution by speaking to the special educational needs of non-English-speaking children in the United States.

Fishman's awareness of the political economy of languages and Howe's attention to educational equality directed at particular minority groups, however, were attenuated by the climate of Cold War nationalism when translating the ideal of bilingualism into policies. One gets a glimpse of this in how legislators rallied around bilingualism that serves US national interests in the Congressional Hearings of 1967. The connections between the domestic discourse of civil rights and the global emergence of the United States as a leader of the "free" world during the Cold War have been discussed by Mary Dudziak among others.[74] Whereas Dudziak focuses on state actions that reflect keen interest in perceptions of the United States as a democracy abroad, the rhetoric of the Latino legislators and expert witnesses who supported bilingual education in the Hearings show that the Cold War climate of shoring up national security through race reform at home also opened an avenue for racial minorities to claim an Americanness previously denied them by aligning the interests of minority communities with those of the nation.[75] In other words, deliberate demonstrations of civic-mindedness and patriotism were a means by which leaders of minority communities tried to facilitate the political and cultural inclusion of the groups they represented. Cold War nationalism permeated the appeals on bilingualism as serving national economic and interests and the purpose of national security. The fact that the National Defense Education Act, signed only about a decade earlier in 1958, included clauses on foreign language instruction and emphasized the importance of foreign language learning for the sake of national security added weight to the appeals on behalf of bilingual education in the 1967 Hearings.[76] In fact, one may even argue that the National Defense Education Act was the precursor to the Bilingual Education Act, which reinforces the idea that non-English languages were essentially "foreign" languages and intimates that the inclusion of bilingualism in the American Dream was about the strategic uses of non-English languages.

## CONTENTIOUS HUMAN CAPITAL IN MULTICULTURALISM

Despite the good intentions of the advocates of bilingual education in the Congressional Hearings of 1967, as an educational policy, bilingual education met with tough challenges. As resistance to bilingual policies gained momentum in the 1980s, the relationship between bilingualism and the promotion of group identity in particular became a focal point of criticism. Former US assistant secretary of education and longtime education scholar Diane Ravitch, for example, criticized court interventions in mandating bilingual education as an act that mistakes "pedagogy" for "civil right."[77] According to Ravitch, the fact that bilingual education, which is a pedagogical method and tool with untested and inconclusive results, can be viewed as a civil right for some attests to the "politicization of the language issue in American education."[78] She also denounced bilingual education as an example of "race consciousness" that promotes "ethnic particularism in the curriculum."[79] Ironically, what was initially a measure of addressing structural inequality that manifested along the line of race became the target of criticism for holding back democracy. In the climate of the new Right, the view that identity-based social movements have taken their demands too far, encapsulated in such phrases as "reverse discrimination," undergirded the neoconservative resistance to race-based policies, including bilingualism.[80] The most visible and popular opposition to public bilingualism that reflected the political climate of the 1980s was the English Only movement, spearheaded by US English, a self-declared "citizen's action group" that Samuel Hayakawa founded with John Tanton in 1983.[81] In 1981, Hayakawa proposed the English Language Amendment in Congress for the first time, which called for a constitutional amendment to make English the official language of the United States. While it never passed, the bill appeared several times in subsequent sessions of the Congress. US English, in addition to supporting the various versions of the English Language Amendment, also supported the organization of popular local movements to repeal state laws that mandated bilingual ballots or bilingual education.

Several scholars have analyzed the populist movement, variously to show it as a white, conservative reaction to Latino immigration, to refute the need to make English an official language, to quell fears that English is under threat, and to understand why English Only gained such support.[82] Here I am most interested in the unexpected twists and turns that the idea of building human capital through bilingual education took in subsequent decades. One of these twists and turns has to do with the strange marriage of human capital and ethnicity in vernacular sociologies by scholars such as Thomas Sowell. Another is the Ebonics debates in 1996, the flash point for the repressed issue of language as capital in bilingual education. While these two examples of the strange career of human capital may seem unrelated at first blush, I suggest that they reveal the fault lines of the reconstitution of bilingual personhood along the terms of possessive individualism.

A seemingly race-neutral concept, human capital, nonetheless, was soon swept up in a new discourse of racialization that essentialized cultural difference. In his critique of human capital delivered in 1985, sociologist Stephen Steinberg suggests that human capital theorists have absorbed controversial ideas about the correlation between ethnic cultures and economic success. "To put it in the vernacular," he says, "'human capital' means having 'the right stuff'"—the values, attitudes, habits that are amenable to socioeconomic success.[83] And the problem with such a vernacular understanding of human capital, according to Steinberg, is that "despite all the trappings of scientific objectivity," it "treats the marketplace as though it were some kind of benevolent society, parceling out its rewards to the culturally deserving."[84] Studies of human capital informed by such a perspective, Steinberg argues, produce and reproduce problematic causal relations between certain ethnic cultures, such as Jewish and Asian, and the aptitude for capital accumulation.[85] In this frame of reference, human capital is not solely about the value of education but more about what ethnic cultures are suited to fast-track economic assimilation. When it is ethnicized in its application and usage, human capital becomes a term for evaluating racial personhood, lives, and experiences in the hands of certain scholars.

The idea of the model minority, which emerged in the late 1960s with its origin often attributed to William Petersen's 1966 article in the *New York Times*, "Success Story, Japanese-American Style," may be a precursor to the ethnicized application of human capital Steinberg criticizes.[86] Citing Gunnar Myrdal's *An American Dilemma*, the epitome of mid-twentieth century racial liberalism, Petersen notes how Japanese Americans go against the "principle of cumulation," in which the cumulatively added effects of discrimination produce "problem minorities."[87] Twenty years beyond the internment camps, "Japanese Americans," Petersen says, "are better than any other group in our society, including native-born whites. They have established this remarkable record moreover, by their own almost totally unaided effort. . . . Even in a country whose patron saint is the Horatio Alger hero, there is no parallel to this success story."[88] In Thomas

Sowell's thesis on the differential human capital of different cultures, best seen in his 1994 publication, *Race and Culture*, Petersen's tentative idea that there may be a cultural explanation to the economic assimilation of a minority group is extended and hardened into an ethnicized understanding of human capital. Rejecting both what he calls the position of cultural relativism that eschews value assessment in cultural difference and the class critique of someone like Steinberg, whom he criticizes for dismissing the evidence of ethnic differences, Sowell argues that "the incidence of economically valuable skills . . . varies from ethnic group to ethnic group and from nation to nation."[89] And it is these ethnic differences that account for the socioeconomic mobility of some groups over others according to Sowell: "Some immigrant groups begin at a lower socioeconomic level than that of the surrounding population and eventually rise above them, due to their skills, work habits, or other economic performance differences. They have changed class precisely because of their skills, capabilities, or performance."[90]

Strangely, a concept that explains the creation of symbolic capital through education in skills, capabilities, or performance in Becker becomes the cause of differential skills, capabilities, and performances among ethnic groups in Sowell. In Sowell's usage of human capital, it is almost as if being born into a certain ethnic group determines the chances of one's upward mobility.[91] One encounters an investment in ethnicity quite different from that of Fishman's in Sowell. While Fishman sought an enrichment of life through the maintenance of ethnic cultures and saw this as crucial to a vibrant democracy in the United States, Sowell is interested in correlating ethnic origin to actions and outcomes measured through the assumption of ethnic homogeneity. Rather than contributing to democracy (through, for example, creating viable options of representations for language minorities as in the case of Fishman), ethnicity becomes a straitjacket in Sowell's usage. The ethnicization of human capital, or the differential distribution of human capital along the line of ethnicity, not only shows the confusion around the concept of human capital but also brings into high relief a way of conceptualizing the relationship between ethnicity and public education contra bilingual education. Instead of associating certain ethnicities with a disadvantage that should be addressed through affirmative institutional acts, such as bilingual education, it naturalizes different performances among different ethnic groups.

Another unexpected turn in bilingual education happened when in 1996 the Oakland School District announced that it would recognize Ebonics (African American Vernacular English) as a language of instruction based on the guidelines of bilingual education, only to be met with an unexpected stream of nation-wide criticism and derision. To summarize the thrust of the criticism directed at the district, which came from a wide swath of the political spectrum, the Oakland School District was viewed as "giving up" on African American students and promoting cultural separatism. When one considers that the principle of the pedagogical use of the student's home language proposed by the district proposed was common to bilingual education, the sheer animosity that was directed at the Oakland School District deserves a second look.[92] And it speaks volumes about the assumptions of language as symbolic capital that were intimated yet never directly addressed in the debates on bilingualism.

In a brief op-ed in the *Los Angeles Times*, legal scholar David Troutt pointed out that the relationship between language and symbolic capital is the crux of the Ebonics debate. Observing that "we treat our fluency like property," Troutt says that "the problem [with Ebonics] is that its public acceptance might throw into question claims of ownership to intelligence and belonging. After all, Ebonics is not as much the language of blackness as it is the only dialect of persistently poor, racially segregated people—the so-called black underclass."[93] Troutt's view of language highlights the fact that language, or fluency, is a tool that can be used for class mobility. In Macpherson's thesis of possessive individualism, "the individual is essentially the proprietor of his own person and capacities, for which he owes nothing to society."[94] From the perspective of possessive individualism, language, including literacy, as it is procured and developed through the educational system, is one of the capacities the individual comes to embody and that can be used to gain economic capital, but that theoretically cannot be alienated from the person. It is a quintessential form of what Pierre Bourdieu calls cultural capital in "the embodied state," a disposition of the mind and the body cultivated over a period of time.[95]

The assumptions of the individual and of language behind the resistance to the Oakland School District's Resolution on Ebonics further come to light when one recognizes that those who criticized the Resolution were responding to and reinforcing the linguistic market in which Ebonics is not valorized as a capacity, or skill, that yields profit. What Bourdieu says about standard language and the role of education in reproducing the symbolic capital of standard language may prove helpful here. According to Bourdieu, standard language does not exist prior to the political relations of governance and the social relations of the market but is produced and reproduced in the systems of the modern bureaucratic state and the free market. What is of particular interest here is his suggestion that "the market in symbolic goods" plays an invisible role in the social determination of what language counts as legitimate and what does not.[96] "The constitution of a linguistic market," Bourdieu claims, "creates the conditions for an objective competition in and through which the legitimate competence can function as linguistic capital, producing a *profit of distinction* on the occasion of each social exchange."[97] The reason Ebonics was not considered a legitimate language in schools, then, is that the linguistic market does not confer on it any distinction that is convertible to economic capital unlike the foreign languages that are being taught in bilingual education. Hence, for the critics of the Oakland Resolution, investing in Ebonics was not only a misappropriation of the time and resources that could go into the cultivation of skills that can more readily be converted into economic capital but also an attempt to disturb the status quo of the linguistic market.

The stigma of Ebonics Troutt notes above—it is a sign of "the so-called black underclass"—certainly evokes the "stigmata of bilingualism" Haugen discussed in 1972.[98] In fact, in his discussion of the peculiar American definition of bilingualism, Haugen even pointed out that in the United States, "the term has enjoyed a semantic development not unlike that of 'minority group,' a term that one would not normally apply to the English aristocracy or to American millionaires."[99] If being bilingual was tantamount to being African American in terms of the social stigma that both language and racial differences carried at the time of Haugen's writing in 1972, it seems like language and racial differences have evolved differently in the popular imaginary in the intervening twenty-plus years. The Ebonics debate came up at a time when public bilingualism was under attack—Proposition 227 banning bilingual education in public schools in California was passed just two years later in 1998—but if the idea of using federal funds to support the educational opportunities of language minority students was being challenged, the idea that being able to speak a foreign language in addition to English increases one's human capital seems to have taken hold.

What the Ebonics debate reveals is not so much the failure of bilingual education as an educational policy but the fault lines in a bilingual American Dream that rests its case on the liberal ideology of
possessive individualism. As appealing as it may have been to those
present at the Hearings, the rationale of *homo oeconomicus* in Fishman's argument assumes a universal human subject in the mold of
a possessive individual that is troubling when viewed in light of the
history of racialization in the United States, in which racialized persons were often relegated to the realm of the non- or subhuman. The
institution of chattel slavery is a stark illustration of how the distinction between the free individual and his property, regarded as a fundamental aspect of American liberal democracy, was buttressed for
white men by the reduction of enslaved African Americans to property.[100] The idea of African Americans as property also appears resid-
ually in the mid-twentieth century liberal state's view that African
Americans are a "problem" that need to be addressed by the state,
most famously encapsulated in Gunnar Myrdal's famous statement
on the "Negro problem" in *An American Dilemma*. Such objectification of racial personhood complicates the distinction between individual and property, between manager and resource, that is taken for
granted in Fishman's characterization of language as symbolic capital, especially when it applies to racialized persons occupying the
place of the possessive individual. The resonance between the terms
employed by Myrdal to characterize African Americans and those
employed by Fishman to characterize bilingualism perhaps best demonstrates this complication. In his much-cited study of the "Negro
problem," published in 1944, Myrdal famously says that "America is
free to choose whether the Negro shall remain her liability or become
her opportunity."[101] Needless to say, the terms of liability and opportunity, applied to African Americans, are metaphors, just as the terms
of liability and asset, applied to bilingualism, are metaphors. Yet
Myrdal's approach to African Americans and Fishman's approach to
bilingualism are both undergirded by an economic rationale in determining the value of racialized subjects and objects to white America. The only difference is that in the case of Myrdal, it is racialized
personhood that is being evaluated, whereas in the case of Fishman,
he may unwittingly be encouraging racialized persons to adopt the
mantle of ethnic entrepreneurship. The irony of this reversal of roles
is hard to miss.[102]

Fishman's enthusiasm for public bilingualism in the 1960s certainly held out a promise enticing enough to counter the long hold of
English as the only language of capital in the United States, something
that Hayakawa firmly believed. Along with the tales of the classroom
that show English-as-a-Second-Language instruction, as in Mohr's
short story, a different kind of classroom like Mrs. Earles's—and with
it a whole new way of being and doing—became imaginable in this
climate of social and cultural change. To imagine that bilingualism
could be a part of the American Dream was to move beyond the cognitive horizon defined by a singular notion of English as the language
of power. Yet the continuity between investing in English and investing in English Plus becomes apparent when one turns to the idea of
personhood that sustains the American Dream, in one or two or however many languages. What made the argument for public bilingualism so persuasive in the 1960s is also what made it vulnerable to the
contentions around human capital in subsequent decades.

## RACE, LANGUAGE, AND CLASS

Now I would like to briefly look at the Chicano writer Richard
Rodriguez's disquisitions on the relationship between bilingualism
and class since they offer some compelling insights on the unresolved
problem of the importance of class in turning the liability of bilingualism into an asset in the post–civil rights era. I discuss the associations between Rodriguez's views on post–civil rights race relations
and his dormant bilingualism in more detail in Chapter 4. Here, I
focus on his remarks on bilingualism in his editorials and interviews
to show his triangulation of race and language through class. On the
one hand, Rodriguez's opposition to bilingual education, for which he
has received ample scrutiny from critics, is based on his view of English as colorblind capital, much like Hayakawa's. On the other hand,
he departs from Hayakawa when he writes of the importance of class
background in attaining linguistic capital, be it in one language or in
two. Even as he subscribes to the same idea of the possessive individual as the backbone of a liberal society, Rodriguez acknowledges that
this idea of possessive individualism is coextensive with class inequality. Some of the contradictions in Rodriguez's views of bilingualism
evince the challenges of bilingual personhood in the post–civil rights
era when the notion of "post-race," the view that race does not really
affect the American Dream, comes up frequently.

Rodriguez's ideas on the relationship among socioeconomic mobility, class, and bilingualism appear most succinctly in a *New York Times* op-ed published in 1985, entitled "Bilingualism, Con: Outdated and Unrealistic." Here Rodriguez makes the provocative statement that "proclamations concerning bilingual education are weighted at bottom with Hispanic political grievances and, too, with middle-class romanticism."[103] In this brief piece, Rodriguez creates a psycho-moral drama of grievance and restitution for the Latino—but mostly Chicano—advocates of bilingual education. "Bilingualism," he posits, "becomes a way of exacting from gringos a grudging admission of contrition—for the 19th-century theft of the Southwest, the relegation of Spanish to a foreign tongue, the injustice of history."[104] The psycho-moral drama of Hispanic vengeance is instrumental for Rodriguez to criticize bilingual education as an intra-Hispanic story of class subordination. That is, bilingual education is problematic not just because Hispanics are trying to get restitution for previous damages through this educational measure but because middle-class Hispanics are holding working-class Hispanic children hostage in doing so. He suggests that for the Hispanic advocates of bilingual education, "bilingualism became proof that one could have it both ways, could be a full member of public America and yet also separate, private Hispanic." These advocates, he continues, "have foisted a neat ideological scheme on working-class children. What they want to believe about themselves, they wait for the child to prove that it is possible to be two, that one can assume the public language (the public life) of America, even while remaining what one was, existentially separate."[105]

Rodriguez creates a nexus of language, education, and socioeconomic mobility in his argument against bilingual education. Assuming a strict division between public and private, while also defining the minority person as someone who is confined to the private, Rodriguez views the aim of education for the minority person as learning how to access the public—a position that dates back to 1978 when he published "Beyond the Minority Myth," an indictment of affirmative action.[106] Because for the minority person, the felt gap between the two spheres seems insurmountably big, Rodriguez suspects the argument that one can be two persons, that one can have both a public and private identity without sacrificing either, does not originate from the minority person but from the middle class: "Middle-class man, unable to celebrate the opportunity for public life and afraid to admit the lessened opportunity for private life, finds his best hope in bestowing on himself a sense of separateness from the crowd while still remaining in public."[107] Hence Rodriguez criticizes middle-class Latinos (Chicanos) as the main culprit in bilingual education. As people who already possess the linguistic capital of English, the middle-class Latinos sell the idea to working-class Latinos—who do not have much by way of any linguistic capital that would help them access a middle-class life, English or Spanish—that they can have double the linguistic capital of English and Spanish. For Rodriguez, this is a lie and he argues that bilingual education takes away, rather than adds to, the symbolic capital one acquires (and has to acquire) through education when one is a minority.

Implicit in Rodriguez's argument against bilingual education is a view of racial identity as something that is both potent and illusory. While racial groups such as gringos and Hispanics have enough coherence in Rodriguez's argument to be given unified psychological profiles, class difference also erodes the idea of group cohesion as middle-class interests clash with working-class interests. Rodriguez's investment in English as the symbolic capital that promises socioeconomic mobility for working-class children from Spanish-speaking homes, then, is based on the idea that race overdetermines the lives of poor Spanish-speaking children whereas it is a matter of choice for middle-class Hispanics. Rodriguez's view of racial identity as something that acquires meaning in tandem with one's class position resonates with Hayakawa's view of the middleman minority's identity as a group. As Hayakawa predicts the middleman minority's disappearance with socioeconomic assimilation, so does Rodriguez seem to imply that the meaning of race as a social constraint will fade with the racialized person's socioeconomic assimilation.

In terms of how one's class background affects the function of bilingualism as liability or asset, Rodriguez presents two interesting counterpoints to his former self as a bilingual child: an elite Mexican bilingual and a middle-class bilingual white American. Recalling the Mexican writer Carlos Fuentes discuss his bilingual childhood during his father's tenure as diplomat in Washington, DC, Rodriguez adamantly asserts in an interview that Fuentes's bilingualism is not the same as his.[108] Even if they both may have shuttled back and forth between a Spanish-speaking home and an English-speaking school, Rodriguez claims that Fuentes's elite background makes his experience of bilingualism fundamentally different from his own experience as a working-class, dark-skinned Chicano child. In fact, according to Rodriguez, Fuentes may have more in common with Larry Faherty, a childhood friend of Rodriguez whom he discusses in his second collection of essays, *Days of Obligation* (1992). Unlike Rodriguez who consciously distances himself from Spanish, his white American friend Faherty seizes Spanish as a way of escaping his banal, middle-class life in the suburbs. Rodriguez cannot help but notice how his white American friend is more "Mexican" than he is with his fluency in Spanish and his frequent trips south of the border with his family.[109] Through the examples of Fuentes and Faherty, Rodriguez suggests that bilingualism, as symbolic capital, was a luxury that he could not afford and that it is something attainable only for those who already have at least middle-class status and wealth.

The vexed relations of affiliation among Fuentes, Faherty, and himself that Rodriguez presents speak to the oscillating meaning of bilingualism between disadvantage and advantage, between liability and asset, in the post–civil rights era. The conclusion Rodriguez seemingly offers is that class matters more than race in what function bilingualism comes to serve and how one can relate to bilingualism. Yet for someone who disavows the significance of race, Rodriguez cannot stop writing about race, even after his socioeconomic ascent. I would like to suggest that the quandaries Rodriguez displays are actually constitutive of a new mode of racialization that prevails in the postwar period. In wrestling with the dilemma of at once being a possessive individual who has used well his property in his person and in his capacities to attain socioeconomic mobility, and a racial subject obsessed with past memories and present predicaments of racialization, Rodriguez's contradictions are characteristic of bilingual personhood in the postwar cultural politics of bilingualism.

Is it better to be bilingual, or is it better to be monolingual in English? This question has been asked time and again in the popular debates on bilingualism over the course of the second half of the twentieth century. While it seems simplistic in its assumptions about what is good (or better) and what being bilingual or monolingual is, this was a key question behind much action and contemplation in the postwar politics of bilingualism. Far from just being about language, this question entailed a cultural struggle about changing ideas about opportunities and advantages. The decades that saw the most vociferous arguments and opinions on bilingualism were also the decades that saw rapid changes in the racial makeup of the society and experienced the stress of the economic transition from Fordism to post-Fordism. As much as the debates on bilingualism were about issues of heritage and identity in a society contending with new waves of immigrants, they were also about what skills or knowledge are required to be a competitive person and a competitive workforce in an era of global capitalism. Bilingual personhood, from this perspective, is a site where anxieties about being an American were played out and mapped in the post-war era.

CHAPTER THREE

# Schooling Bilinguals In and Against Multiculturalism

The 1967 Congressional Hearings on the Bilingual Education Act included the testimony of Piri Thomas, author of *Down These Mean Streets* (1967), a memoir that chronicles his struggles with drugs, gangs, and crime while growing up as a dark-skinned Puerto Rican American man in the New York of the 1940s and '50s. Invited to give his opinion on bilingual education from the perspective of someone who grew up bilingual, Thomas made a statement in support of bilingual education that employed what seems like a prototypical rhetoric of multiculturalism: "Like all ethnic groups aside from those who speak English, outside they [language minorities] speak English, but in their homes and families and communities they speak the tongue that is the joy of their heart, whether it is Jewish, Italian, Spanish, Russian, Chinese, Japanese, and all the others. That does not make them any less Americans. I think it makes them better Americans if they can have the liberty and freedom of choice in expressing the beauty of their culture and their heritage."[1] Thomas's emphasis on respect and appreciation of cultural and linguistic difference resonates with what Charles Taylor calls "the politics of recognition," which is based on the presumption that "a person or a group of people can suffer real damage, real distortion, if the people or society around them mirror back to them a confining or demeaning or contemptible picture of themselves."[2] Instead of a deficiency, a lack, bilingualism is the sign of sufficiency and abundance in Thomas's vision of multiculturalism, a rectification of the misrecognition of before.

His essay, "Sounds from a Street Kid," appended to his statement before Congress, however, offers a slightly different take on the significance of bilingualism. Bilingualism, here, appears not so much based on an evenness between the languages of the private sphere, of "the homes, families, and communities" and that of the public sphere but on a recognition of the anarchic tendencies of marginal languages to threaten the processes of linguistic standardization that construct linguistic capital. A street kid's address to the "Olders" about how they could work toward social harmony together, "Sounds from a Street Kid" employs street slang, a far cry from standard English, to make its case. The few instances where a Spanish word appears, its English equivalent is given in parentheses immediately after, and the Spanish words are incorporated into the street vernacular. Thomas uses this street vernacular, the language of the street kid, to communicate an epochal shift in the tides of power. "We're born faster," proclaims the street kid, "live faster, learn faster and really travel faster. We live in an age of bobby terms, 'like for real,' 'monsters,' 'molecules,' and 'split atoms.' And like in your long English, 'an age of power.' One beyond our normal kicks and imagination, with fears, uncertainties, of forced mananas [sic], as the ever present game time flares out and fades out via La Bomba."[3] The kid asserts that the destructive power of advancements in technology, like the atomic bomb, shapes the language of the everyday on the streets and creates an acute awareness of the relations of power in one's environment. This is the matrix of bilingual subject formation from the street kid's perspective.

In retrospect, the two different kinds of bilingual experiences Thomas delivered at the Hearings can be read as forecasting future debates on multiculturalism, especially as to whether multiculturalism's emphasis on identity directs attention away from structural problems of inequality.[4] Thomas's support for the "liberty and freedom of choice in expressing the beauty of their culture and their heritage" imagines democratic society as a place where individuals and groups can live authentically according to their cultural heritage without being stigmatized or discriminated against. In this sense, his vision accords with Joshua Fishman's ideal of cultural pluralism discussed in the previous chapter. However, in his literary representation of the bilingual child, Thomas complicates the democratic vision in his public congressional statement. Thomas's street kid, a literary example of the very children under discussion at the Hearings, shows the elusiveness of multiculturalism for democracy when it is detached from the material concerns and power relations that create an equivalence between the terms of bilingual children and children of the streets. When viewed separately, Thomas's congressional testimony may seem like an endorsement of multiculturalism as a politics of recognition. Yet when viewed alongside his appended literary essay, one comes to realize that the politics of recognition he partakes in is one that not only sees "the supposed links between recognition and identity" but also links recognition to redistribution.[5] The vision of democracy that motivates Thomas's ideas of authenticity, freedom, and mutual respect is not so much a democracy that exists but democracy as a horizon of promise.

In this chapter I read Américo Paredes's *George Washington Gómez* (1990, written between 1935 and 1940) and Maxine Hong Kingston's *The Woman Warrior* (1976) through the two layers of meaning Thomas attributes to multiculturalism. Both texts are considered representative examples of bicultural coming-of-age narratives in the discourse and curriculum of multiculturalism. Paredes's novel portrays the development of a Mexican American boy in a small town on the United States–Mexican border. Kingston's memoir, now considered a canonical work of twentieth-century American literature and a foundational text for Asian American literature, shows the struggles of growing up for a Chinese American girl in Stockton, California. While George Washington Gómez was written much earlier than *The Woman Warrior*, it was published much later in 1990 due to Paredes's personal circumstances.[6] Ramón Saldívar suggests that this time lag between composition and publication gives *George Washington Gómez* a "polytemporal" quality.[7] One way of approaching the novel's "polytemporal quality" may be to situate it within the recovery projects in ethnic studies that focus on excavating the unpublished or out-of-print texts by writers of color and putting them into circulation. These recovery projects could be said to carry out in the realm of literary representation multiculturalism's politics of recognition.[8] These recovered texts testify to the exclusions in the making of an American literary tradition that parallels the exclusions that created racial injuries in the social and political realms, and they build an ethnic literary tradition that speaks specifically to the ethnic group's history while also supplementing the extant literary tradition. Yet if the recovery projects perform a politics of recognition that largely conforms to the tenets of multiculturalism, the recovered texts themselves often reveal complex worlds whose cultural politics cannot be reduced to multiculturalism. Despite the differences in their times of composition, Paredes's and Kingston's texts are both informed by the ethos and practices of multiculturalism that have prevailed in the teaching of ethnic literatures in US universities. As multicultural literary models of growing up in two languages, *George Washington Gómez* and *The Woman Warrior* offer a unique opportunity to examine the vagaries of bilingual ethnic formation.

My objective in reading Paredes's novel side by side with Kingston's widely discussed text is to illuminate contradictions of literary multiculturalism that are in play for readers engaging with representations of the bilingual child. These contradictions, I suggest, can best be seen in the multiple valences of bilingualism for ethnic formation that Paredes and Kingston portray. Paredes's active engagement with the regional specificity of the United States–Mexico border and the history of border conflicts imbue *George Washington Gómez* with a keen awareness of the relations of power behind the valorization or the stigmatization of bilingualism. In the course of the novel, the bilingual child Guálinto goes through the affects of racial shame and pride regarding his Mexican heritage to surprisingly end up a proverbial race traitor as an adult, utilizing his bilingualism in the service of the US government as a spy. The much-discussed controversy around *The Woman Warrior* recapitulates in the real world the fictional controversy over Guálinto's betrayal in *George Washington Gómez* as Asian American cultural nationalists accused Kingston of "selling out" by misrepresenting Chinese American experiences. By reading Kingston's seminal text through Paredes's insights on the bilingual child, I revisit this controversy as ultimately symptomatic of the competing visions of bilingualism as cultural and human capital in multiculturalism. I excavate the yellow bilingual body in Kingston's text to foreground the material conditions of bilingual conflicts, which, in comparison to Paredes's text, are displaced in an aesthetic of biculturalism. Behind the aesthetic concerns of biculturalism, *The Woman Warrior* points to the strictures of language as property for the bilingual child. Together, the two texts reveal a syncretic composition of bilingual personhood in which various anxieties of language's value as property are worked out in relation to an ethnic subject's formation as a key element of literary multiculturalism.

## THE PRICE OF INCORPORATION IN
## GEORGE WASHINGTON GÓMEZ

*George Washington Gómez* is the coming-of-age story of the novel's namesake, George Washington Gómez, or Guálinto as he is called for most of the novel. Set between the 1910s and the 1940s in the United States–Mexican border town of Jonesville, Paredes's novel shows what it was like to grow up Mexican American in the mode of realism. Bearing the burden of his deceased father's wish that he become "a great man among the Gringos," Guálinto struggles to overcome the social disadvantage of his Mexican heritage—including discrimination in school, poverty, and segregated neighborhoods—at the same time he develops friendships and suffers from unrequited love.[9] Were it not for the strange ending, *George Washington Gómez* would be an unsurprising ethnic bildungsroman. In the penultimate chapter, the reader sees Guálinto renew his faith in and commitment to the Mexican American community. While he has felt shame over his family's economic and social status and doubted his uncle's character in his adolescent struggles, Guálinto realizes that he had been in the wrong as his uncle's background as a Seditionist who not only fought for the rights of Mexicans but also honored the lives of the poor and the vulnerable in doing so is revealed to him. This realization prompts him to change his mind about the future. He will go to college and receive an education that he will use to benefit the Mexican American community so that his father's wish and his uncle's sacrifice will not go to waste. After such a gratifying moral resolution to Guálinto's inner struggles, the last chapter of some twenty pages is a severe disappointment and seems to be an incongruous conclusion to the story. Instead of the return of a hero—a homeboy who made it good in the larger world and now returns to lift up his people—Guálinto's family and friends are confronted with a traitor. Guálinto returns as an army intelligence officer sent to spy on any possible Mexican American antistate activities on the border as the United States prepares to enter World War II.

Why did he do it? The ethnic bildungsroman takes on the qualities of a mystery novel with such a question. But unlike the mystery of the perpetrator in the whodunits, the mystery at hand is the mystery of Mexican American assimilation. I suggest that the answer to this question lies in the economy of bilingualism Paredes portrays in the novel. In the rest of this section, I examine the premise of liberal inclusion for Mexican Americans in *George Washington Gómez* to show that Guálinto's rechristening as "George G. Gómez" and his transformation into an agent of the state is actually anticipated in the narrative.[10] Guálinto's struggles between racial shame and pride exemplify a politics of recognition prior to the naming of this politics as multiculturalism and pushes the reader to reexamine multiculturalism as a mode of inclusion within the larger frame of liberalism. The politics of recognition that Guálinto is embroiled in prior to leaving his hometown of Jonesville is unable to address the economization of bilingualism, especially for the economically deprived Mexican Americans. At odds with the enthusiasm for bilingualism as human capital that legislators and the community leaders displayed in the 1967 Congressional Hearings of the Bilingual Education Act, the act of capitalizing on one's bilingualism is beneficial for neither the individual nor any larger community in Paredes's novel. Guálinto's (mis)management of his racial difference at the end, if we could call it that, is then not so much an aberration from his younger self but a variation of the mode of managing his difference within the same spectrum of liberalism.

The border town of Jonesville, where more than three quarters of *George Washington Gómez* is set, depends on English-Spanish bilingualism for commerce and politics. Guálinto's uncle Feliciano decides to move Guálinto's family from San Pedrito, where violent clashes between the Seditionists and the Texas Rangers are an everyday occurrence, to Jonesville because the town holds out the promise of a comparably peaceful existence. The seemingly balanced relationship between the English-speaking and the Spanish-speaking people accounts for the initial attraction Feliciano feels toward Jonesville. A town that has seen an influx of different kinds of Anglos, from the early "English-speaking adventurers . . . [who] married into Mexican landowning families, and became a ruling élite allied with their Mexican in-laws" to the "real-estate men and the land-and-title companies" after the railroad, Jonesville is a town where "even the Gringos spoke Spanish."[11]

Under the appearance of the Anglo accommodation of Spanish and of Mexican culture, however, is a power structure that is dominated by Anglo capital and political power. Nothing illuminates this better than the characteristics of the local elite's bilingualism, which I term situational bilingualism. Robert Norris, Feliciano's patron who is also the local judge and leader of the political party, the

Blues, engages in a situational bilingualism where he can employ either English or Spanish, depending on his audience and the situation, to advance his economic and political interests: "He [Norris] was bilingual," Paredes mentions, "with blood ties to his constituents. His grandmother, if you were speaking in English, had been Spanish. Pure Castilian, daughter of a hidalgo family. If you were speaking in Spanish, she had been Mexican. Even Judge Norris himself said so when he was making campaign speeches in Spanish."[12] Norris uses his Spanish fluency to create a bond between him and the Spanish speakers of Mexican descent that form his political base. However, the content of his speech changes depending on what language he speaks and the audience he addresses as his heritage fluidly moves between a Europeanness that is acceptable to Anglos and a Mexicanness that attaches him to darker-skinned, working-class Mexicans. While residents of such racially segregated neighborhoods as the one Guálinto lives in have limited exchanges with English speakers and struggle with illiteracy in Spanish, Judge Norris can utilize his access to two languages both to make himself acceptable to the Anglos in power and to mobilize working-class Mexican Americans for his individual goals.[13] Norris's ethnic affiliation and his bilingualism are forms of ethnic capital in the bilingual town of Jonesville much in need of brokers to go between the English-speaking and the Spanish-speaking communities.

The situational bilingualism of the local elites raises questions about the role of minority elites in racial uplift, especially regarding the recurring motif of Guálinto's mission to become "a great man who will help his people."[14] Judge Norris's bid for local political power partly fills the need for Mexican Americans, as a dominated group, to mobilize. Yet his example also draws attention to the fact that Mexican American elites may benefit from the structure of Anglo domination. Through his appropriation of a "Spanish" identity, Norris evades the crippling effects of Mexican American racialization that plague his less fortunate brethren. A fundamental dilemma of political representation crystallizes around bilingualism as ethnic capital. Can someone like Norris who is dependent on the status quo of race relations for his ethnic capital represent the dispossessed Mexican Americans? The mission that Guálinto has been given to lift up his people contains the same unresolved tension between the individual and the collective, a tension that becomes visible when bilingualism functions as ethnic capital.

Compared to Judge Norris, another example of the local elites, the Osunas, demonstrate a much more blatant form of ethnic exploitation. Grandfather Osuna is said to have grown rich by cooperating with the "'cattle barons' [who] came down like a plague on the Mexican ranchers of south Texas."[15] By siding with the powerful Anglos and disregarding the violence leveled against other Mexican Americans, Grandfather Osuna is able to join the ranks of the wealthy. As is the case with Norris, Grandfather Osuna also becomes a "Spaniard" with his wealth and influence: "Grandfather Osuna himself was no longer a Mexican. He was now a Spaniard."[16] The disavowal of a Mexican identity, however, does not mean that the Osunas cease to profit through their local relations with Mexican Americans. An important part of the grandson's business is renting poorly maintained, shabby tenement houses to Mexican Americans, "*Los cuartos de Don Onofre*," as the Spanish-speaking residents call them.[17] While Mexican Americans provide the backbone of the Osunas' wealth, through rent and through cheap labor as ranch hands, the Osunas employ a strictly individualistic view of capital accumulation that makes them exploit their racial group yet sever any ties that may become a hindrance to their success. The Mexican American elites' notion of language is not to view it as an essential element of identity but to flexibly use it to maximize personal gain.

Against such an individualistic notion of language and identity, Paredes presents another example of the relationship between language and identity that is based on collectivism though a fictionalized account of El Plan de San Diego, an aborted revolution by the Spanish-speaking people of Mexican descent in Texas in the early twentieth century.[18] In San Pedrito, the seat of Seditionist activities where there are frequent violent confrontations between the Seditionists (*los sediciosos*) and the Texas Rangers, a militarized distinction between English and Spanish prevails. For example, in describing a retaliatory attack by the Rangers on the Seditionists, Paredes shows them as directing their violence on Spanish speakers indiscriminately, regardless of whether they took part in the initial attack against the Rangers or not: "The next day the Rangers would come. To kill everyone they found close to the scene of the ambush, that is everyone who could not speak English."[19] In this space that is akin to a war zone, one's linguistic identity it taken for a sign of which side one belongs to. A nationalist ideology underwrites such construction of equivalence between one's language and her national affiliation. Because the language one speaks is taken to be a transparent sign of one's group allegiance, an individual's bilingualism, in this context, is tantamount to treachery and viewed with suspicion. Feliciano looks at the white priest, who tries to gain the trust of the "Border Mexican" by speaking "understandable Spanish," with distrust, and Lupe, another uncle of Guálinto who leads a faction of the Seditionists, accuses an Anglo merchant who knows Spanish of being a spy for the Rangers.[20] While the nationalistic outlook on language and identity certainly emphasizes the common fate of the collective, the rigid condemnation of the enemy's language perpetuates a cycle of hatred and casts as bleak the prospect of any meaningful relations between Spanish and English speakers.

Born in this militarized border space of San Pedrito, Guálinto's name is the sign of the impossibility of bilingualism under the condition of war. The naming of Gumersindo's newborn son occasions the family members to reveal the values they hold dear, a part of which includes their hopes for the future of the "Border Mexican."[21] In her astute analysis of the implications of the names each family member suggests for the infant, María Saldaña-Portillo points out Feliciano's "Mexican revolutionary nationalism" in the names of the Mexican revolutionary leaders he puts forth (Venustiano and Cleto) and the grandmother's rootedness in a traditional, Catholic, and patriarchal world of Mexican peasants (José Ángel and Gumersindo after the father).[22] In this proliferation of viewpoints, Gumersindo decides that his son be named after "the great North American, he who was a general and fought the soldiers of the king," the man who "drove out the English and freed the slaves."[23] As Saldaña-Portillo argues, Gumersindo's "desire to interpellate his light-skinned son into a legacy of liberty (driving out the English) and of equality (emancipating the slaves)" is coupled with a skewed understanding of the achievements of great Gringo men.[24] Gumersindo conflates George Washington, the man who "drove out the English," with Abraham Lincoln, the man who "freed the slaves," and ends up naming his son after the man who supported the institution of slavery.[25] The contrast between Gumersindo's idealism and the racial violence embedded in the signification of the name George Washington succinctly illustrates how the militarized border prohibits the development of a hybrid Mexican American identity that can adequately combine a racialized person's aspirations for national inclusion and a deep understanding of the historical complexities of that inclusion. The orthographic variations of "George Washington" in this scene intended to deliver the family members' Spanish-inflected pronunciation of the English name—Gumersindo's "Jorge Wachinton" and grandmother's "Guálinto"—capture the limits of English to represent the experiences and dreams of a "Border Mexican."[26]

The departure of Guálinto's family from San Pedrito suggests that Paredes does not view militant nationalism—or the propensity to defensive monolingualism it gives rise to—as a viable alternative to the situational bilingualism of the Mexican American elite. Rather than propose militant nationalism and a consequent ideology of monolingualism as solutions to the unequal distribution of wealth and power among working-class Mexican Americans, Mexican American elites and Anglos, Paredes examines the social mechanism by which marginal bilinguals are incorporated into the mainstream. For Spanish speakers in Jonesville, developing a relationship with English is crucial to having a public voice and presence since the dominant power structure is English-speaking, and as an institutional apparatus that shepherds Spanish speakers into the English-speaking world, the public school in Jonesville is at the center of this social mechanism. Structurally, the public school is a two-tier system with the first two grades divided into "high" and "low" sections based on a social hierarchy of English speakers on the top and Spanish speakers on the bottom. Paredes takes care to point out that this tiered system actually takes place in a so-called integrated school environment. While racial segregation is the norm for Texas schools in the 1920s, in Jonesville, "schools were fully integrated from first grade up through high school, a fact always pointed to with pride by local politicians whenever they ran for re-election."[27] The seemingly progressive side of public education in Jonesville complicates the meanings of segregation or integration in the abstract, as the integration that is touted by politicians as a sign of racial progress in the novel actually masks enduring racial inequalities between the Anglos and the Mexican Americans.

While segregation openly employs a biological notion of race to create groups of affinity, Jonesville's integrated schools use language-cum-academic performance to divide their students:

> Low first and low second served the great majority of entering pupils, who were of Mexican origin and knew little or no English when they came to school. They were taught bilingually by teachers who knew both English and Spanish and who had the job of teaching the English language to their charges, along with all the other skills first and

second graders were supposed to know. High first and high second accepted those children fortunate enough to know the English language before they entered school, and who for religious or economic reasons were not sent to private schools run by the Catholic church. The highs and lows became fully integrated in the third grade, taught entirely in English. The idea seemed an excellent one, giving the Mexican children the chance to learn English during their first two years in school as they were worked into the Angloamerican school system.[28]

The system, which seems to be "excellent" in the abstract, turns out to be disastrous for Guálinto, who finds himself in low first, the charge of Miss Cornelia, notorious for her hatred of Mexican American students despite her shared racial background with them. While in theory the division of students into Spanish-dominant and English-speaking groups may make sense, in reality, the Spanish-dominant classes are given less qualified teachers and fewer material resources, which, like a self-fulfilling prophecy, results in lower academic performance for Spanish-speaking students. By highlighting the discrepancies between the façade of integration and the reality of segregation, between the theory of transitioning Mexican American students into English classes through temporary bilingual instruction and the practice of discrimination against them, Paredes reveals the social conditions of educational inequality that fueled the debates undergirding the *Brown* decision and the Bilingual Education Act discussed earlier. At the same time that he points to the social matrix from which the juridical and legislative measures of educational redress takes place, Paredes also clearly shows the limits of the law alone to actualize racial equality.[29] The sly transformation of a racial hierarchy into an academic and social hierarchy in Jonesville's public school shows that racial hierarchy can work its way around the appearance of equality and accommodation. In this school environment, Guálinto learns that his background, including his mother tongue, places him in a socially inferior position.

Given this hierarchical world he lives in, the sense of "a divided personality" that Guálinto admits to once he is moved out of Miss Cornelia's class after a traumatizing beating and when he finds himself in the hands of more capable teachers who "gently [prod] [him] toward complete Americanization" is hardly an admittance of cultural confusion.[30] Rather, this trope of "a divided personality" registers the effects of liberalism's hailing of bilinguals. On the surface, the two selves of Guálinto echoes the identity crisis of a subject caught between two divergent currents of culture, commonly seen in the literary representations of hyphenated identities. Guálinto's "twin," George Washington Gómez, is a "product of his Anglo teachers and the books he read in school, which were all in English," whereas "the Mexican side of his being" "rebel[s]" against Americanization.[31] In his sophisticated interpretation of the border subjectivity that Guálinto represents, Ramón Saldívar cautions against the idea that Guálinto's "divided personality" is the effect of two different systems of culture, Mexican and American. In this line of thinking, "Guálinto the American would thus be seen as the product of a pluralist American melting-pot ideology, while, simultaneously, Guálinto the Mexican would be the shaped product of a sustaining traditional world."[32] Such an interpretation, Saldívar argues, is to impute a "full subjective agency" to Guálinto when what Paredes pursues is "the simulation of fullness and agency experienced acutely as the in-betweeness of the borderlands of culture."[33] Saldívar's poststructuralist and postcolonial interpretation of Guálinto as "an elegant prefiguration of the bordered subject of postmodern Chicano and Chicana narrative" offers a way of understanding the American and Mexican selves as not fixed, determinate systems but as flexible effects of the conditions of subjectivity in the border, constantly in the making.[34]

The border subjectivity that Saldívar attends to is worth elaborating on. On the one hand, it is clear that Paredes presents a "Mexicotexan" subjectivity, rooted in time and place, in contradistinction to an abstract immigrant subjectivity, even if it is somewhat unclear how Guálinto becomes conscious of his Mexicotexan self.[35] "Immigrants from Europe can become Americanized in one generation," Paredes explains. "Guálinto, as a Mexicotexan, could not. Because, in the first place, he was not an immigrant come to a foreign land. Like other Mexicotexans, he considered himself part of the land on which his ancestors had lived before the Anglotexans had come."[36] Paredes seems at times to imply that there is a vernacular imaginary, which is based on the lived experiences and oral history of the Mexican American community and which allows Guálinto to see himself as part of a larger organism of land, people, history, and customs.

On the other hand, several textual signs also suggest that Guálinto's consciousness as a Mexicotexan does not exist independently from the hegemony of an English-mediated ideology of liberal pluralism. To put it slightly differently, the counterhegemonic identity of the border subject is an effect of hegemonic identity. When one looks at the generation of Guálinto's resistant identity, it seems very much a reaction to hegemonic action—specifically, the unjust and injurious actions of authority he encounters at school. In stark contrast to his mother's expectation that the public school would aid Guálinto in achieving the prophecy of his name, the school is the site that gives rise to a counterhegemonic identity in Guálinto through racialized psychological injury.[37] For example, as a way of absorption into institutional authority, Guálinto is conferred an indigenous identity as Miss Cornelia (willfully) misinterprets his name as Indian in origin.[38] In the course of Guálinto's schooling, this misrecognition ends up being symbolic of the development of a resistant identity on the part of Guálinto. Miss Cornelia's misrecognition is corrected when Guálinto's mother, María, informs the teacher that Guálinto is named after George Washington, whose heroic story Guálinto had just recited at a school performance in front of the parents. Miss Cornelia openly derides what she sees as the pretentious ambition of a working-class Mexican family, embarrassing the liberal, white American teacher at the scene and infuriating María. As Miss Cornelia turns her knowledge of Guálinto's real name into a private joke, calling him "'Mr. George Washington Gómez whenever she spoke to him in class, emphasizing every syllable," Guálinto grows to "hate his name, as well as the real George Washington who was supposed to be the father of his country."[39] This hate leads him to claim the Indianness of his name. At this point, his claim to an Indian name is no longer just a misrecognition but a misrecognition that transforms into a self-recognition of his own wrongful victimization and a consequent identification with the oppositional moral authority of an indigenous identity.

Another example of textual ambivalence in the signification of a Mexicotexan identity is the spectral presence of the Seditionists and their demand for a unified, monolingual, and nationalist identity. The counterhegemonic element of Mexicotexan identity echoes the militant separatism of the Seditionists. Yet, as an aborted rebellion, the Seditionist movement only remains a spectral presence at best for Guálinto, a legend with no material traces until his uncle Lupe appears in town, only to be stoned in misrecognition by Guálinto. Additionally, the nationalist ideology's demand of monolingualism is impossible for the already bilingually constituted Guálinto. Paredes indicates that Guálinto's relationship to English parallels his relationship to Spanish. It is not just a second language but a second mother tongue, as can be seen in Paredes's metaphor of schooling as mothering and Guálinto's liberal, white American female teacher as "the mother of the Mexicotexan's American self."[40] Through the metaphor of schooling as an unconscious embrace of the world mediated through the near-familial affinity of the Anglo teacher and English, Paredes disables a clear distinction between a Spanish-mediated psyche and an English-mediated one.

Reading Guálinto's bilingual subjectivization through Louis Althusser's concept of interpellation offers a way out of the bind of determining what is Mexican and what American culture, or what is resistance and what assimilation. Here I turn to a part in Althusser's "Ideology and Ideological State Apparatuses" that has received ample critical attention: the part where Althusser employs the scenario of someone being hailed by the police to explain the operation of ideology, its function of interpellation to transform the individual into a subject.[41] The scenario goes like this. A police calls out "Hey, you there!"[42] The individual who is hailed turns around. "By this mere one-hundred-and-eighty-degree physical conversion," Althusser says, "he becomes a subject. Why? Because he has recognized that the hail was 'really' addressed to him, and that 'it was *really him* who was hailed' (and not someone else)."[43] Althusser's compelling scenario of subjectivization assumes a monolingual unity between the police and the hailed individual. But what if the hailed individual does not speak the same language? Introducing linguistic dissonance into Althusser's scenario complicates and elucidates his idea of interpellation. If Guálinto's Spanish-speaking, Mexican self is a subject that exists independent of hegemony, I would argue that he would not understand the police's hailing and, therefore, not turn. However, as a bilingual, Guálinto's hypothetical refusal to turn and address the police would be a conscious act and, therefore, still be a recognition of the hailing as "'really' addressed to him." From this perspective, Guálinto's recognition of his "divided personality" is not really outside the ideology of liberalism but a mode of subjectivization that exists as liberalism's interpellation of bilinguals. As much as his Mexican self may seem to be at odds with his other self, it is not each or both of these selves that create him as a subject of the liberal state but the conscious management of the differences that mark these two selves that makes him one. Guálinto's bilingualism, in this sense, is integral to the border subjectivity Saldívar reads in him.

The above interpretation places the racial pride that Guálinto cultivates while he is in school with his tightly knit group of Mexican

American friends not at a variance from but within the spectrum of liberalism. In fact, the identity of the fiery cultural nationalist that Guálinto adopts may be an illustration of what Wendy Brown claims are politicized identities based on racial injury. Such a politicized identity, she says, "emerges and obtains its unifying coherence through the politicization of exclusion from an ostensible universal, as a protest against exclusion, a protest premised on the fiction of an inclusive/universal community, a protest that reinstalls the humanist ideal insofar as it premises itself upon exclusion from it."[44] Guálinto's expressions of racial pride—his intellectual arguments with his classmates on the omissions and falsifications of history in textbooks, his rejection of passing as a "Spaniard" to enter a segregated club, his solidarity with darker-skinned Mexican American friends—signify what Brown terms Nietzschean ressentiment, "the moralizing revenge of the powerless."[45] According to Brown, such an identity "becomes attached to its own exclusion" and is therefore incapable of generating a vision of the future.[46] Not only is it "premised on this exclusion for its very existence" but it also has to continuously look back on its racial injury to affirm its existence.[47] The inextricable link between the universal and the excluded appears in Guálinto's psyche as an oscillation between racial pride and shame.

Guálinto's American self secretly harbors the desire "to be a full-fledged, complete American without the shameful encumberment of his Mexican race."[48] Paredes presents this racial shame as accompanying Guálinto's formation in English, the superior language associated with a superior culture within the hierarchical world he lives in: "Before he knows it the little Latin is thinking in English, and he can feel infinitely dirty if he forgets to brush his teeth in the morning."[49] The production of Mexican identity as stigma, what Erving Goffman calls "spoiled identity," is a form of difference management in liberalism.[50] As brutal as the racial hierarchy that governs Guálinto's world seems, it operates under the banner of rule by law. The oppositional identity of the cultural nationalist Guálinto adopts is another form of claiming difference in liberalism in that what it purports to do is to redress the hierarchy through building a group identity, through which both the individual and the group can rise in social status.[51]

At the end of the novel, when Guálinto returns as George, years after he left Jonesville for college, married to a liberal, white American woman and working for the army intelligence, he disavows his past self as a defender of Mexican Americans. For his friends and Feliciano who remain steadfast in their politicized identity as Mexican Americans, Guálinto's transformation bespeaks the ultimate betrayal of the promise of racial uplift. Yet what Paredes shows so well in the novel is not so much the moral bankruptcy of assimilation but the tenuous ability of a bilingual subject who is already interpellated as a liberal subject to resist the lure of individualist socioeconomic success. Guálinto's turning his bilingualism into an asset as a native informant echoes the enterprises for political and economic power by the Mexican American elites like Judge Norris or the Osunas. His transformation into an ethically suspect agent of the state, however, is all the more disconcerting because it shows that even the most vocal critics of Anglo-American dominance may still be incorporated into the system that perpetuates racial violence. Elodia, Guálinto's high school friend and staunch defender of Mexican American rights, is seen as having opened a restaurant and club, La Casita Mexicana, in Jonesville. Conceived as a "rival establishment" to La Casa Mexicana, the club that does not serve Mexican Americans despite employing stereotypical folk images of Mexicans to market the business to tourists, Elodia's small business holds out the promise of vindication.[52] It will provide Mexican Americans with a restaurant and club they can frequent without fear of racism and promote authentic ideas and images of the Mexican people. As good as the business idea sounds, the novel leaves unanswered the question of whether Elodia's venture can escape the same fate of individualist incorporation that Guálinto surrenders to. If *George Washington Gómez* is a prefiguration of the emergence of the Mexican American middle class, as Paredes himself states in an interview and as several critics reiterate, then the trope of bilingualism in the novel asks us to examine the price of incorporation.[53] Kingston's text suggests that this price just might be that there is little freedom for the bilingual subject outside the logic of economic liberalism that transforms the expression of cultural difference itself into a mode of economic belonging to and an affirmation of the liberal order.

## MULTICULTURAL BILINGUALS AND THE FREE MARKET ECONOMY IN THE WOMAN WARRIOR

The reception of Maxine Hong Kingston's *The Woman Warrior: Memoirs of a Girlhood among Ghosts* (1976) certainly suggests that cultural sensibilities on hyphenated identities may have changed since the 1930s depicted in *George Washington Gómez*. Kingston's first book was a critically acclaimed bestseller that was embraced by literary critics and feminists for its nuanced portrayal of the struggles of growing up a Chinese American girl in Stockton, California, during the mid-twentieth century. Such warm reception in the mainstream literary market and by academics, however, was not replicated among Asian American writers and academics.[54] The most vociferous critic of Kingston, Frank Chin, labeled Kingston a sellout for negative portrayals of Chinese men and established a strident division between "real" and "fake" Asian American literature based on his criteria of antiracism and the artistic integrity of Asian Americans. While the controversy has been primarily discussed within the parameters of the nascent field of Asian American studies, the significance of the controversy Kingston's text provoked goes well beyond Asian American studies. The controversy, as I show, was really about the stakes of ethnic self-stylization in the era of multiculturalism when racialized groups are expected to engage in self-representation.

While the ethos of multiculturalism may create more space for a variety of ethnic memoirs, still the dilemma for racialized groups is that self-representation is intrinsically tied to the politics of group representation. There is often only a fine line that separates the celebration of an original ethnic voice from the indictment of cultural inauthenticity or misrepresentation in the cultural politics of multiculturalism. These two sides of the cultural politics of recognition can succinctly be seen in how Asian American critics view the narrative's biculturalism, or its "divided personality" to borrow *George Washington Gomez*'s phrase. For those who appreciate Kingston, the narrative's biculturalism is a "double-voiced discourse" characteristic of a minority person's necessity to move between two "subcultures" and indicative of Kingston's sophisticated artistry.[55] For those who are critical, however, the same narrative illustrates the pathology of "dual personality," an ascriptive construct that is applied to Asian Americans to turn social issues of racism or inequality into issues of individual psychology.[56] On the one hand, the standoff between the defenders and critics of Kingston may seem to resemble the standoff between George and Elodia or Feliciano at the end of Paredes's text, with the cultural nationalist accusing the bilingual broker of selling out. On the other hand, the stakes of these standoffs are quite different.

In *George Washington Gómez*, George, as the bilingual broker, is engaged in a conscious act of espionage that is likely to have material consequences for the Mexican Americans of Jonesville. At stake in the controversy over Kingston's publication are epistemological and aesthetic questions of cultural difference. The harm that Kingston's detractors allege her text causes is real to the extent that one believes "a person or group of people can suffer real damage, real distortion, if the people or society around them mirror back to them a confining or demeaning or contemptible picture of themselves."[57] In this sense, the debate over *The Woman Warrior* accords with the basic tenets of multiculturalism Charles Taylor outlines with the links between recognition and identity at it heart. The vehemence with which Kingston was attacked, more than anything else, attests to the level of felt injury on the part of her attackers, their sense that the book "was a form of oppression, imprisoning [them] in a false, distorted, and reduced mode of being."[58]

One way of resituating the critical discourse on *The Woman Warrior*, then, may be to actively pursue the connections between Kingston's text and the material world. That is, we need to ask how the aesthetic of the hyphen in Kingston's text, its literary biculturalism, relates to the racial politics of incorporation in multiculturalism. To this effect, my analysis of Kingston's text in this section is premised on the idea that in addition to the qualities that are internal to the text that make it a nuanced articulation of being bicultural, *The Woman Warrior* also attracted so much critical attention because its aesthetic of biculturalism corresponded with tough questions on inclusion and difference management that were being worked out in the social realm through such initiatives as bilingual education. The hybrid aesthetic Kingston employs to express a bicultural identity speaks to new cultural sensibilities on understanding and discussing minority subjectivities. But at the center of this hybrid aesthetic lies a concern about the tenuousness of the freedom that authorizes such aesthetic experimentation and the continual erosion of resistance that can be defined against systemic oppression. Here I show that Kingston's trope of bilingualism, which relies on figures of cultural anomie and anxieties of disability, registers such an underside of her much-lauded hybrid aesthetic.

Kingston's adaptation of the Chinese story of Fa Mu Lan exemplifies her hybrid aesthetic that draws on the myths and tropes of Chinese culture to show the inner, everyday life of a Chinese American girl. It is also an important piece of evidence for Frank Chin in labeling Kingston as a "fake" Asian American writer. In "Come All Ye

Asian American Writers of the Real and the Fake," Chin argues that Kingston "rewrites the heroine, Fa Mulan, to the specs of the stereotype of the Chinese woman as a pathological white supremacist victimized and trapped in a hideous Chinese civilization."[59] King-Kok Cheung, among others, has pointed out that Chin misses "the narrator's insistent admissions of her own penchant for fabrication and her inability to discern fact from fiction" in such accusations.[60] But even if we acknowledge that Kingston's adaptation of Fa Mu Lan is more about a young girl's imaginative recreation of herself as a warrior than a faithful recounting of the Chinese tale, Chin's discomfort of Kingston's Fa Mu Lan deserves a second look in terms of what Chin calls "the stereotype of the Chinese woman."[61]

What troubles Chin the most about Kingston's Fa Mu Lan is that he sees it as exhibiting symptoms of white supremacy. "The tattoos Kingston gives Fa Mulan, to dramatize cruelty to women," Chin exclaims, "actually belong to the hero Yue Fei, a man whose tomb is now a tourist attraction at West Lake, in Hanzhou city."[62] These tattoos are words that the woman warrior's parents carve on her back before she leaves for the battlefield, the "oaths and names" that signify "revenge" and that are meant to serve as a reminder of communal "sacrifice."[63] Kingston describes the process of bodily inscription in detail:

> My mother caught the blood and wiped the cuts with a cold towel soaked in wine. It hurt terribly—the cuts sharp; the air burning; the alcohol cold, then hot—pain so various. I gripped my knees. I released them. Neither tension nor relaxation helped. I wanted to cry. If not for the fifteen years of training, I would have writhed on the floor; I would have had to be held down. The list of grievances went on and on. If an enemy should flay me, the light would shine through my skin like lace.[64]

To some extent, it is understandable that Chin bristles at the violence in this passage. The yellow, female body in pain comes across so vividly in Kingston's description. But while Chin reads this violence as the masochism of internalized racism, which displaces the violence of white supremacy to the violence of Chinese patriarchy, there is little indication in the text that the cause of the narrator's suffering is Chinese men. The greedy, feudal, misogynist baron is doubtless a warmonger who exploits peasants, but he is too much of an archetypal villain to represent Chinese men at large. Actually, it is the lack of an easily identifiable cause of the woman's bodily suffering that I think causes Chin to misrecognize the perpetrator as Chinese men.

While the fantasy's melodramatic moral binary of good and evil suggests that the narrator's suffering may be a sign of her martyrdom, the realist narrative that frames the narrator's fantasy of becoming a woman warrior offers another way of interpreting the bodily violence. With the sentence, "my American life has been such a disappointment," the narrator alludes to the burden of excellence, of having to "do something big and fine," due to her fear that she will otherwise not be appreciated as a girl in a patriarchal culture.[65] The fear that her "parents would sell [her] when [they] made [their] way back to China," however, is not a realistic fear but a fear that reflects the distance between the English-language world of the narrator and the Chinese-speaking Old World.[66] The narrator's increasing distance from the world of her parents is compounded by the racism she experiences, a reminder of her nonbelonging in America.[67] The lack of belonging in both the Old World and the New is manifested in her felt lack of ownership over both Chinese and English. Chinese is the language that represents the "invisible world the emigrants built around our childhoods" rather than the language of "solid America."[68] It is "the language of impossible stories" her mother tells her.[69] English, on the other hand, continuously denies her a voice and a place of belonging as a language that mediates racism and exclusion. The narrator can only talk back to her employer making a racist joke about "nigger yellow" in her "bad, small-person's voice that makes no impact," and her voice turns "squeaky and unreliable" each time she stands up for the rights of minorities.[70] The grown-up narrator confesses to an abiding stress when it comes to speaking in public: "A dumbness—a shame—still cracks my voice in two, even when I want to say 'hello' casually, or ask an easy question in front of the check-out counter, or ask directions of a bus driver. I stand frozen, or I hold up the line with the complete, grammatical sentence that comes squeaking out at impossible length."[71] The narrator lives with this sense of shame that leaves her either speechless or verbose and always inadequate to the occasion of speech. The suffering represented by the carved writings on the fantasy woman warrior's back, then, is not so much suffering imposed by Chinese men, but the suffering of a bilingual child who lives in a world that doubly denies her a sense of self through language. One may even suggest that the narrative of progress from silence to voice in Kingston's text—something that made the text an ideal of feminist development—repeats in literature the imperative of representing the bilingual children behind the Bilingual Education Act.

Once we recast the yellow, female body in pain as the bilingual body in pain, we can see that the fantasy of the woman warrior is that of a child in need of creating a language for herself out of the remnants of the disappearing Chinese and what can be salvaged from hostile English. At the end of the chapter "White Tigers," which contains the fantasy of Fa Mu Lan, the narrator returns to the image of the carved words on the body after denouncing both the devaluation of women among the Chinese and the racism of American society. Claiming that "what we [the swordswoman and I] have in common are the words at our backs," the narrator discusses writing as an act of taking revenge: "The reporting is the vengeance—not the beheading, not the gutting, but the words. And I have so many words—'chink' words and 'gook' words too—that they do not fit on my skin."[72] The narrator's sentiment of vengeance echoes Guálinto's resentment at the discrimination against Mexican Americans, a familiar "moralizing revenge of the powerless" mentioned earlier.[73] However, whereas Guálinto's resentment was expressed through group bonding among Mexican Americans and the voicing of an alternative Mexican American history and identity, the narrator's resentment folds back on the self. The bodily pain that the woman warrior of the fantasy has to suffer is a transposition of the psycholinguistic injury the narrator suffers in her impossible bilingual life.

Kingston's turn to the psychology of the bilingual child as the site of conflict between contending forces is a sign of the tenuousness of the freedom offered to minorities after the end of legal racism. For example, the narrator's fight in The Woman Warrior is different from that of the Civil Rights movement, the heroic protests and sit-ins in the face of police brutality whose images decorated the media in the 1960s. Given the terms of the debate between Frank Chin and Kingston on authentic representations of cultural difference, the struggles of self-representation in The Woman Warrior is closer in sentiments to the self-determination struggles that followed the Civil Rights movement than to the Civil Rights movement itself.[74] The narrator's fight to acquire a "personality" illustrates the stakes of self-determination as well as the illusory qualities of such a pursuit.[75] A much-commented-on moment in the text, the narrator's bullying of a Chinese American classmate, can actually be read as an allegory of the pitfalls of self-determination, as the narrator resorts to violence in her attempt to impose her own view of personhood onto another Chinese American girl.[76] At school, the narrator corners a quiet Chinese American girl, a girl she has observed with mounting anxiety because she reminds the narrator of all the traits that mark herself as deviant from mainstream norms of sociality, such as athleticism and lack of self-expression, and indulges in a session of interrogation and coercion. All to make her speak. "If you don't talk," the narrator says to her classmate, "you can't have a personality. You'll have no personality and no hair. You've got to let people know you have a personality and a brain."[77] This statement strings together a number of seemingly incoherent aspects of personhood that combine in the narrator's mind as what makes one a socially desirable person: speech (emphasized as primal), physical beauty (hair), and mental power (brain).

Compared with Guálinto's struggles with a "divided personality," though, what is most striking about the narrator's case is the doubling of herself as the bully. If Guálinto's bully was manifestly exterior to him—particularly in the character of Miss Cornelia—the bully outside becomes the bully within in the case of Kingston's narrator. This difference is not just a difference in characterization but a difference that reflects the terms of racial inclusion in multiculturalism. The problem of a "divided personality" in *George Washington Gomez* is unequivocally a problem of a racial hierarchy whose history goes back to armed conflict between the English-speaking and the Spanish-speaking peoples and invokes the tropes of colonial conquest and the subordination of conquered people. In Kingston's text, the same predicament of "divided personality" becomes a problem of individual social adjustment and communication issues within the family, particularly between the mother and the daughter. For example, the narrator points to the predicament of the bilingual child as having to choose between two rivaling sets of social norms represented by the two languages through the orthographic differences between Chinese and English. Asked to read a passage from a book at school, the narrator comes to a halt when she comes across the word "I": "The Chinese 'I' has seven strokes, intricacies. How could the American 'I,' assuredly wearing a hat like the Chinese, have only three strokes, the middle so straight? . . . I stared in at the middle line and waited so long for its black center to resolve into tight strokes and dots that I forgot to pronounce it."[78] Such bilingual reflection results in the narrator's being penalized, as the teacher fails to recognize the fact that the narrator's pause in reading is an existential inquiry into the exigencies of being bilingual.

The problem with Kingston's representation of the bilingual predicament is not that the young Chinese American girl's confusion has no merit or value but that it leads to a misrecognition of the bilingual predicament as something that can be solved by a promotion of multicultural awareness. This misrecognition is actually an effect of the particular understanding of culture as a domain that is evacuated of political and economic implications in multiculturalism.[79] And it leads to a diagnostic that looks like this: Since the narrator's wrongful penalization at school resulted from the teacher's inability to understand the sensibilities of a Chinese American bilingual child, the most pressing issue is to develop an awareness of Chinese language and culture in teachers to avoid future errors of this kind. This approach, however, displaces the structural and systemic basis of the bilingual child's injuries, so aptly foregrounded in *George Washington Gómez*, onto the plane of individual cultural negotiations. Unlike the diagnostic multiculturalism I mention above, Kingston does allude to the problem of uneven power relations between variously racialized groups in *The Woman Warrior*. It is there in her portrayal of residential segregation, the hate speech of white Americans, and the proliferation of stereotypes about people of color. Yet these references are diffuse and the source of the narrator's psychological suffering is neither monolithic nor unified. If there is cultural confusion in *The Woman Warrior*, it is not the confusion between Chinese and American cultures that matters but the one between the sure sense of a resistant subjectivity in the era of legal racism and the unmoored sense of self that is at once too free and not free enough to represent oneself in liberal multiculturalism.

The topoi of Asian American displacement and belonging that the grown-up narrator voices to her mother relate this tenuous freedom of the post–Jim Crow Asian American to an erosion of collective rights and identity for racialized groups. To the grown-up narrator who has come back home to visit, the mother tells the story of the loss of their family land in China. With the giving up of this family land, the idea of not going back to China takes on a concreteness that is hard for the mother: "We have no more China to go home to."[80] In the mother's mind, the family land is the equivalent for the country of China. Losing this land, hence, is tantamount to losing home. The narrator consoles with a view of belonging and citizenship that goes beyond nation-states and gestures to the planetary: "We belong to the planet now, Mama. Does it make sense to you that if we're no longer attached to one piece of land, we belong to the planet? Wherever we happen to be standing, why, that spot belongs to us as much as any other spot."[81] This moving statement on planetary citizenship is a marked contrast to the mother's premodern notion of belonging to a place, as well as to the politics of land ownership in *George Washington Gómez*, where Mexican American dispossession of the land forms the basis of their collective struggle to reclaim ownership. An easy way of explaining these contrasting views on land might be to evoke the distinction between immigrants and the groups that Will Kymlicka calls "national minorities."[82] Kymlicka suggests that whereas immigrants, as voluntary migrants in search of the American Dream, cannot claim dispossession, historical minorities who have been subject to historical wrongs of slavery, conquest, and exclusion are subject to racial formations that reflect particular histories and struggles of systemic dispossession.[83] This distinction, however, does not quite hold up in the case of *The Woman Warrior*, as the textual clues on Chinese exclusion and Japanese internment explicitly reference the racial formation of Asian Americans. A more textually truthful explanation of the idea of planetary belonging, then, might be that it is the narrator's provisionary answer for articulating belonging at a time when a firm sense of group identity or rights is eroded by new paradigms of accounting for difference and an alternative basis for articulating racial injuries is yet to be found. In other words, the trope of planetary belonging is the psychological predicament of multiculturalism as Kingston sees it.

Meanwhile, the racial injuries turn inward and are marked on the mind and body of the narrator. The proliferating images of disability in Kingston's text, especially in the way many of them link the mind and the body in a chain of dysfunction, point to the narrator's displaced anxieties about her uneven bilingualism and the lack of a platform to articulate such anxieties. If the hybrid aesthetic of the Chinese Americanizing of Fa Mu Lan shows the potential of the narrator's bilingualism, the underside of her bilingual anxieties can be seen in the images of disability. Anne Cheng, in her reading of the figure of hypochondria in *The Woman Warrior* as "an expression of assimilatory anxiety," shows how the grief of the racialized body translates into somatic symptoms in Kingston's text.[84] If Cheng focuses on the intertwined dynamic of the mind and the body in the

Chinese American girl's struggles of assimilation, I turn to the division effected between self and society in my analysis of how the racial injuries that originate in the social realm are displaced onto the mind and body of the individual through images of both cognitive and bodily disabilities. From this perspective, the yellow, bilingual body that had to suffer the pain of having words carved on the back in the Fa Mu Lan fantasy returns as the narrator's disabled body after her bullying of her classmate. The searing physical pain in the fantasy becomes "a mysterious illness" in ordinary life, but the temporary incapacitation of the body remains the same.[85] The fact that bodily trial leads to a state of heightened understanding of the self's relationship to the world also remains the same. Just as the fantasy woman warrior is able to understand her role as a witness of the people's grievances through the words on her back, the narrator is able to revise her assumptions about her Chinese American classmate after her illness: "I was wrong about nobody taking care of her. . . . She was protected by her family, as they would normally have done in China."[86] The temporary experience of disability allows the narrator to adopt a more flexible approach toward social norms, allowing the space for another way of life even if she does not fully comprehend the meaning or the implications of this other way. Bodily disability functions as a check on the self's indulgence in unencumbered violence as the fantasy woman warrior's physical power is bridled by the inscription of the communal mission and the narrator's potential as a bully is tempered by her "mysterious illness."

At the same time that they adumbrate the narrator's anxieties about her uneven bilingualism, the images of disability also presage the neoliberal emphasis on competence, or skills, commonly understood in an economic sense, in the evaluation of a person's value, which I look at in detail in Chapter 4. Nothing shows this better than the trope of the narrator's cut tongue. This trope links the narrator's anxieties about becoming existentially surplus, as Grace Hong puts it, in a neoliberal, skills-oriented free market economy to bodily and cognitive disabilities.[87] The narrator's confession that her mother cut her tongue when she was young follows a conversation between siblings that undermines the veracity of memory. As two siblings try to piece together the accounts on the day their aunt, Moon Orchid, met her estranged husband, they cannot agree on what they remember. To further blur the line between fact and fiction, the narrator insinuates that the story of Moon Orchid she recounted in the previous chapter

might be "twisted into designs," like the knots made by China's out-
law knot-makers.[88] Such admission of a penchant for embellishment
and an identification with authority-defying artists as a preface to the
story has led critics to read the tongue-cutting as a primal scene of
the narrator's coming into voice.[89] I would like to focus here, though,
on the mother's reason for this violation of the daughter's organ of
speech. While it is overlooked in most critical examinations of the
narrator's cut tongue, I believe it is important in reading the deficient
tongue as a socially produced disability. In response to the narrator's
questions about why she did it, the mother says "I cut it so you would
not be tongue-tied. Your tongue would be able to move in any language. You'll be able to speak languages that are completely different
from one another. You'll be able to pronounce anything. Your frenum
looked too tight to do these things, so I cut it."[90] Despite the casual
manner of delivery, the mother's reason for cutting her daughter's frenum (to give her linguistic excellence) is hardly unwarranted given the
frequent clinical misdiagnosis of bilingual children as linguistically
deficient. As I have examined elsewhere, the mother's performance
of frenectomy on the narrator is a reminder of how bilingualism was
often seen as a cause of stuttering, and frenectomy proposed as a
cure.[91] Instead of wishing away the narrator's bilingualism, though,
the mother actually yearns for her daughter's multilingualism and her
freedom to express oneself and code-switch at will. Implied in the
mother's reason for lingual mobility might be an unarticulated desire
for socioeconomic mobility for her daughter. If the narrator learns to
be fluent in both English and Chinese ("languages that are completely
different from one another") with her loosened frenum, she could
possibly turn her liability of bilingualism into an asset like the Mexican American elites of *George Washington Gómez*.

For the narrator, the economic evaluation of bilingualism appears
obliquely in her continuous felt need for an appraisal of self-worth
through language both at school and at home. At the English-
speaking school, she is constrained by the inability of the teachers
and school authorities to understand her differences from the norms
of speech, misrecognizing her silence for lack of intelligence or a
troubled psychology. Regularly sent to speech therapy at school, the
narrator struggles with the stereotypes of her bilingualism and the
misleading ideas of her abilities that they engender. It is only when
she "invent[s] an American-feminine speaking personality" that she
is released from the grip of such stereotypes that turn her bilingualism

into a liability.[92] The Chinese school, which she attends after school, is not a haven from the worries about language that plague the narrator either. While some of her Chinese American peers who are "silent at American school [find] voice at Chinese school," the narrator is suspicious of the demands made on her by the Chinese school.[93] "You can't entrust your voice to the Chinese, either," she says, "they want to capture your voice for their own use. They want to fix up your tongue to speak for them. 'How much less can you sell it for?' we have to say. Talk the Sales Ghosts down. Make them take a loss."[94] If the narrator is disappointed with the English-speaking school's unremitting misrecognition of her linguistic abilities, she remains likewise deeply skeptical of the abilities the Chinese try to cultivate in her, which primarily involves translation to promote the economic interests of Chinese adults. Her worth, the narrator realizes, lies in how she avails herself of her languages to navigate the demands on the demonstration of her abilities made by various groups.

At home, which also doubles as a workplace for the family business of the laundromat, the narrator worries about her exchange value for her parents both in the United States and in the hypothetical scenario of a return to China. As Erin Ninh demonstrates, these worries about "disownment" are a sign of the daughter's dependence on her parents, or of "sovereign parental power," to borrow her words.[95] The narrator plays many roles in the family economy, as unpaid labor for the laundromat and as designated translator (being the oldest) to sort out cultural misunderstandings between the parents and English-speaking business owners.[96] For example, when the mother receives an errant delivery from the neighborhood pharmacy, the narrator is sent to "rectify their crime" for "taint[ing] [the narrator's] house with sick medicine," a task that calls for such daunting cross-cultural explanation that the young narrator is already set up for failure.[97] It brings out her deepest linguistic anxieties. Despite her contributions to the family economy, the narrator constantly worries about her worthlessness to her parents, assessing and reassessing her value in the family economy. "But if I made myself unsellable here," the narrator ruminates after noticing her approximation of social deviancy, "my parents need only wait until China, and there, where anything happens, they would be able to unload us, even me—sellable, marriageable."[98] Trying to assess her worth bilingually, for both the English-speaking and the Chinese-speaking, adds to the narrator's burden of figuring out her self through language. When a Chinese

American patron of the family laundromat, a woman of wealth and influence in the immigrant community, criticizes the narrator's "pressed-duck voice," which, according to her estimation, makes her a poor candidate for marriage, it is a shrill reminder that the narrator's "American-feminine speaking personality" is not sufficient to meet the demands of her bilingual world.[99]

Perhaps it is the ceaseless myopic and unrealistic calculations of her exchange value, or her human capital, that drives the narrator to return again and again to the image of insanity, the ultimate breakdown of mental ability. Language is crucial to the narrator's drawing the line between a healthy, high-functioning person and an unhealthy, dysfunctional one. "I thought talking and not talking made the difference between sanity and insanity," the narrator says. "Insane people were the ones who couldn't explain themselves."[100] The faith in such rational usage of language, however, dissipates in the face of the closeness the narrator sees between herself and the so-called deviant subjects of Stockton's Chinatown, such as Crazy Mary and Pee-A-Nah. These women are the redundant women of Chinatown U.S.A. in that, like their predecessors in Victorian England, who were considered as having little to no economic value to the industrializing nation, they are not considered to be contributing to the economic functions of the narrator's world. For all her rejection of these redundant women—"I did not want to be our crazy one"—the narrator's uneasiness about mental disability is heightened when she believes her parents are considering a match between her and a mentally disabled Chinese American boy.[101] "I studied hard, got straight A's but nobody seemed to see that I was smart and had nothing in common with this monster, this birth defect."[102] The narrator's words against the boy reveal her anxieties about her precarious position as a devalued subject who can easily slide into the category of Chinatown's redundant women. Mentally disabled as he is, the wealth of the boy's family and the privilege of being a male will protect him in ways that the narrator cannot be protected.

Finally, the narrator shows her verbal fluency in a list of grievances she airs in front of her family, quelling any suspicion of deficiency in her human capital and vowing to dissociate herself from the grueling labor that characterizes Chinese immigrant lives and to exercise her right to upward mobility through education. "I'm going away anyway. I am . . . I may be ugly and clumsy, but one thing I'm not, I'm not retarded. . . . Do you know what the Teacher Ghosts say about me? They tell me I'm smart, and I can win scholarships. I can get into colleges."[103] The assertion of smartness, of mental ability, is seemingly demonstrated by her flood of words, and the narrator builds a web of associations between the family and a lower economic position and between school and a higher economic one to arrive at the imperative of "going away." While the mother may have wished multilingualism and attendant socioeconomic mobility on the daughter, the narrator's convoluted understanding of her own human capital in the isolated social environment of Chinatown leads to a disavowal of her bilingualism. "It's your fault that I talk weird," she claims. "The only reason I flunked kindergarten was because you couldn't teach me English, and you gave me a zero IQ. I've brought my IQ up, though. . . . I don't need anybody to pronounce English words for me. I can figure them out by myself. I'm going to get scholarships, and I'm going away."[104] In her strained logic, she overcomes the inheritance of mental disability, associated with maternal Chinese, and climbs up the hierarchy of languages to arrive at high performance in English in a feat of meritocracy. This individual achievement, it is implied, is what she views will promise her a sense of security and self-worth outside Chinatown.

After this outburst, the narrator reconciles with her mother. Her many misunderstandings of her family's views of her, including the pathologization of her speech—"You can't stop me from talking. You tried to cut off my tongue, but it didn't work"—are somewhat cleared in the aftermath of the outburst.[105] The biggest misrecognition of the narrator, though, is neither the mother's motives nor the lack of opportunities for the limited-English-speaking Chinese to move up in the socioeconomic ladder. Rather, it is her understanding of bilingualism as a liability that proves the biggest misrecognition when, in fact, the entire book itself is a demonstration that it could be an asset. A profound reflection on language as human capital from the perspective of a Chinese American bilingual girl, *The Woman Warrior* still leaves the reader with the challenge of reconciling the narrator's insights on the limitations of bilingualism with the text's value as cultural capital.

In closing, I would like to briefly discuss the excesses of bilingualism in fantasies. Above, I have examined Kingston's fantasy of Fa Mu Lan as an example of her hybrid aesthetic, an aesthetic that demonstrates her mixing of Chinese and American cultures. Needless to say, such a view of biculturalism assumes a tidiness around the boundaries of cultures that does not exist. What can be pinpointed as "Chinese" or "American" cultural traits are usually caricatures of Chinese or American culture. Still, these cultural boundaries, or the feeling that they exist, may play a bigger role in the complex negotiations of cultural pluralism today than we would like to admit. Frank Chin's comparison between the story of Fa Mu Lan and the English nursery rhyme "London Bridge Is Falling Down," which he comes up with in an effort to expose Kingston's ethnic inauthenticity shows this well.[106] With his claim that among Chinese Americans Fa Mu Lan's story is "as popular today as 'London Bridge Is Falling Down,'" Chin actually erodes the ground for Chinese Americanness that is neither Chinese nor white American as the cultural distinction that is important seems to be that between Chinese and Anglo-American.[107] That this comparison informs Chin's discussion of "real" Asian Americanness is an irony of Asian American cultural nationalism. But if Chin's way of critiquing "fake" Asian Americanness seems ineffective, maybe a way to sidestep a too-easy reduction of culture into behavioral patterns or categorical values is to turn our attention to how language mediates culture.

Viewed as a bilingual fantasy, a fantasy that requires the deployment of one's relationship to both languages of her world, Kingston's story of the woman warrior is an excessive use of the narrator's bilingualism in that the story does not play a part in proving the abilities of the young narrator to those in her immediate surrounding, whether Chinese or English speaking. The fame of Kingston's story, in the form of the publication *The Woman Warrior* and coming years after the supposed fantasizing took place in the young narrator's mind, is sweet revenge. It proves her abilities by exceeding the utilitarian expectations of the young narrator's quotidian world and showing the capacity for a former bilingual child to become a writer who commands considerable cultural capital. Of course, not all bilingual fantasies have such real-life results. A comparably impotent bilingual fantasy, Guálinto's fantasy of leading the Mexican side in the reenactment of the United States–Mexican War, otherwise called his "mother-loving dream," taps into his repressed relationship with his mother tongue to accomplish in dreams what his life cannot.[108] In his fantasy, he leads the Mexican army, which includes "Irishmen and escaped American Negro slaves" to a heroic victory.[109] History is reversed in his dream world, as the suppressed resentment of the

Mexicotexan against Anglos rears its head. While in his waking life, Guálinto goes on disavowing his Mexican heritage and his relationships with his Spanish-speaking family and friends, this bilingual fantasy breaks the peace of his seemingly white American, middle-class life. After this recurring dream, Guálinto asks "Why do I keep doing this? Why do I keep on fighting battles that were won and lost a long time ago? Lost by me and won by me too?"[110] These questions may well be what the literary excesses of bilingualism leave us with so that we can continue to reflect on the gains and losses of the liberal inclusion of bilinguals.

CHAPTER FOUR

# Dormant Bilingualism in Neoliberal America

In his memoir cum scholarly study of civil rights jurisprudence, *Covering* (2006), Kenji Yoshino includes a brief discussion of the relationship between language and race he intuited when he attended Phillips Exeter Academy:

> The stereotype that plagued me the most was the portrait of the Asian-American as the perpetual foreigner. I came to hate the question 'Where are you from, *really*' that followed my assertion that I had grown up in Boston. I washed away this tincture of foreignness with language. I wish to be careful here, as my pleasure in language feels largely independent of any other identity. Yet my racial identity did spur my will to command English. I could see my parents struggling with a language in which neither of them would ever swim. And my own failure at Japanese gave me direct experience of illiteracy. I collected English words like amulets. At Exeter, I noticed this mastery whitened me.[1]

I begin with this lengthy quote because this fleeting moment of Yoshino's reflection on how his adolescent self understood the correspondence between mastery of standard English and racial difference underscores the subject I examine in this chapter: the relationship between language and race in the post–civil rights culture and politics of assimilation. Yoshino judiciously suggests that his linguistic and racial identities are not commensurate yet indisputably related. The fact that he is viewed as a foreigner due to his racial difference pushes him to prove his Americanness through English. It would be beside the point to ask to what degree the soft racism he encountered is responsible for his avid cultivation of English. The two metaphors in the above passage of being fluent in English as swimming and English words as amulets bring to mind common expressions in teaching English as a second language: the pedagogy of teaching English through immersion that is referred to as the sink-or-swim method and the idea of English acquisition that assumes language is an object to be acquired. As someone from a language minority household, Yoshino's confession of his ardent desire for unaccented English reveals his inadvertent interpellation as a subject by the pedagogy of English as a second language. Ironically, even as he tries to shed the suggestion of foreignness through mastery of English, the very fact of his doing so actually positions him as a foreigner when one considers the ideological operation of English.

Looking at it through an Althusserian lens, Yoshino's exploration of "covering," the act of veiling from social scrutiny a trait that is socially unaccepted or controversial, can be read as a sustained engagement with the interpellative force of the juridical apparatus to produce subjects that voluntarily play down certain elements of their identity that may make them hypervisible in the public when they perform their social identities.[2] As a term that indexes the predicament of post–civil rights jurisprudence for Yoshino, covering hinges on the idea that some identities—such as one's language of origin or sexual orientation—can be covered whereas some—such as the color of one's skin—cannot. As a legal scholar Yoshino's interest lies in how this distinction between identities results in an uneven application of the equal-protection clause in civil rights laws to socially vulnerable groups.[3] Compared to other strategies for minority inclusion, such as conversion (which requires the transformation of a core identity) and passing (which requires the hiding of a core identity), covering, Yoshino suggests, is generally viewed as less harmful, if at all, to the minority person since the person who covers is not prohibited from engaging in public activities or from reaping the benefits of such and since it is generally viewed as applied to peripheral elements of a person (or a noncore identity). His primary example for the differential legal demands made on minorities to cover is the widespread belief that one's sexual orientation can be covered (as opposed to a trait like skin color) and the subsequent lack of legal protection afforded sexual minorities in this context. Language minorities parallel sexual minorities in Yoshino's work as an employer can ask a bilingual employee to cover her non-English language at work without legal consequences just as an employer can expect a gay employee to refrain from activities or expressions that are explicitly related to his sexual identity at work without legally being considered discriminatory.

What social pressure does such legally sanctioned covering of non-English languages have for bilinguals? The psycholinguist François Grosjean's concept of dormant bilingualism is helpful in thinking through such a question. In his study on bilingualism, Grosjean says that "people undergoing this process [language forgetting] can be termed 'dormant bilinguals' in the sense that one of their languages is no longer used regularly."[4] The post–civil rights politics of assimilation, one can say, actually encourages dormant bilingualism through the legal nonintercession on the social expectations of language covering. The dormant bilingualism of racial minorities such as Asians and Latinos, then, is inexorably tied to the rollback of civil rights legislation and policy in neoliberal multiculturalism. I place the writings of the contemporary writers Richard Rodriguez and Chang-rae Lee in such a context in this chapter to examine the relationship between language and race in neoliberal America. As literary accounts of post–civil rights linguistic assimilation, Richard Rodriguez's memoirs—especially *Hunger of Memory: The Education of Richard Rodriguez* (1982) and *Brown: The Last Discovery of America* (2002)—and Chang-rae Lee's debut novel, *Native Speaker* (1995), reflect the social concerns on multilingualism and civic disunity that permeated the last two decades of the twentieth century and locate the immigrant's loss of the mother tongue in this context. Yet Rodriguez's and Lee's narratives are distinct from what could be called a prototypical narrative of language assimilation in US literature in that their representations of dormant bilingualism appear in the shadows of racial tropes. Building on the use of the rhetorical figure of analogy employed by bilingual plaintiffs—that language is "like race"—in the legal briefs on English-only workplace rules, I show the relation of contiguity Rodriguez and Lee embed in their representations of language and race.[5] While the analogy between language and race mostly fails in the courtrooms, I argue that it is a productive rhetorical move for investigating the contingencies of bilingualism in post–civil rights America for Rodriguez and Lee. Through their exploration of the intersections of language and race, Rodriguez and Lee show that language is prone to be influenced by the same capitalist logic that commodifies race. The complex web of relations among language, race, and capital in their writings brings into high relief how illusory such terms as freedom and choice are in neoliberal America for racialized subjects.

## COVERING BILINGUALISM IN POST–CIVIL RIGHTS JURISPRUDENCE

Here I look at three well-known lawsuits involving English-only policies, including *Garcia v. Gloor* (1980) and *Garcia v. Spun Steak* (1993), two cases that legal scholar Cristina M. Rodriguez suggests "set the parameters of the debate in the language context," and *Dimaranan v. Pomona Valley Hospital Medical Center* (1991).[6] These cases have been studied in depth by legal scholars who disagree with the verdicts, which do not extend the equal-protection clause to the bilingual plaintiffs' right to speak a language other than English at work.[7] Most often a lawsuit of this kind takes place when one employee, or several, violates or refuses to comply with the employer's English-only rules at work, is penalized for such actions, and seeks legal redress under Title VII of the Civil Rights Act of 1964, which "makes it illegal to discriminate someone on the basis of race, color, religion, national origin, or sex" in employment.[8] I trace the arguments of bilinguals who refuse to cover their language and those of the employers respectively before offering an interpretation of why the plights of these bilinguals seem to elide the civil-rights rationale of the law in the post–civil rights era. The breakdown of civic harmony at the heart of these cases boils down to two contrasting views of language: the plaintiffs' view of language as a cultural right versus the employers' and the courts' regard of language as a skill. As these very different views of language impede a satisfying resolution of the social conflict, the rhetorical figure of analogy serves as a prosthetic for the bilingual plaintiffs who seek legal redress. They argue that unlike the courts' view that language use is a matter of individual will and choice, language is "like race," not necessarily reflective of individual will or choice and prone to discrimination based on prejudice.[9] This analogy, however, commonly fails to hold up as the courts subscribe to the view of language as a skill and of the worker as what anthropologist Bonnie Urciuoli calls "a bundle of skills."[10]

In *Garcia v. Gloor*, Hector Garcia, a twenty-four-year-old Mexican American man at the time when he was fired from his job as a salesperson at Gloor Lumber Supply, Inc., in 1975, sued his former employer for language discrimination. Located in Brownsville, Texas, which has a high population of Spanish-speaking people, Gloor Lumber's employee demographic also reflected the linguistic diversity of the area.[11] The company had a total of thirty-nine employees, thirty-one of whom were Hispanic. Of the thirty-nine employees, eight were salespersons, and seven of them were Hispanic.[12] The company had an English-only rule with some restrictions: the English-only rule did not apply to breaks; the employees could speak Spanish to customers on the job; and the English-only rule did not apply to the few Spanish-speaking employees who had no or limited English proficiency and worked in the lumberyard. Garcia, a third-generation Mexican American, grew up speaking Spanish at home and identified as a bilingual whose primary language was Spanish. When a supervisor found him answering a coworker's question about the availability of an item in Spanish, Garcia was let go. Gloor Lumber argued that the decision to fire Garcia was based on a number of reasons pertaining to job performance of which noncompliance with the English-only rule was only one. The court sided with Gloor Lumber, saying: "Mr. Garcia was fully bilingual. He chose deliberately to speak Spanish instead of English while actually at work," and denied Garcia relief under Title VII.[13] *Garcia v. Gloor* is often cited as setting the precedent for, in Yoshino's words, "us[ing] immutability as a gatekeeping mechanism" in language discrimination cases.[14]

*Garcia v. Spun Steak* shows a similar conflict between Spanish-speaking employees and an employer who has an English-only rule at work. The conflict took place in a south San Francisco poultry-packing company, Spun Steak, which had thirty-three workers, twenty-four of whom were Spanish-speaking. The company established an English-only rule after it received complaints against two of its employees, Priscilla Garcia and Maricela Buitrago, that they "made derogatory, racist comments in Spanish about two coworkers, one of whom is African-American and the other Chinese American."[15] The company also recommended against the use of hurtful language at work at the same time. After ineffectively protesting the English-only rule, Garcia, Buitrago, and Local 115, their labor union, filed a discrimination charge against Spun Steak with the Equal Employment Opportunity Commission, which found the company's actions to be in violation of Title VII. While the district court agreed with the EEOC opinion, the appellate court reversed the decision and found the company to not be in violation of Title VII based on the reason that it could not find adverse effects of the English-only policy on Spanish-speaking workers.

*Garcia v. Spun Steak* is often cited as the case that tested the application of the disparate impact theory for English-only rules on bilingual employees. Legal terms that often appear in legal battles concerning civil rights laws, disparate impact and disparate treatment can be viewed as tools in the legal discernment of what discrimination is. Both basically assume that a plaintiff has been treated differently by certain policies or practices at work. However, to make a disparate treatment claim, the plaintiff has to demonstrate discriminatory intent on the part of the person who enforces these policies or practices. In a disparate impact claim, the plaintiff just needs to demonstrate that a supposedly neutral policy adversely affects an individual or a group. Needless to say, plaintiffs who make disparate treatment claims often bear a higher burden of proof as they need to show evidence of the other party's intent. The plaintiffs in *Garcia v. Spun Steak* argued that Spun Steak's English-only rules disparately impacted the employees who speak Spanish, most likely adopting the disparate impact claim because it is close to impossible to show discriminatory intent in workplaces policies that do not contain racism or prejudices in their explicit wording. Accepting that the company's English-only rules applied differentially to the Spanish-speaking employees, the court still placed the evidentiary burden of showing that the English-only rule had created adverse working conditions for a certain group of employees on the bilingual plaintiffs and decided that in this case disparate impact did not amount to undue discrimination. While these may seem like legal jargon, terms such as disparate treatment or disparate impact actually index the challenges of sorting out what constitutes differential treatment that is acceptable and what not in post–civil rights culture. The courts' refusal to see the disparate impact of English-only rules as discrimination shows that language covering at work is viewed as not only legal but also socially and culturally advisable.

Another challenge to addressing language conflicts through civil rights laws is that an English-only policy is often presented as a neutral solution to racial conflicts in multiracial work environments. The complaint leveled at the bilinguals, Garcia and Buitrago, by their coworkers in *Garcia v. Spun Steak* illustrates this well. It is hard not to notice how the company takes on the role of the race-neutral mediator of conflicts by establishing English-only rules as a solution to the lack of civility among minorities at work. A slightly different case that nonetheless frequently comes up in critical discussions of language discrimination, *Dimaranan v. Pomona Valley Hospital Medical Center*, also allows the reader to place the clash between bilingual and monolingual employees in the context of a breakdown of workplace civic culture. In this case, Adelaida Dimaranan, a Filipina nurse who held the title of assistant head nurse, was demoted for speaking Tagalog at work with fellow Filipina nurses and for allegedly breeding divisiveness in her unit. While Dimaranan claimed the hospital had an unlawful English-only rule under which she was penalized for noncompliance, the court interpreted the conflict between Dimaranan and her supervisors as going beyond the speaking of Tagalog and viewed the hospital's policy as more of a No-Tagalog rule than an English-only rule. At once rejecting Dimaranan's request that the court view the hospital's management of her as a Title VII violation in which the hospital used her language (Tagalog) as a proxy for her national origin to discriminate against her, the court accepted her demotion as a retaliatory act on the part of the employer for Dimaranan's resistance to the hospital's language policy and ordered remedies. The question of bad faith in the bilingual employee's interactions with other employees and supervisors reappear in other legal cases as language is attributed with the power to exclude or include in abstraction from the speakers and the concrete situations of language use.

Hector Garcia, Priscilla Garcia, Maricela Buitrago, and Adelaida Dimaranan are all bilinguals who refused to cover their bilingualism at work despite obvious pressure. What led them to believe that they had the right to speak a non-English language at work? On what grounds did they not only refuse to comply with the company's workplace rule but decide to take their cases to court to argue for their right? An expert witness's statement in *Garcia v. Gloor* summarizes the answer to these questions. On behalf of Hector Garcia, the expert witness said that "the Spanish language is the most important aspect of ethnic identification for Mexican-Americans, and it is to them what skin color is to others."[16] This analogy between language and race recurs in the arguments of the bilinguals who seek refuge from language discrimination at work.[17] Basically, such analogy suggests that language cannot be covered just as race, an immutable and visible trait, cannot. On the one hand, the "like-race" argument resonates with the strategy adopted by many plaintiffs in discrimination cases who resort to Title VII protection in its implicit view that race is the paradigmatic trait that Title VII is designed to protect from discrimination.[18] On the other hand, it acknowledges the common view that language is a sign of ethnicity, associated more with a distinctive group's way of life than a biologically oriented view of a group such as skin color. In this aspect, the analogy operates not to suggest that language and race are similar to each other regardless of context but to emphasize the symbolic significance of such traits as skin color and language in the social perceptions of minority groups in the United States. Spanish, in other words, is the kind of group trait used by non-Latinos to identify and place Latinos the way that skin color is used by white Americans to identify and place African Americans.

The rigidity of the legal category of race in civil rights laws of course fails to fully address the experiences of racialized bilinguals. At the same time, the bilingual plaintiffs also cannot escape the existing legal categories that shape the social expression and acceptance (or nonacceptance) of their bilingualism. In this context, one may think about the figure of analogy in the legal defense of bilinguals as a rhetorical adjudication of the different identities that constitute the bilingual person. That is, in the like-race arguments, language becomes a noncore identity that functions as a screen upon which another, presumably more vulnerable part of one's identity is projected. In terms of legal protection against discrimination, it creates a hierarchy of identities, effectively reinforcing the subordination of language difference to racial difference that has long characterized American culture.[19]

However, when one attends to the rationale of the free market in the court decisions on these workplace language disputes, one can also see a neoliberal logic that seems distinctively turn-of-the-twenty-first century. Almost uniformly, the courts viewed the English-only rules as justified based on "business necessity" and dismissed the argument that language is a protected category like race or national origin by emphasizing the will and choice of the bilingual.[20] Interestingly, the *Gloor* court conceded that "to a person who speaks only one tongue or to a person who has difficulty using another language than the one spoken in his home, language might well be an immutable characteristic like skin color, sex or place of birth."[21] "However," the *Gloor* court went to say, "the language a person who is multi-lingual elects to speak at a particular time is by definition a matter of choice."[22] By viewing language as either a mutable or an immutable trait based on contingency, the *Gloor* court made it possible to adopt an expansive, if elusive, definition of choice in ruling in favor of language covering. To the bilinguals who argued that they were denied the privilege to express themselves in the language of their choice, a privilege of employment that monolingual English speakers enjoyed, the courts responded with quite a different view of privilege. The *Gloor* court, for example, rejected the idea that an employee has the privilege to express herself in a language of her choice. "An employer's failure to forbid employees to speak English," it said in reference to the monolingual English employees, "does not grant them a privilege."[23] While being more receptive to the idea that certain forms and expressions of speech at work, such as small talk between coworkers, may be a privilege of employment, the *Spun Steak* court still maintained that bilinguals do not suffer from unlawful denial of privilege as "a privilege . . . is by definition given at the employer's discretion; an employer has the right to define its contours."[24] Faced with the argument that language is a proxy of national origin, the courts agreed to it in the most general sense but refused to see its applicability in the particular cases in front of them. Instead, the courts emphasized such terms as "preference" and "inconvenience" in their decisions. The *Gloor* court argued that all that Gloor Lumber did with its English-only rule was to "restric[t] [Hector Garcia's] preference while he was on the job and not serving a customer," something within the purview of an employer's right.[25] Just as the *Gloor* court used preference to downplay the bilingual plaintiff's complaint, the *Spun Steak* court also regarded the English-only rule as a matter of inconvenience for the bilingual plaintiffs, saying that, "Title VII is not meant to protect against rules that merely inconvenience some employees, even if that inconvenience falls regularly on a protected class."[26] Ironically, the *Spun Steak* court ruling has the effect of legalizing disparate treatment by sending the message that differentially inconveniencing a protected class is justified as part of the liberal rule of law. Where the court draws the line between convenience and necessity, between inconvenience and discrimination, remains unspecified.

Whereas the bilingual plaintiffs view language as more or less a cultural right, such a view holds little to no sway as the courts attend to the prerogatives of the businesses and view the English-only rules in the context of the employer's decisions about what is best for business practice. What is less obvious than the prominence of business interests in these juridical decisions but nevertheless is still important for the purpose of understanding the nature of language covering is the courts' view on language as a potential skill that can be commandeered by the employer. The *Gloor* court's view of Hector Garcia's bilingualism shows this best. The *Gloor* court points out that Garcia was "hired by Gloor precisely because he was bilingual."[27] But instead of using this fact as the basis for why his bilingualism should be respected at work, the court draws a very different conclusion on the power of the employer to curtail his language use. "His preference in language," the *Gloor* court says, "was restricted to some extent by the nature of his employment. On the job, in addressing English-speaking customers, he was obliged to use English; in serving Spanish-speaking patrons, he was required to speak Spanish."[28] The advantage that Garcia may have had for the business as a bilingual employee becomes evidence for the court to conclude that Gloor Lumber was already restricting Garcia's use of his two languages. Such restriction almost seems like a condition of employment to start with.

The *Gloor* court's view of Garcia's bilingualism as a skill that is subject to business interests and dictates, I suggest, reflects a neoliberal understanding of the worker and of language, which calls for analyzing these juridical decisions on bilinguals who refuse to cover their linguistic difference not in isolation from other social processes but in relation to changing social views on the economic demands on the workforce. In "Skills and Selves in the New Workplace," anthropologist Bonnie Urciuoli presents what she calls "the notion of 'worker-self-as-skills-bundle'" as the image of the worker in the neoliberal economy.[29] "Not only is the worker's labor power a commodity but the worker's very person is also defined by the summation of commodifiable bits" in this view of the worker as a bundle of skills, which Urciuoli suggests is a "social construction cumulatively produced by years of skills discourses in business and education."[30] According to Monica Heller's research on ethnolinguistic minorities, language is one of the skills that constitute this bundle. "The globalized new economy," Heller argues, "has resulted in the commodification of language," which she defines as that "which renders language amenable to redefinition as a measurable skill, as opposed to a talent, or an inalienable characteristic of group members."[31]

From this perspective, the bilinguals who refuse to cover their bilingualism are inflexible workers who question and defy the reduction of their ethnic language into just another skill in the bundle that they are. In her research, Urciuoli includes the example of immigrant and migrant workers in the United States to illustrate how the neoliberal idea of the worker as a skills bundle affects bilingual workers and bilingualism as commodifiable skill. In US factories, she says,

"Filipino, Korean, and Central American workers" are often blamed for failings of the production lines they work at because they lack "English skills," even though these failings are due to a "much more complex nexus of events."[32] In this particular workplace, their skill in their mother tongue is unrecognized or viewed as a potential liability.

The legal conflicts between bilingual workers and their employers around English-only rules can also be examined through the new conception of the worker in a neoliberal economy and how this affects bilingual workers, an examination that highlights the neoliberal logic underwriting the court rulings. Because the courts are more receptive to the need for a flexible workforce that drives the new economy, the bilingual plaintiffs' argument that language is analogical to race and deserves protection under Title VII is brushed aside. The demands on a bilingual to cover her mother tongue, as well as the legal battles over the legitimacy of such demands, take place within such a context of the neoliberalizing economy and the ideal of the flexible worker who views herself as a bundle of skills and uses each and every one of those skills in accordance with business interests and workplace demands. While the analogy of language and race may not be accepted in court for bilinguals who want to bare their mother tongue at work, the associative link between language and race characterizes the representations of dormant bilingualism in the writings of Richard Rodriguez and Chang-rae Lee. What we see in the figuration of the contiguity between language and race in these writings is a sustained attention to when and where bilingualism becomes a liability or asset in the logic of neoliberal multiculturalism.

## DORMANT BILINGUALISM AS BROWN IN RICHARD RODRIGUEZ

Richard Rodriguez's most well-known publication, *Hunger of Memory: The Education of Richard Rodriguez*, can be read as a text of language covering. Some critics have delivered strong critiques of what they read as Rodriguez's subscription to a liberal narrative of assimilation; some have tried to look into the indeterminacies and the contradictions that lace the binaries in the text; some have criticized the heterosexism implicit in the critique of Rodriguez by Chicano nationalists.[33] Regardless of where one stands on the spectrum, the assumption seems to be that *Hunger of Memory* is Rodriguez's musings on his felt need to cover his home language of Spanish (and, by extension, his heritage culture and his sexual identity), and the differences in interpretation primarily lie with whether he reinforces the binaries of public and private, of Mexican and American, or plays with them. Since the publication of *Hunger of Memory*, Rodriguez's views on cultural difference have softened with each subsequent book. *Brown: The Last Discovery of America* (2002) is a text that uncovers what was previously covered as Rodriguez openly discusses his gay identity and embraces the racial term of brown as his main conceit. If language is viewed as analogous to race in the bilinguals' legal defenses of their right to use their mother tongue at work, dormant bilingualism is contiguous with the racial trope of brown in Rodriguez's evolving cultural politics. The contiguity between dormant bilingualism and race in Rodriguez acutely shows that there is a collapsible distance between race and language and that whether bilingualism is an advantage or not depends on one's agency over this distance.

While Rodriguez presents liberalism as the dominant mode of subject formation in *Hunger of Memory*, he explores the new lexicon of multiculturalism in *Brown*, testing its compatibility with his investment in liberalism and with his (uncovered) interest in ethnicity.[34] Since multiculturalism is what legitimates Rodriguez's change of views on Spanish, from the language of shame and guilt in his first memoir to a language of potential and coolness in his third collection of essays, it is worth attending to the contours of multiculturalism in *Brown*, especially in terms of how it relates to his primary trope of brown. Rodriguez engages in what scholars would call "comparative multiculturalism" (i.e., examining the character and impact of state-led multicultural endeavors across different nation-states) to situate his observations on multiculturalism in North America.[35] He compares US multiculturalism with that of Canada and Mexico, charting a region that one cannot help but notice is coterminous with the region covered by the North American Free Trade Agreement.[36] He suggests Canada, the United States, and Mexico exist on a spectrum of individualism, with Canada being the most given to individualism and Mexico the least. "In Canada-after-Trudeau," Rodriguez says, "one can be Chinese and fully Canadian."[37] Lest the reader mistake this for an endorsement of the Canadian brand of multiculturalism, Rodriguez emphasizes the Anglo Saxon bias of such a model.[38] According to him, the Canadian version of multiculturalism is too sanitized, disjunctive with the realities of many "brown immigrant children in

today's Canada" and "propound[ing] a most unerotic notion of society" in the way it assumes that *"you* will never inextricably entwine
with *I.*"[39] At the other extreme is Mexico, "a brown idea that we
[the United States] would rather not discuss," a country that Rodriguez says "is only learning the meaning of eighteenth-century individualism."[40] Without excusing Mexico's blatant preference for light
complexion or its suppression of "indigenous peasants in Chiapas,"
Rodriguez points to *"mestizaje"* or "the marriage of races," as Mexico's brand of multiculturalism that is possibly more attractive than
Canada's due to its embrace of interracial mixing.[41] Rodriguez places
US multiculturalism in the middle, between the extremes of Canadian
and Mexican multiculturalism.

Yet Rodriguez's interest in comparative multiculturalism is hardly
neutral. The fact that he is specifically interested in the place of ethnic-
ity in the national community can be seen succinctly in his response
to the often-drawn comparison between Latinos and the Quebecois.
He does not think the circumstances of the Spanish-speaking in the
United States parallel those of the French-speaking in Canada.[42] His
response to the question from a French Canadian media station,
*"Are Hispanics in the Southwest destined to forge some sort of new
Quebec,"* is an unhesitant no.[43] No matter how anti-assimilationist
Latinos may seem, he says that Latinos ultimately have faith in "the
ancient Spanish pronoun, the first-person plural, the love-potion
pronoun—*nosotros.* We."[44] "Try as we will to be culturally aggrieved
by day," he continues, "we find the gringos kind of attractive in the
moonlight."[45] The main challenge Rodriguez faces in straddling multiculturalism and liberalism is that multiculturalism, when managed
the Canadian way, can turn into separatist cultural nationalism (like
the example of Quebec), where the appearance of the recognition of
difference masks the lack of willingness to "entwine with," as he says,
the other. His way of getting around this dilemma, then, is to infuse
liberal nationalism with a sense of ethnicity. Spanish emerges as the
method of amalgamation here as Rodriguez resorts to the Spanish
first-person plural, *nosotros,* as a "love-potion" capable of solving the
problem of ethnic division. Rodriguez suggests that the Mexican way
of life is sufficiently open to differences, to the extent that interracial
intimacy and relationships flourish, by using the Spanish language as
a vehicle of connection.

Rodriguez's use of the Spanish first-person plural should be read
alongside his discussion of the Spanish second person, *tu,* in a 2003

interview with David Cooper. In this interview, Rodriguez returns to an idea he first presented in *Hunger of Memory*, as he reflects on his first memoir and the responses it garnered, to elaborate on his art and craft of writing and mentions that there is something called the "personal" between private and public life.[46] According to Rodriguez, the critics who faulted him for "tak[ing] one life and pos[ing] it against the public language that was being used to describe it" did not get the fact that his memoir was about "mak[ing] the private personal."[47] Rodriguez elucidates the elusive distinction between the private and the personal by bringing up *tu*: "In a way, in my own mind I distinguished between those things that are private, which exist within the realm of the intimate, the realm of *tu* in Spanish, and those things that are so personal that they can only be described to someone in public, those revelations that you cannot share with those you love."[48] Rodriguez also uses a textual moment from *Hunger of Memory* to illustrate the distinction between private and personal. He had previously written into his memoir his mother's letter asking him not to divulge family matters in his writings, and he uses this example to illustrate the risks of making the private personal: "When I took my mother's letter, which for her existed within the realm of *tu*, within the realm of the private, and then published it, I was violating her privacy in the service of the personal."[49] As in the case of his use of *nosotros* to signify a collectivity undergirding the nation-state, Rodriguez uses *tu* here to reference the private that is defined against the public and that can be deployed to create the space of the personal in the public realm. His recourse to Spanish personal pronouns, I suggest, shows Rodriguez trying to rhetorically construct varying kinds and levels of interpersonal relationships. In other words, he mobilizes Spanish personal pronouns to rhetorically perform the relationships that he believes are the bedrock of a liberal polity.

Of course, his use of the Spanish word *nosotros* to refer to a public collective reflects a dramatic change of view on Spanish, a language that he previously called "the language of the alien."[50] Despite such change of view, Rodriguez's ideas of relationships and community remain at the level of semantics and fails to penetrate the more—or at least equally—significant concerns about the material conditions of existence that galvanize Chicano and Latino activism, including its support of bilingualism. Rodriguez's departure from those who view Chicano or Latino as a political identity that achieves coherence through historical experiences of marginalization and structural

inequities can clearly be seen in his trenchant critique of the Chicano/
Latino nationalists, whom he calls "neo-nationalists," as being imitative of African Americans in articulating their identity and claims of
rights to the state.[51] He also suggests that this imitative move is motivated by self-interested group politics:

> Not so long ago, Hispanics, particularly Mexicans and Cubans,
> resisted the label of "minority." In a black-and-white America, His-
> panics tended toward white, or at least tended to keep their distance
> from black. I remember my young Mexican mother saying to her
> children in Spanish, "We are not minorities," in the same voice she
> would use decades later to refuse the term "senior citizen." One day
> in the 1980s, my mother became a senior citizen because it got her on
> the bus for a nickel. One day, in the 1960s, the success of the Negro
> Civil Rights movement encouraged Hispanics (along with other
> groups of Americans) to insist on the coveted black analogy, and thus
> claim the spoils of affirmative action.[52]

Rodriguez creates a simple narrative of comparative racialization
between black and brown in the aftermath of the Civil Rights movement. Whereas Latinos strove to identify with the white top (or strove
to not be identified with the black bottom) in the binary racial hierarchy before, they started to stake out a claim to a minority identity
once the Civil Rights movement created social and structural support for the reparative claims of African Americans. This imitative
move on the part of the Latinos, their wanting to be a minority the
way that African Americans are, Rodriguez calls "the coveted black
analogy." And he sees a petty politics of envy in this move. Rodriguez's overall take on post–civil rights black-brown relations partly
echoes what Stephen Steinberg calls the politics of "comparative suffering," wherein the history and narrative of black American suffering becomes the prototype of minority experience in the United States
against which other minority groups' experiences are measured.[53]

Rodriguez's critique of "the coveted black analogy" deserves a
careful look, especially in light of the argument that language is "like-
race" that prevails among the legal cases on language covering. On
the one hand, Rodriguez argues that the black analogy used by Latinos is a wrongful substitution, a creation of similarity where there is
none. Ironically, though, his own refutation of the black analogy relies
on another analogy, the analogy between his mother's claim on the
identity of "senior citizen" for reduced bus fare and the Latino claim
on a minority identity for the benefits of policies geared to rectifying

racial inequality. According to Rodriguez, just as his mother takes on the identity of the senior citizen once the state endows on it certain entitlements to take advantage of the system, Latinos clamor to be interpellated as a minority once the state associates it with (limited) material benefits. Such rhetorical move on Rodriguez's part makes his judgment of "the coveted black analogy" somewhat suspect. Instead of showing the fallacy of the analogy between Latinos and African Americans, it brings into high relief Rodriguez's own political position and morals that are projected onto his contradictory use of analogy. If the salience of "like-race" arguments made by bilingual plaintiffs contesting English-only rules at work shows the inadequacy of the black-white racial binary in amending the breakdown of civic harmony, then Rodriguez's condemnation of the black analogy among Chicano/Latino cultural nationalists can be viewed as an attempt to shore up the black-white binary in the face of the challenge it faces in the post–civil rights era. We can surmise here that analogy may be more of a function as opposed to something that carries substantial meaning. That is, it is not so much that an analogy is true or untrue but that an analogy serves a particular function determined by the purpose and the contingencies of its deployment.

It may seem strange that Rodriguez relies on a racial binary in a book that is titled "brown" and in which he consistently extols the virtues of brown to "blee[d] through the straight line, unstaunchable— the line separating black from white."[54] But such contradiction is actually not a contradiction when one understands the dual function of brown as a trope to both conserve the sense of collectivity that buttresses Rodriguez's idea of a liberal polity and make room for ethnic difference that does not disturb this ideal of the liberal polity. From this perspective, the analogy between Latinos and African Americans becomes a problem because the black-and-brown comparison enables imagining a "we" that presumably competes with the "we" of the liberal polity, the "we" that "the love-potion pronoun—*nosotros*" is meant to consolidate. While the "we" that emerges from a black-brown coalition potentially presents a collective that is set against white privilege, Rodriguez's own narrative construction of "we" adheres to a particular, liberal narrative of US history that takes slavery as America's original sin, views the wrongs heaped on African Americans over time as incomparable to what other racialized groups have undergone, and seems to endorse black exceptionalism.[55]

In *Brown* black exceptionalism is the narrative that allows Rodriguez to maintain his view of civic culture that he first presented in *Hunger of Memory*, despite his embrace of brown as the ultimate sign of "impurity" in his later publication.[56] In *Hunger of Memory*, Rodriguez argues that initiatives such as bilingual education are "attempts to make the language of the alien the public language" when it is the public language that should be taught to the minority children so that they do not continue to stay "alien[s] from public life."[57] The emphasis on a civic culture that unites the nation likewise appears in *Brown*, although it is tempered by a much stronger acknowledgement of the troubled history of race in the United States than in *Hunger of Memory*. "When Americans organize into subgroups," Rodriguez says, "it should be with an eye to merging with the whole, not remaining separate. What was the point of the Negro Civil Rights movement of the early twentieth century, if not integration?"[58] Just as he resorted to "the love-potion pronoun—*nosotros*" to diffuse the dangerous possibility of the Spanish-speaking in the United States forming a separate bloc like the French-speaking in Canada, Rodriguez uses a narrative of black exceptionalism that could serve as the story of racial injury and suffering for the nation as a whole, while simultaneously promoting interracial and intercultural mixing through the trope of brown.

In fact, the trope of brown potentially forms another narrative of race in the United States that complements the narrative of black exceptionalism with its neat plot of sin and atonement. In this vein, Rodriguez's paean to the bilingual woman, Pocahontas, can be read as his paean to the transformative power of the trope of brown. Rodriguez offers the story of Pocahontas as "a Puritan parody," the other "colonial tale" to the well-rehearsed tale of the Puritans.[59] Rodriguez presents a brief but romantic and exuberant picture of Pocahontas, "the American princess": "As a child, Pocahontas saves the life of an Englishman. As an adult, she marries an Englishman, a different Englishman. She 'goes native'; . . . With her husband she travels back in time to London, toward her new innocence; assumes a title there. She is presented to Queen Anne."[60] In the fairy-tale sketch, Pocahontas is a courageous and adventurous person, who reaches out across racial and cultural boundaries, tries out assimilation into Anglicism with gusto, and who revises the myth of the New World as innocence by attaining innocence in, of all places, the seat of the Old World Empire.

To be fair, Rodriguez is careful to indicate in several places in *Brown* the historical proscription on interracial mixing, the fact that "the erotic history of America kept pace with segregation."[61] His epistemology of brown is about valorizing interracial mixing in the face of such a troubled history. If "one of the first lessons in America, the color-book lesson, instructs that color should stay within the lines," Rodriguez's lesson in *Brown* is that color cannot, and should not, stay within the lines since "desire and sympathy" will naturally run afoul of the arbitrary lines of color demarcation.[62] Not only is Rodriguez's support of interracial mixing directed against the ideology of white supremacy that has historically proscribed interracial relationships but it also seems to take to task the racial and cultural essentialism that can be seen in cultural nationalist circles. As he intimates, it is true that the bilingual women, like Pocahontas and La Malinche, the mistress of Hernán Cortés, who bridged their native cultures with that of the white settlers with their forked tongues, and mothered mixed-race children, have become symbols of racial betrayal for cultural nationalists.[63] In an interview conducted in 2003, Rodriguez offers an explicit identification with Pocahontas and what she embodies: "The feminine history of the Americas is full of stories of women, African, Indian, white, becoming bilingual, bicultural, falling in love outside their tribe. No coincidence either was it, I think, that Richard Rodriguez as a boy—a queer little boy—was enchanted by the legend of Pocahontas. I was enchanted by the subversion of eroticism."[64] Unlike in the world of Rodriguez's childhood in *Hunger of Memory* where bilingualism is a liability, in the world of *Brown*, bilingualism is an asset.

In that it opposes rigid and unchanging ideas of identity, Rodriguez's trope of brown shares a lot in common with the poststructuralist critiques of essentialism. Yet the trope of brown, despite its seeming espousal of freedom of being and doing, actually limits the horizon of such freedom by focusing on individual freedom that pertains to the private realm. Rather than challenge structural inequities and social injustices that often apply a differentiated notion of freedom to people of color, Rodriguez treats freedom as primarily a matter of individual choice, even if that means attaining it by covering. Elsewhere I have examined Rodriguez's notion of brown as the racial undertone of the third language he discusses in an attempt to free himself from the binary of bilingualism and discussed the limitation of his brand of hybridity.[65] Extending that critique a bit further here, I argue that Rodriguez's epistemology of brown is undergirded by the morphing of a postcolonial sense of hybridity into a neoliberal

consensus-building rhetoric. Arguably the most well-known pro-
ponent of postcolonial hybridity, Homi Bhabha, uses the idea to
explore the in-between places and positions of being and doing that
go unexamined in binaries of power such as that of the colonizer and
the colonized.[66] But, as David Theo Goldberg summarizes, even as
hybridity may be an "outward expression" of the powerless, it tends
to "assum[e] some of the hierarchical aspects of power," and particularly in what he calls "racially marked states," institutions tend
to foster difference as long as it contributes to the state's aim of creating homogeneity at a larger level.[67] Henceforth, Goldberg submits
that "it is the value invested in the concept [of hybridity] in relation to
the material historical contexts in which it is embedded accordingly
that will determine hybridity's capacity in specific space-time conditions."[68] What needs to be further examined for Rodriguez's cultural
politics of brown, then, is its "material historical contexts," and I
think Rodriguez's change of views on Spanish in *Brown* from *Hunger
of Memory* serves as a telling sign of the vulnerability of his trope of
brown to neoliberal multiculturalism.

In *Hunger of Memory*, Spanish represents shame and poverty.
Rodriguez's opposition to using Spanish in public is based on the fact
that he associates the language with his working-class environment
and origin. Perhaps one of the most painful memories related in the
book is the young Rodriguez's reaction to his father's broken English. When his father has a hard time communicating with the gas
station attendant, this so diminishes the father's stature in the mind
of the young boy that he rejects his father's hand on his shoulder, the
smallest gesture of physical closeness, as they return home. "I cannot
forget the sounds my father made as he spoke," Rodriguez recounts.
"At one point his words slid together to form one word—sounds as
confused as the threads of blue and green oil in the puddle next to
my shoes."[69] Rodriguez's description of his father's accented English
metaphorizes his inarticulacy. The borders of words dissolve and the
words touch each other like the different shades of the slivers of oil on
the ground. Without appropriate boundaries, Rodriguez intimates,
making oneself intelligible is impossible for the Mexican immigrant
and his children. Just as he sets up a border between himself and his
father, Rodriguez also sets up a border between the public language
of English and the private language of Spanish: "I'd hear strangers
on the radio and in the Mexican Catholic church across town speaking in Spanish, but I couldn't really believe that Spanish was a public

language, like English. Spanish speakers, rather, seemed related to me, for I sensed that we shared—through our language—the experience of feeling apart from *los gringos*. It was thus a ghetto Spanish that I heard and spoke."[70] At the same time that he describes Spanish as the language spoken by those he views as isolated from the mainstream society, Rodriguez also ghettoizes Spanish by refusing to see the Spanish-speaking social and cultural spaces as part of what constitutes the public.[71]

Spanish is no longer a ghetto language in *Brown*. Actually, Rodriguez seems to acknowledge that Spanish has virtually become the second language of the United States. "Pragmatism," he says, "leads to Spanish signage at government offices, hospitals, parking lots, bus stops, polls . . . virtually all instructions in America are in Spanish as well as English."[72] While he says he "remain[s] skeptical of the effect pragmatic Spanish might have on the assimilation of Latin American immigrants," he "marvel[s] at the middle-class American willingness to take Spanish up."[73] In fact, in California where he lives, Spanish is so widely used that it even "occurs to [him] that the Chinese-American couple in front of [him], by speaking Spanish, may actually be speaking American English."[74] Whereas the memory of the "ghetto Spanish" of his childhood may have held back Rodriguez from recognizing the cultural capital of Spanish, middle-class Americans who are not impeded by such memory are eager to be a part of the second most widely used language in the United States. The spread of Spanish in the United States, Rodriguez goes on to suggest, has even given birth to "a new, North American Spanish accent . . . meant to be decipherable (and inoffensive) alike to Cubans, Mexicans, Dominicans, and blonds like you, because it belongs to none."[75] The use of the second person here directly singles out a potential group of readers—blonds—and aligns them with three ethnic groups within Latino pan-ethnicity, a move that syntactically supports the influence of this new Spanish to bring together groups that previously have not had common ground. It also illustrates Rodriguez's seemingly contradictory claim that "Hispanic Spanish" is at once "hybrid, uniform."[76] As a language that is accessible to as disparate users as "Cubans, Mexicans, Dominicans" and "blonds like you," Hispanic Spanish is hybrid and diverse. Yet the reason that it can be these things is because it is uniform, because the various Latin American Spanish accents disappear into a new "accentless" accent for communicability's sake in the United States.[77] A language that reflects Rodriguez's observations

and vision of Spanish's migration to and new formation in the New
World, this Hispanic Spanish may well be a quintessential brown language. It is hard not to notice, though, how ethnicity becomes tantamount to hair color in the participatory logic of Hispanic Spanish, the
histories of oppression presumed in ethnic nationalist articulations of
race dissolved into a visual sign of fashion.

The simultaneity of hybridity and uniformity in Hispanic Spanish distinguishes it from the father's broken English that made the young Rodriguez cringe. While both Hispanic Spanish and the father's broken English
might blur and remake the borders in a language, Hispanic Spanish has
a uniformity that is recognized by virtue of being used as a medium of
communication by a significant number of speakers whereas the father's
broken English remains in the realm of the incommunicable. In other
words, Hispanic Spanish has a socially recognized value, whereas the
father's broken English does not. Another example of a hybrid language
that distinctly shows Rodriguez's views on language and value is black
English. In *Brown*, black English epitomizes the resilience, creativity,
and vitality of American English and culture. "Despite laws prohibiting
black literacy in the nineteenth century," Rodriguez says, "the African
in America took the paper-white English and remade it (as the Irish and
the Welsh also took their English), wadded it up, rigmarolled it, rewound
it into a llareggub rap, making English theirs, making it idiosyncrati-
cally glamorous (*Come on now, you try it*), making it impossible for
any American to use English henceforward without remembering them;
making English so cool, so jet, so festival, that children want it only
that way."[78] In addition to highlighting the cool factor of black English,
Rodriguez also acknowledges a debt to the language as an American
writer: "I cannot imagine myself a writer, I cannot imagine myself writing these words, without the example of African slaves stealing the English language, learning to read against the law, then transforming the
English language into the American tongue, transforming me, rescuing
me, with a coruscating nonchalance."[79] Such a view of black English is
a dramatic change from *Hunger of Memory* where he expresses disap-
proval at the black teenagers speaking to each other in black English
on a bus for propagating the wrongheaded idea that "the language of
the alien" could be "public language."[80] The glamor of black English he
noted but checked himself against in *Hunger of Memory* returns with
full force and out of the closet in *Brown*.

While Rodriguez's valorization of such hybrid languages as black
English or Hispanic Spanish may seem progressive, there is an implicit

acknowledgement of the relationship between language and value in his appraisals of these languages. He gravitates to Hispanic Spanish after it has acquired social capital, just as he applauds black English for its cultural capital. The loose association among a language, the power of its speakers, and capital in Rodriguez's views deserves critical attention because the relationships among the elements are still in the process of being formed. While Rodriguez does not admit this, it may well be that the same force of capital that creates political capital in the identity of Latinos, which he adamantly criticizes, is what changes the status of Spanish in the public, making room for Hispanic Spanish to take root and to grow. In criticizing the Latino appropriation of the minority identity, their use of "the coveted black analogy," Rodriguez brings to attention the imbrication of ethnic identity in corporate profit-making that he identifies in the coherence Latinos acquire as a minority: "The notion of African Americans as a minority is one born of a distinct and terrible history of exclusion. . . . To say, today, that Hispanics are becoming America's largest minority is to mock history, to pervert language, to dilute the noun 'minority' until it means little more than a population segment."[81] Rodriguez continues, "This is exactly what Hispanics have become—a population segment, an ad-agency target audience, a market share."[82] If Rodriguez is critical of the co-optive force of capitalism to distort the historical meaning of minority, he is strangely silent on the fact that the rise of Spanish to a public language is likewise contingent on the growth of Latino political capital and social visibility. In a somewhat different but related vein, Rodriguez is silent on the divorce between the literary capital of black English and the enduring structural inequalities and racism that African Americans face in the post–civil rights era, when, arguably, these inequalities are seminal to his own narrative of black exceptionalism.

Rodriguez's cultural politics, which stand at the crossroads of neoliberal multiculturalism and an uncertain, but more critical, awareness of the politics of race, are best described, I think, as the politics of dormant bilingualism. In a 2003 interview, Rodriguez offers the following statement on his dormant bilingualism, his most direct commentary on this subject so far:

> People say to me, "Surely you can, surely you are able to [speak Spanish]," and I tell people, "No, it's not possible." It is not possible; there *is* some impediment. I cannot explain it. Maybe in my inability is a kind of lesson that I just felt so profoundly that I was switching social

allegiances that I just felt forever stigmatized. I remained my grandmother's favorite grandchild. She would speak to me and would mock
me for not speaking back to her, but we spent many, many hours
together and I was her translator in public. To this day I am eared,
but not mouthed. I will venture, or I will float through Mexico, or
through Latin America, or through Spain, all ears, and I can understand everything said around me, or all eyes, I can read everything
around me, but it is like I am asleep, because I don't speak.[83]

Rodriguez eloquently describes what he sees as an asymmetry in his
phenomenological engagement with the world through language.
He is, in his words, "eared, but not mouthed." The racial trope of
brown suggests Rodriguez's desire to come to terms with the inexpli-
cable "impediment" that created his dormant bilingualism in the first
place, an impediment that I dare say goes beyond individual psychology and becomes an impediment to advocating social change. At one
point in *Brown* Rodriguez mentions that "the price of entering white
America is an acid bath, a bleaching bath—a transfiguration—that
burns away memory."[84] One cannot but notice the allusion to the liberal education he received as an overwhelmingly immersive and hurtful experience. While the psychological scar of language loss appears
in a much more subdued manner in the works of Chang-rae Lee, a
similar awareness that language is potential human capital in neoliberal multiculturalism can be seen in *Native Speaker*. Having lived
most of his adult life asleep in a figurative sense, Henry Park wakes
up to the possibility of bilingual capital. However, he first needs to
contend with the racial politics of multiculturalism before he can reap
the benefits of such capital.

## THE DORMANT BILINGUAL AS MODEL MINORITY IN CHANG-RAE LEE'S NATIVE SPEAKER

My starting point for examining Henry Park, the main character of
*Native Speaker* (1995), as a dormant bilingual is an essay that Chang-
rae Lee published two years prior to the novel, "The Faintest Echo
of Our Language" (1993). One of the two essays that Lee published
around the time of *Native Speaker*'s release, "The Faintest Echo"
delivers a painful and beautiful sketch of Lee's relationship with his
mother during her last days of illness through his reflections on the
meaning of language difference and bonds of affection. I read this
essay as a subtext for *Native Speaker*, a subtext in the commonly used
sense of underlying meaning but also with an allusion to the archaic

sense of "a text appearing below another text on a page."[85] While "The Faintest Echo" is not physically appended to *Native Speaker* in any way, I think reading the novel, which has received much critical attention since its release, in relation to the essay foregrounds the subject of dormant bilingualism in the novel and shows the dual meaning of being under(-)cover in the text—to be a spy who conceals his identity and to be a dormant bilingual who covers his mother tongue.[86]

If language difference is subordinated to the more prominent theme of racial difference in *Native Speaker*, "The Faintest Echo" is exactly the opposite. Language difference is the difference that is salient in this brief piece on a son's complex emotions about his inability to fully communicate with his mother as he watches her dying. At a first glance, the only explicit reference to race is Lee's mention of the history of Japanese colonialism in Korea, which comes up as he imagines what his mother's childhood would have been like: "And as she would speak of her childhood, of the pretty, stern-lipped girls . . . who could only whisper to her sisters in the midnight safety of their house the Korean words folding inside her all day like mortal secrets, I felt the same burning, troubling lode of utter pride and utter shame still jabbing at the sweet belly of her life, that awful gem, about who she was and where her mother tongue and her land had gone."[87] Interestingly, this point about his mother's loss of her language is followed by a different situation of mother tongue loss: Lee's loss of Korean in the United States as he grows up in an immigrant household. In response to the mother's worries "that I was losing my Korean," Lee says "what she didn't know was that it had been whole years since I had lost the language, had left it somewhere for good, perhaps from the time I won a prize in the first grade for reading the most books in my class."[88] The duress of involuntary language loss under colonialism is contrasted with a different mode of language loss—a voluntary submission to the enticements of academic achievement in liberalism.

Yet Lee also seems to suggest that the social conditions of language loss cannot simply be explained away through a binary of colonialism and liberalism. This comes up in a striking scene in the essay when the young Lee goes over to Tommy's with his mother before his friend moves away. The only other Asian at Lee's childhood school, Tommy is Japanese and the young Lee's best friend. On what would be his last visit to his best friend's house, the young Lee overhears the mothers' conversation, "half of it in profoundly broken English, the other half in what must have been Japanese." Looking back on this moment, Lee thinks that "for the momentary sake of her only son and his departing friend, she was willing to endure those two tongues of her shame, one present, one past. Language, sacrifice, the story never ends."[89] With this terse observation, Lee suggests that for his mother both Japanese and English were "tongues of her shame." The temporal distinction between the colonial past and the immigrant present becomes moot in the affect of language as the mother's public world is always defined by the language that does not belong to her. The language that shames her. Throughout the essay Lee shows the mother as only being free from the constraints of the public language when she is in private space, the epitome of which is her bedroom—the place she retreats to when her son, the young Lee, pointedly expresses his frustration at having to be her voice in the public—a sanctuary where "her words sang for her, they did good work, they pleaded for my life, shouted entreaties, ecstasies, they could draw blood if they wanted, and they could offer grace, and they could kiss."[90] Through such attention to the pain of linguistic alienation Lee shows an ambivalence toward the idea of language as a matter of individual will and choice. Additionally, one can see Lee's suggestion that the category of Asian American is a pan-ethnic category born out of a reaction to racism in the friendship he portrays between his young self and Tommy. The language of Asian America, it is implied, is necessarily multilingual and wrought with its own internal conflict among languages with colonial histories.

Similar to Rodriguez's *Hunger of Memory*, in "The Faintest Echo" bilingualism is also consistently depicted as more of a liability than an asset. Following the transcription of a bilingual conversation between himself and his ailing mother, which consists of simple sentences that pertain to checking basic needs, Lee says that "this will be our language always. To me she speaks in a child's Korean, and for her I speak the same child's English."[91] While he discovers a minimalist intensity in the children's language of mother and son, which enables "the minute discoveries in the mining of the words" Lee's doubt that "our union is handicapped by [our language]" is hard to shake off entirely.[92] Instead of an individual matter, Lee presents bilingualism through the kinship of mother and son, with the mother being deficient in English and the son being deficient in Korean. The emphasis on mutual deficiency is what possibly creates a "handicap" in the bond of mother and son. *Native Speaker* starts out with the premise that bilingualism for Asian Americans is a liability, a handicap.

At the heart of Henry Park's midlife crisis, both in his personal life after he loses his son to a tragic accident and in his professional life as he becomes skeptical of his job as a spy for a private intelligence firm, Glimmer & Company, lies his insecurities of being a nonnative speaker, a newcomer to the land of opportunities who is constantly viewed as not belonging due to his race. Henry's story is intertwined with another story of New York City's upcoming mayoral race as the person he is assigned to, John Kwang, is the rising star of New York politics.[93] His relationship with Kwang, which grows close beyond his assignment, occasions Henry to question his assimilation and provokes ethical quandaries about his job as a spy. But more importantly for my purpose, Henry comes to see a new possibility of bilingualism through Kwang, that of bilingualism as asset. Such breakthrough, however, is ultimately frustrated by the terms of Asian racialization as model minority in neoliberal multiculturalism that refuses serious engagement with the issues surrounding the transformation of language into human capital.

In *Native Speaker* Lee explores the idea of ethnic capital first and foremost through the figure of the immigrant small business owner and that of the culturalization of ethnic capital through the stereotype of the model minority. At the same time that he follows the mode of sociological realism in portraying the world of Korean small-business owners in New York City, Lee also emphasizes the institution of *ggeh*—"a privatized welfare program or informal bank" according to Daniel Kim—to draw attention to a culturally foreign institution brought over by the immigrants as the basis of ethnic capital accumulation.[94] Henry's father, Mr. Park, whose name is only given at one point in the text as George Washington Park, the English name he wanted to adopt but never quite did, typifies the post-1965 Korean immigrant man in his reason for immigration.[95] He has a good education from his home country, having been trained as an engineer, but he sees a greater opportunity for socioeconomic mobility in the United States and he immigrates. His "personal lore" of success conforms to the narrative of the American Dream: "He started with $200 in his pocket and a wife and baby and just a few words of English."[96] Lee is careful not to simplify the causes of Mr. Park's financial success. Mr. Park worked hard; he had an indomitable will and a single-minded focus to succeed; and he relied on cheap immigrant labor. But he does suggest that an operational aspect of the ethnic community, one which is often overlooked in discussions of post-1965 Asian immigrant economic assimilation, is crucial to Mr. Park's success, which, in the end, amounts to five stores in New York City.[97] "The truth," says Henry, "is that my father got his first infusion of capital from a *ggeh*, a Korean 'money club' in which members contributed to a pool that was given out on a rotating basis. Each week you gave the specified amount; and then one week in the cycle, all the money was yours."[98]

Whereas Rodriguez suggests that Latinos are constructed as an ethnic group by corporate marketing and consumerism, Lee shows that an ethnic community can also attain coherence and significance through an ethnic institution of capital accumulation. The tightly knit community of Korean small-business owners and their employees is not just based on the mere fact of ethnicity but also on their mutual exclusion from English-speaking institutions of capital accumulation. That is, Lee presents the Korean immigrants' reliance on other members of their ethnic community (like *ggeh*) or other non- or limited-English-speaking immigrants (as cheap labor) as an economic model that becomes viable because of their shared exclusion from economic activities that are solely conducted through English. At the same time that they offer the benefits of providing a platform for recent immigrants to engage in economic activities with a degree of autonomy, ethnically based institutions are also presented in the novel as perpetuating class division within their own group, and exploiting the comparably less well off. His father's "rule of thumb" for hiring employees, Henry recollects, is "to hire somebody if they couldn't speak English, even blacks from Haiti or Ethiopia, because he figured they were new to the land and understood that no one would help them for nothing."[99]

At the same time that Mr. Park is determined to achieve economic success, relying on his Korean and immigrant network to grow his business, it seems that he is fully aware of how his limited English deprives him of sociocultural capital. Despite his economic success, Mr. Park's dream, Henry imagines, is "to enter a place and tender the native language with body and tongue and have no one turn and point to the door."[100] Like Richard Rodriguez who uses bodily metaphors to refer to what he thinks is his half fluency in Spanish—"I am eared, but not mouthed"—Lee also creates a bodily image for native comfort in a language. In Henry's imagination, speaking a language to the effect of demonstrating belonging is not just about communicating meaning through words but more about assuming a unity between speech and the speaking body, wherein meaning is created and communicated through a smooth circuit of flow between the mind and the body. Such a view of language likens not being a native speaker of a language to a disability. Rodriguez's phrasing of being "eared, but not mouthed" compares lack of fluency in speech to muteness, the fact of muteness made stark in contrast to the fact of hearing. Henry suggests that the effect of this disability of not being a native speaker is social rejection or, to be more literal about what he says, ejection from social spaces. Saddled with what in Henry's mind is a perpetual disability, Mr. Park sees in his American-born son, Henry, the possibility of attaining the sense of belonging he never had and its attendant sociocultural capital. When Henry was young and working at his father's grocery store on the weekends, his father would try to show off his English, "to make a display of it, to casually recite 'some Shakespeare words.'"[101] While the young Henry rebuffs his father's requests, mainly attributing them to his pursuit of profit— "it might be good for business"—Mr. Park's pride in his son's English is not so much about its immediate monetary yield but more a recognition of the sociocultural capital his son would command due to his English.[102] The performance of Shakespeare the father asks of the son is a particular kind of "tender[ing] the native language with body and tongue," a deliberate show of the mastery of the most widely recognized canonical writer in English literature. Of course, such striving for cultural capital also shows that the pursuit of cultural capital itself depends on keeping the myths of cultural value intact. While Shakespeare is certainly not native to the United States, and Shakespearean English at quite a variance from contemporary American English, Henry's father equates being a native speaker with using English like Shakespeare, affirming a set of assumptions about belonging in a language that accentuates his own foreignness.

Henry, however, belies his father's expectation of native belonging in English. He moves away from the mainly Korean-speaking ethnic community, but his accentless English is hardly a sign of his American belonging. Lee suggests this from the very beginning through the story of Henry's relationship with his wife Lelia, whom he first meets at a party when he had just started working for Glimmer & Co. They are attracted to their differences, and their different relationships to language, in particular, become the topic of an intriguing exchange. Against the backdrop of El Paso's multilingualism of English, Spanish, and *"mixup"* that is reflected in the party attendants' conversations,

Henry and Lelia use their perceptions of the other person's language as a way of understanding each other.[103] They realize that they both are very careful with language, albeit for different reasons. Henry's attentiveness is due to his being a nonnative speaker, whose uncertain claim over the language is compounded by his racial identity, whereas the care that Lelia takes with the language is due to her being the "standard-bearer," as she calls it, which is also related to her profession of speech therapist.[104] Henry is attracted to the confidence Lelia exudes in what he sees as her "execut[ion]" of the language: "She went word by word. Every letter had a border. I watched her wide full mouth sweep through her sentences like a figure touring a dark house, flipping on spots and banks of perfectly drawn light. The sensuality, in certain rigors."[105] Lelia's English symbolically shows the tenets of English monolingualism with order, propriety, and control. The way she speaks, for example, is the polar opposite of what young Rodriguez hears in his Mexican immigrant father whose words have no borders.[106] The somewhat strange metaphor of Lelia's articulation as a tourist of a dark, unlit house is worth attending to as it suggests Lee's view on teaching English as a second language, a largely feminized profession in the United States and also Lelia's chosen profession. According to the metaphor, Lelia's articulateness is like bringing light to the dark corners of the spaces she enters. By implication, she also has the power to withhold light. While it is not stated, the dark house of inarticulacy is presumably inhabited by people like Rodriguez's father. Yet the metaphor only brings into focus the "tourist" of the dark house, the native speaker who enlightens the linguistic others, as the beneficiaries of this enlightenment become invisible as undifferentiated darkness. Given that the location where Henry meets Lelia is El Paso, a border town, and that Lelia works as a volunteer for a relief agency, delivering food and used clothing to "illegals, Mexicans and Asians," the metaphor also brings to mind the image of the night border patrol.[107] Of course, her liberal politics place Lelia at the opposite end of the political spectrum on the issue of immigration and border control. The ambivalence in Lee's metaphor of Lelia's power of articulation, however, suggests that the two ends of the political spectrum may still exist within the larger political philosophy of liberalism, which reinforces, or at least does not challenge, the cultural myth of the hierarchy between the native and the foreigner.

In contrast to the almost natural ease with which Lelia assumes authority and power over her language, Henry continuously runs into stereotypes that deny him the same kind of authority and power. Lee presents the stereotype of the model minority as the stereotype that plagues Henry the most and that persistently denies his identity as American, treating him as foreign to American customs and mores. Lee makes the father figures in Henry's assimilated life, such as his father-in-law, Stew Boswell, and his boss at Glimmer & Co., Dennis Hoagland, wield the stereotype of the model minority to emphasize the paternalism behind the seeming extolling of (misunderstood) Asian cultures and values. Stew Boswell, Lelia's father, typifies the white American businessman who is a power broker, the kind of man who is "all balls and liver," the kind of man who comes from elite schooling and who has "neatly clipped silver hair and tailored suits and unmitigating stare of eyes and trim old body," the kind of guy who communicates through his comportment and grooming that he is "Chief Executive Officer."[108] And Boswell indulges in the idea of the model minority, which Henry presumes partly accounts for his acceptance of a son-in-law of different racial origin. Lelia "needs someone like you," Boswell remarks to Henry at one point in the text, "There's so much that's admirable in the Oriental culture and mind. You've been raised to be circumspect and careful. It's no wonder we're getting our heads handed to us. It's a new world out there. Different players now. Different rules."[109] Boswell's business acumen makes him see the changes in the global economy—most likely the rise of the Asian tigers as the media hype had it in the 1980s—which he, in turn, associates with the economic success of Asian immigrants like Henry's father. One can see a full-blown culturalist explanation for economic success in Boswell's express admiration of "Oriental culture and mind." Dennis Hoagland, the head of Glimmer & Company, also evinces a similar view of Asian culture's compatibility with success. Complaining about how white American culture encourages transparency of identity that "ma[kes] the worst spies," Hoagland suggests that Asian culture produces a discipline of identity ideal for his line of work. "If I were running a big house like the CIA," he says, "I'd breed agents by raising white kids in your standard Asian household. Discipline farms."[110] Boswell's and Hoagland's valorization of Henry's Asianness adheres to the loosely constructed idea that certain groups "—notably Jews and Asians—who have the 'right stuff' overcome every impediment of race and class to reach the economic pinnacle."[111] As sociologist Stephen Steinberg argues, such misguided notion of culture underwrote the concept of human capital used by certain economists.[112] While Boswell's and Hoagland's misrecognition of Henry's human capital places him in their favor, Henry can only maintain this favorable position by pretending an identification with the culture and language that he has long left behind. Ironically, it is only as a dormant bilingual that Henry can assume the position of the model minority that white men like Boswell and Hoagland project onto him.

On the surface, the idea that Asians are a model minority makes Henry an ideal marriage partner for his white in-laws and an ideal employee for his boss. But his assimilation turns out to be just an appearance. While Henry at one point confesses that his job as a spy made him think he "had finally found [his] truest place in the culture" as he feels that the duplicity required for the job comes effortlessly to him, such aptitude for the job recedes after Henry loses his son in an accident.[113] In fact, the death of Mitt can be viewed as a trigger that sets Henry off on a path of uncovering what he has covered. Emile Luzan, the Filipino psychiatrist he has been assigned to spy on, initiates the return of the repressed for Henry. For the first time, Henry falters and loses the distinction between his real identity and his identity for the job, digging into his childhood memories of the "invisible brother with no name," a figure he invented with all the qualities he wanted for himself, and using "story-forms" upon Luzan's encouragement to relate to the painful events of the past.[114] Luzan awakens in Henry a dormant connection with the immigrant world he left behind. He realizes that he can no longer write the registers he wrote daily on his assignments, narratives of his assigned subjects, praised by Hoagland as "textbook examples" to be emulated.[115] He realizes that Luzan might have taught him that he "no longer can simply flash a light inside a character, paint a figure like Kwang with a momentary language, but that [he knows] the greater truths reside in our necessary fictions spanning human event and time."[116] Echoing an earlier use of the associative link between knowledge and light, Lee once again suggests that knowledge instantly attained through a shine of light is an imperial mode of enlightenment and is prone to misrecognition. One can read the realization Henry arrives at as a rejection of the stereotypes that have restricted his own understanding of where he comes from, his race, culture, and home language. Once he rejects the stereotype of the model minority, Henry can look back on his assimilation as a sham:

> It's the prerogative of moles, after all, which only certain American lifetimes can teach. I am the obedient, soft-spoken son. What other

talent can Hoagland so prize? I will duly retreat to the position of
the good volunteer, the invisible underling. I have always known that
moment of disappearance, and the even uglier truth is that I have
long treasured it. That always honorable-seeming absence. It appears
I can go anywhere I wish. Is this my assimilation, so many years in
the making? Is this the long sought sweetness?[117]

The "talent" that Hoagland so prizes, Henry points out, is not so
much a result of his having been raised on a "discipline farm" of an
Asian household but the result of growing up Asian in the United
States, the "American lifetime" that is so often warped in the model
minority discourse. The lack of transparency that Lelia finds so hard
to tolerate in Henry is a product of the social valorization of covering
one's Asian differences that do not conform to the stereotype and of
becoming the "good volunteer, the invisible underling."

But even after he learns the limits of stereotypes and their one-
dimensional language to render truthful representations, Henry still
needs to find "story-forms" that can represent his life and experiences. John Kwang, the rising star of New York city politics and the
next subject Henry is assigned after Luzan, offers a new possibility of
representing one's Asian difference in public without covering by virtue of being "effortlessly Korean, effortlessly American."[118] Despite
his economic success, Mr. Park cannot be a model of Asian American
life for Henry since his success is limited to the private realm. Mr.
Park, in other words, is "bound to 600 square of ghetto retail space"
and even when he can "duplicat[e] the same basic store in various
parts of the city," these "stores defin[e] the outer limit of his ambition,
the necessary end of what he could conceive for himself."[119] Kwang,
on the other hand, is and aims to be "a larger public figure who was
willing to speak and act outside the tight sphere of his family."[120]
The dichotomy of the public and the private that Lee alludes to here
is similar in nature to that in Rodriguez's writings, especially *Hunger of Memory*. It is only in *Brown* that Rodriguez softens his view
on the separateness of the private and the public somewhat and turns
to viewing the public as not solely fixed and static but also changing
and dynamic. Just as the increasing power of Spanish in the public is
what allows Rodriguez to rethink his position on the dichotomy of
the public and the private, Lee also uses Henry's changing attitude
toward bilingualism to challenge the separation of the two spheres.
The possibilities of representation, both political and narrative, that
Henry sees in Kwang are encapsulated in Kwang's bilingualism. By

identifying a new horizon of Asian American ontology in Kwang, Henry wakes up from his dormant bilingualism to the possibility of bilingualism as an asset.

Unlike Mr. Park and many other immigrant entrepreneurs like him whose ambitions are limited due to their lack of English, John Kwang can aspire to be a public person because he speaks English fluently. One of the first things Henry notices about Kwang, in fact, is that "he spoke a beautiful, almost formal English."[121] This fluency in English, Lee implies, is behind Kwang's political ambition. That is, Kwang can be Henry's idea of "an ambitious minority politician," with "the adjutant interest groups, the unwavering agenda, the stridency, the righteousness," instead of being "afraid like [Henry's] mother and father, who were always wary of those who would try to shame us or mistreat us" because of his fluency in English and the accompanying sociocultural capital.[122] However, Kwang is also a promising minority politician because he has also maintained his Korean language and the ties to the immigrant community knit together through a shared language. One can see Kwang's fluency in Korean language and culture functioning as his political capital most succinctly in the way he adopts *ggeh*, the operational strategy of Korean small businesses, for his political campaign. If *ggeh* reflects the self-sustaining resourcefulness of Korean immigrant small business owners, Kwang's transposition of the money club to the political realm shows his vision to use a grassroots strategy of capital accumulation to reform city politics.

Kwang's mode of politics, then, could be called a bilingual invention. In a rare moment of Korean in the text, Lee points to Kwang's bilingualism as a political asset:

> But then he [Kwang] loved the pure idea of family as well, which in its most elemental version must have nothing to do with blood. It was how he saw all of us, and then by extension all those parts of Queens that he was now calling his. All day and all night we worked without stopping, knowing we'd get to be with him at the end of the day. *Oo-rhee-jip*, he'd say then, just before the eating and drinking, asking for our hands around the table, speaking *oo-rhee-jip* for Our house. Our new life.[123]

The metaphor of "our house," bilingually represented in the text, illustrates Kwang's vision of paternalism. Whereas *ggeh* as a business strategy was premised on ethnicity as the common ground among the participants, Kwang expands membership in his own *ggeh* to anyone who seeks political representation from him. As the ideological counterpart to the operational strategy of *ggeh*, Kwang's paternalism ensures the smooth functioning of his political club. As a charismatic patriarch who makes everyone feel that "you were the faintest brother to him, perhaps distantly removed by circumstance or blood but a brother nonetheless," Kwang promises to bring the best of his ethnic knowledge to remake politics as something that would benefit the underrepresented.[124] Instead of a biological group, family becomes coterminous with a unit of political representation in Kwang's bilingual invention. While the legal disputes between the bilinguals who refuse to cover their mother tongue and the employers who prefer an English monolingual workplace are about the juridical adjudication of conflict in a liberal society, Kwang's model of political society relies on the benevolent patriarch and the members' good faith to moderate among conflicting interests. Kwang's bilingual invention finds an ideal audience in the dormant bilingual Henry as the romance of the mother tongue powerfully draws him to Kwang's political vision and the two men bond over their presumable native access to the meaning of "*Oo-rhee-jip*."

Ultimately, though, Lee suggests that we might not be ready for a society where bilingualism can be an asset for sociopolitical advancement on the part of minorities. While the most apparent reason for Kwang's failure is his personal flaws, Lee also offers a number of ways to contextualize the frustration of Kwang's political vision. First, the racialization of English as white and the naturalization of the so-called broken English as Asian perpetually create doubt in Henry with regard to how far Kwang's fluency in English can go. For example, Henry cannot but feel tentative in the English-speaking public, as can be seen in his recurring sense of doubt when he encounters an English-speaking Asian. When having a conversation with Kwang, Henry notices that he is listening to their conversation as they speak. "For despite how well he spoke," says Henry, "I kept listening for the errant tone, the flag, the minor mistake that would tell of his original race."[125] The same foreignness he listens for in Kwang Henry also attributes to himself even after he has assimilated into English. He thinks: "I will always make bad errors of speech. . . . I always hear myself displacing the two languages, conflating them—maybe conflagrating them—for there's so much rubbing and friction, a fire always threatens to blow up between the tongues."[126] Such element of doubt actually becomes a self-fulfilling prophecy when Henry witnesses Kwang on his downward spiral and hears "his Korean accent

getting thicker and heavier."[127] Henry's doubting Kwang is different
in kind from the self-serving Orientalist liberalism of someone like De
Roos, the city mayor and Kwang's political rival, who gleefully turns
to a trope of yellow peril when the media scandalizes Kwang's practice of receiving donations from undocumented immigrants. Simultaneously saying that he envied Kwang's "amazing mystical energy,"
De Roos presents himself as the paragon of the rule-of-law over the
lawless foreigner, emphasizing that "everyone in this town has to follow the rules."[128] In contrast to De Roos's racism, Lee suggests that
Henry's doubt of Kwang is like self-doubt, "the face of a recognition,"
if I may, that marks the encounters between the Asian Americans in
the text who have to cover their ethnicity and their mother tongue in
the public.[129]

Secondly, Lee hints at the limits of the patriarchal model of governance Kwang promotes by showing the exclusion of Korean immigrant
women from having a public voice, women such as the hospitality girl
of the Korean bar and May, Kwang's wife, in addition to the Parks'
live-in maid "Ahjumma" (a Korean term of address for an older, usually married woman).[130] The failure of Kwang's brand of politics is
most acutely felt when Kwang's political career virtually comes to a
halt after he crashes his car while driving drunk and kills the underage Korean sex worker in the passenger seat. Of course, Lee slowly
builds up to this moment of crisis, and the reader notices Kwang's
human flaws one by one. The brief moment of possible abuse Henry
witnesses when he sees Kwang yelling at his wife within the enclosed
space of his private vehicle is confirmed as abuse when Henry later
notices "the faintest patch of redness" on May's cheek and wonders if
someone slapped her.[131] As he becomes closer to Kwang, Henry finds
out that Kwang is having an affair with his Chinese American female
campaign worker, that Kwang himself had ordered the bombing on
his campaign office after discovering that Eduardo, one of the most
prized members of Kwang's campaign team, was in fact a spy, and
that he frequents a Korean bar that has underage sex workers. On
the other side of benevolent paternalism lies the abuse of women and
an excessive demand of loyalty. Despite the appearance of unity and
harmony in the household of Kwang and his "Oo-rhee-jip," unequal
relations of power and disaffection surface to disturb Kwang's bilingual invention. It is useful to keep in sight the fact that "Oo-rhee-
jip" already reflects a layer of translation as a Romanized term. The
Korean script has already undergone transformation into the Roman

alphabet, thus refuting any idea of authenticity in the Korean language being used. From this perspective, it might be better to think of Kwang's bilingual invention as not so much translation between two discrete languages but a continuous series of negotiations between two languages for a new mode of being and doing. While his bilingual invention may have had potential, Kwang's patriarchal biases bring an end to these negotiations between the two languages of his life.

Rather than return to any rhetoric of liberalism that creates the condition of dormant bilingualism for American-born Asians like Henry or hurriedly suggest an alternative to Kwang's bilingual political vision, I think Lee chooses to ponder the challenge of bilingualism as a sociocultural way of life in the aftermath of Kwang's political demise. In observing the two Laotian children who come to Lelia to correct their English pronunciation, Ouboume and Bouhoaume, whom he compares to Romulus and Remus, Henry wonders what the future of New York City will be, using the myth of Babel. "Ancient Rome was the first true Babel," he says, "New York City must be the second. No doubt the last will be Los Angeles. Still, to enter this resplendent place, the new ones must learn the primary Latin. Quell the old tongue, loosen the lips."[132] Kwang's enterprise possibly projected a bilingual New York, if not in a linguistic sense than in a cultural and political sense, and the demise of his political career suggests that the "old tongue" still holds sway in the city of immigrants. To go back to Richard Rodriguez's change of heart regarding Spanish, from a language of shame in *Hunger of Memory* to a language of potential in *Brown,* one may ask why Henry's views on Korean did not undergo a similar transformation after his encounter with the bilingual Kwang. Is it just because Kwang did not live up to his promise of becoming a new breed of minority politician who will bring change to New York's city politics and represent the underrepresented? While that may account for it partly, I suggest that Henry's views on Korean could not change significantly because Korean does not have the same political and cultural capital that Spanish does, as Rodriguez amply shows in *Brown.* Korean remains a private language at the end of *Native Speaker*; it is still a language one is asked to cover in the public.

The bilingual plaintiffs who refuse to cover their other language in the legal analysis and the trope of dormant bilingualism in Rodriguez's and Lee's writings show the codependence of socially produced dormant bilingualism and language as a form of capital. Contradictory as it may seem, the simultaneous existence of these two phenomena may actually best characterize the intersections of language and race at the end of the twentieth century. It is interesting to think of what the future holds for the young bilinguals like Ouboume and Bouhoaume whose home language of Laotian has neither the cultural capital of English nor Spanish. Will they grow up to become monolingual in English under the social pressure to cover their home language? Will they hold onto their home language of Laotian and become bilingual in English and Laotian? Or will they become bilingual in English and Spanish, the two most widely used languages in the United States? The spirit of neoliberal multiculturalism in Rodriguez's and Lee's representations of dormant bilingualism suggest that economic calculations may be what determine the answers to these questions.

CHAPTER FIVE

# Global English and the Predicament of Monolingual Multiculturalism

In a 1999 article, "On Global English and the Transmutation of Post-colonial Studies into 'Literature in English,'" Rita Raley draws our attention to a phenomenon that she calls the transmutation of postco-lonial studies into Literature in English. A phenomenon that obliquely points to the fact that "Postcolonial Studies is still primarily a study of the *English* empire," this transmutation, according to Raley, reg-isters the declining significance of postcolonial studies as the site of critique of "Western epistemologies and their attendant assumptions about the world" and shows global English and its implicit universal-ism as crucial challenges for postcolonial studies.[1] Most insightful in Raley's analysis is her keen awareness of economic globalization and the emergence of Literature in English as interlocking systems. The continuity Raley sees in the imperial English of the British empire and the global English of the present day allows her to view with skep-ticism the idea that the diversification of English into various Eng-lishes makes global English a sign of democratic communication. In that both the English of the British empire and global English sanc-tion dialectal variants of English (which includes postcolonial Eng-lishes of previous British and US colonies) as long as they are alterities defined against the norm of standard English, neither really interro-gates the hegemony of English as the language of power and capital. Colin MacCabe's statement that "English literature is dead—long live writing in English," which Raley includes as epigraph to her article and also refers back to later in the essay, takes on a whole different meaning from what he intends in this context. While the death of the canon in English literature signals the flourishing of multiple voices, experiences, styles in MacCabe, Raley astutely shows that "writing in English" informs a cultural politics that is not all that different in kind from the cultural politics of the English literary canon.

The critique of multiculturalism may seem an unlikely counterpart to the critique of global English. Yet Raley's concerns on the transmutation of postcolonial studies into Literature in English are echoed by Werner Sollors in his dissatisfaction with US multiculturalism's monolingualism. In his introduction to the collection of scholarly essays, *Multilingual America*, Werner Sollors advances a trenchant critique of how US multiculturalism failed to account for multilingualism, a failure that becomes manifest in the English Only movement. "The absence of 'language' as a variable in the debate [on multiculturalism]," Sollors suggests, "may have contributed to the dominance of racially based identifications and the pervasiveness of identity politics."[2] Multilingualism, according to Sollors, should be a fundamental element of multiculturalism because language lies at the heart of identity. "How can one advocate a better understanding of others without learning the others' language," Sollors eloquently asks.[3] While the immediate sets of critical issues that provoke Raley's critique of World Literature in English and Sollors's critique of US multiculturalism may be different, their critiques converge on the common observation of the power and influence of English. For Raley, English comes to replace other languages in representing the lives and experiences of those from the former British and American colonies in World Literature in English. Similarly, for Sollors, English becomes the medium of expression for the lives and experiences that are not always necessarily in English in US multicultural literature.

The connection between Raley's critique of World Literature in English and Sollors's of US multicultural literature becomes palpable when we turn to a small group of bilingual writers of color that are based in the United States and who publish in both areas of World Literature in English and US multicultural literature. Typically, these writers are immigrants or 1.5 generation, and they defy a straightforward affiliation with a single nation-state by publishing writings that are both set in their countries of origin and dwell on the political, social, or cultural dimensions of life in these countries, and set in the US and based the motifs of immigration, assimilation, or racialization. In this chapter, I examine the writings of Julia Alvarez and Ha Jin as examples of literary bilingual brokering in the age of global English. How these bilingual brokers come to straddle the two publishing fields of US multicultural literature and World Literature in English shows that the predicament of monolingual multiculturalism, which Sollors laments, is not isolated from the regime of global English that Raley identifies but a piece of a larger process of a global concentration of literary capital in English.

A writer of Dominican origin, Julia Alvarez made her novelistic debut in1991 with *How the García Girls Lost Their Accents*, which portrays the assimilation of four girls in the García family who, much like Alvarez's own family, find themselves in exile in New York away from the political turbulence in their native Dominican Republic. Since then, she has published a second novel that features the García sisters, *¡Yo!* (1997), as well as a number of novels that draw from various historical heroines of the Spanish-speaking world, such as *In the Time of the Butterflies* (1994), which was adapted for the screen and produced by Metro Goldwyn Mayer, and *In the Name of Salomé* (2000) and *Saving the World* (2006). She has also published collections of poems, several young adult fictions on both contemporary Latino issues—*Return to Sender* (2009)—and modern Dominican history—*Before We Were Free* (2002)—and three essay collections.

A writer who sometimes has been called an exile but who himself prefers the term migrant, Ha Jin moved to the United States in 1984 for doctoral work in English, which he completed at Brandeis University. In interviews, Ha Jin has pointed to what he saw as an extreme form of state violence in the Tiananmen Square Uprising of 1989 as the catalyst for his decision to remain in the United States.[4] While he started his publishing career with a collection of poems, just as Alvarez did, Ha Jin's big break came when his first short story collection, *Ocean of Words*, won the PEN/Hemingway Award in 1997. Since then two other works of fiction by Ha Jin have won major literary awards. *Waiting* won the National Book Award in Fiction in 1999, and *War Trash* won the National Book Award in Fiction once again in 2005 as well as the PEN/Faulkner award and was a finalist for the Pulitzer Prize in Fiction. All his works of fiction up to *War Trash* are set in Communist China and portray Communist party bureaucracy as a farcical yet violent force in everyday life. His more recent works, such as *A Free Life* (2007) and *A Good Fall* (2009) are set in the

United States and generously employ motifs common to immigrant literature.

These brief introductions are probably enough to show that Alvarez and Ha Jin are writers of very different backgrounds. Not only are their countries of origin in different regions of the world but the political circumstances that led to their relocation to the United States and their age of relocation are also different. Despite such differences, I bring together these two writers in this chapter under the premise that we can note their common ground when we turn our attention to the institutional apparatuses of literature, the systems by which literature is classified, taught, and consumed and which place these writers' works largely in the categories of World Literature in English and US multicultural literature.

It might be helpful for me to explain here how bilingual writers such as Alvarez or Ha Jin differ from bilingual writers of an earlier generation like Carlos Bulosan and Younghill Kang since these writers also wrote about both their countries of origin and their adopted country.[5] What is new about the millennial bilingual writers of color? Such question alludes to the fact that migrant writers have existed in all periods of US literature and that these writers, understandably, have written about both their old and new lives. My interest in this chapter, however, does not lie in examining the common tropes of immigrant fiction in US literature. Rather, I am interested in how the writer's bilingualism and bilingual sensibilities—qualities that are related to her migration but not necessarily coterminous with such— are mobilized differently according to the demands of the literary system in which she participates. Henceforth, the millennial bilingual writers of color are essentially different from the interwar bilingual writers I examined in Chapter 1 because the institutional structure of placing and appreciating these bilingual writers have evolved with the development of postwar liberalism.

Whereas the interwar bilingual writers of color such as Bulosan and Kang contended with the legacy of Orientalism in the literary institutions of the early to mid-twentieth century, shaped in the social context of Asian exclusion, Alvarez and Ha Jin are not faced with the kind of legal racism that constrains the writer's self-presentation to a limited range of racially determined styles of difference and that sets up the stakes of literary acceptance in relation to national inclusion. To borrow from Jodi Melamed's periodization of postwar liberalism into the three stages of "racial liberalism (1940s to 1960s), liberal multiculturalism (1980s to 1990s), and neoliberal multiculturalism (2000s)," Bulosan and Kang were cultural brokers during the time of budding racial liberalism, whereas Alvarez and Ha Jin pursue their roles as literary brokers at the onset of and within the tides of neoliberal multiculturalism.[6] If racial liberalism, in Melamed's schema, refers to the state's adoption of an antiracist stance in the midst of the Civil Rights movement and the growing international awareness of the discrepancy between US ideals of democracy or freedom and the reality of racial oppression, neoliberal multiculturalism refers to the stage when the state is no longer as active or deliberate an actor in the management of racial difference, its role taken over by what Melamed identifies as "neoliberal sovereignty," a more flexible form of sovereignty for the neoliberal economic order.[7] The material conditions of writing and publishing for the millennial bilingual writers of color are pretty much shaped by the regime of neoliberal multiculturalism that Melamed describes.

The alleviation of the conditions of legal exclusion and discrimination, however, does not mean that the millennial bilingual writers of color are free of literary constraints related to the management of racial difference. To the contrary, I argue in this chapter that the coexistence of World Literature in English and US multicultural literature in these bilingual writers' works means that their representations of political oppression and human rights abuse abroad are inevitably placed within the pedagogy of neoliberal multiculturalism at home that is geared toward an individualistic understanding of freedom and rights. Even as Alvarez and Ha Jin seek to claim belonging in the homeland of language outside the narrow confines of national literature, that choice itself is circumscribed by the cultural politics of writing in English at a time of global English hegemony.

In the following, I first examine the conditions of circulation for a literary text that is classified as either World Literature in English or US multicultural literature by turning to the institutional apparatuses of literature that are seminal to these fields: the postwar US publishing industry in literary translations and the institution of higher education. The imbalance between literary works that are translated into English and the translation of literature in English into other languages has been pointed out by translation scholars such as Lawrence Venuti. Yet such weak demand for literary translations is a paradox when viewed from the perspective of the growth of demand for multicultural curriculum in higher education. The paradox of a weak demand for cultural difference in literary translations and a strong demand for cultural difference in multicultural curriculum, I suggest, demonstrates the parameters of cultural difference that find acceptance in neoliberal multiculturalism.

Against this backdrop, I read the writings of Julia Alvarez and Ha Jin, first their works that are set abroad and about exposing the tyranny of totalitarian governments and the culture of violence they breed and then their *Künstlerromane* where they reflect on the making of a bilingual writer of color. I suggest that Alvarez and Ha Jin engage in a cultural politics of circulation whereby flexible alliances that uphold universal ideals of individual freedom and rights are valorized over collectively conceived freedom and rights. The effect of such cultural politics of circulation is the creation of what Emily Apter calls a "transnationally translatable monoculture" that reflects American liberal values.[8] Alvarez's and Ha Jin's turn to language as the homeland takes place in this context of the emergence of a transnational monoculture as the other side of neoliberal multiculturalism. Their portrayals of the bilingual writer of color, though, also implode the idea that language can be a homeland by showing the mistranslations that trouble the idea of language as an anchor of any kind.

## UNEVEN TRANSLATIONS IN NEOLIBERAL MULTICULTURALISM

The dominance of English as a global language can be seen succinctly in the uneven global market of literary translation. Trade imbalance, arguably, is the defining feature of the translation industry in the postwar US literary market according to Lawrence Venuti. "Since World War II," he says, "English has been the most translated language worldwide, but it isn't much translated into."[9] Venuti estimates that translations only account for 2 to 4 percent of the total number of British and American books published between 1950 and 1990.[10] Needless to say, literary translations comprise only a tiny portion of these numbers. Relying on the assessment of an international writers' association, Emily Apter writes that "though Anglophone publishing statistics reveal a virtual absence of translations on any bestseller lists, PEN estimates that less than 2 percent of literary market share is devoted to works in translation."[11] Compared to other countries, the percentage of literary translations among all translations in the US publishing industry is also smaller. According to Apter, "literary translations in the United States between 1993 and 2000 made up approximately 37 percent of the national translational market," which "stands in moderate contrast to" countries "where the market share of literary translations consistently made up more than half of the overall translation market"—"India (59%), Denmark (55%), the Netherlands (53%), France (55%), Germany (53%), the Czech Republic (61%), and Russia (63%)."[12] We can speculate based on the information above that literature in English is what dominates the literary market in the United States.

Itamar Even-Zohar's structuralist approach to the literary system may be helpful here in cognitively mapping the postwar literary scene in the United States. The problem of English dominance in the literary market that Venuti's sociological account acutely draws attention to goes beyond the purview of individual writers, readers, or even texts. Tracing the conditions of possibility for publishing and the dissemination of published texts may yet yield a better understanding of the postwar paucity of literary translations. Revising Roman Jakobson's model of the functions of language, Even-Zohar presents a schema of the literary system that includes the following six elements: the reader, the writer, the institution, the dominant literary styles (what Even-Zohar calls "repertoire"), the market, and the text (or the "product"). Even-Zohar takes care to develop the definition of each element in his schema. For example, instead of viewing it as a monolithic entity, he says that the institution is an "aggregate of factors involved with the maintenance of literature as a socio-cultural activity" such as "'critics' (in whatever form), publishing houses, periodicals, clubs, groups of writers, government bodies (like ministerial offices and academies), educational institutions (schools of whatever level, including universities), the mass media in all its facets, and more."[13]

It is within such schema of the literary polysystem that Even-Zohar analyzes the position of literary translations in a given society. Contrary to the widespread belief that translations are inferior or insignificant compared to original works—a belief that explains the lack of interest in translations within literary criticism—Even-Zohar suggests that the position of translations "depends on the specific constellation of the polysystem under study."[14] In Even-Zohar's literary polysystem, a body of literature occupies a central position when it wields cultural and literary influence and a peripheral position when it fails to. If translated literature is viewed as offering new innovations in literature that are not offered by nontranslated literature and are likely to be associated with significant events in literary and cultural history, then it occupies a central position in the literary polysystem. In contrast, if innovations in literary practice—the literary avant-garde, so to speak—are primarily associated with nontranslated literature, then translated literature occupies a peripheral position in the polysystem. Under the assumption that translations are selected on the basis of the target audience's needs and demands, Even-Zohar suggests that there are three circumstances under which translations come to be central in the target society's literary polysystem: when the literature of the target society is "young," or still being formed as opposed to being established; when the literature is "weak" or when it has not yet acquired canonicity; "when there are turning points, crises, or literary vacuums in a literature."[15]

Following Even-Zohar's line of analysis, we can postulate that the US postwar literary system was mature and strong with literary innovations led by English-language writers as literary translations were small in number and lacked influence.[16] From this point of view, the development of multicultural literature as a field of literary publishing is a sign of the strength of the postwar US literary system to create markets for literature traditionally considered nonmainstream. Likewise, the growth of United States–based writers who participate in the field of World Literature in English may attest to the attractiveness of the United States as a literary and cultural center for writers worldwide. Yet the question of what cultural effects this burgeoning of the US literary polysystem has still remains. Given that critics point to literature as the primary site in which debates on multiculturalism in higher education were waged, it is reasonable to assume that English-language literature's dominance in the literary polysystem affects the kinds of cultural difference being sanctioned as acceptable and desirable and the kinds of approaches to cultural difference that are being promoted.[17]

Both John Guillory and Jodi Melamed, for example, point to the canon wars of the 1980s and the 1990s as the example par excellence of literature's seminal place in institutional multiculturalism. Presented in the media as "a battle between irreconcilable antagonists," the canon wars ended up caricaturing the spectrum of varying positions on the significance of literature and of education among humanists into two camps: "In one corner Great Books advocates defended excellence against mediocrity and national unity against cultural relativism. In another corner those who advocated for diversifying curriculum argued that our common culture was a multicultural one with all constituencies deserving representation."[18] Guillory's and Melamed's analyses of the canon wars are instructive here as both place the phenomenon within the context of postwar liberal pluralism and view it as symptomatic of bigger, unresolved issues about the role of literary education at a time when higher education is increasingly leaning toward corporate models of knowledge production and consumption, wherein knowledge that is valued is knowledge that translates more or less immediately into generating profit in the market. Here I trace two parameters of cultural difference that become prominent through the canon wars discussed by Guillory and Melamed: the nation-state as the horizon of cross-cultural communication and exchanges and the primacy of a consumerist model in handling cultural difference.

Guillory argues that the canon wars essentially relied on a heuristic of inclusion and exclusion, a model borrowed from the lexicon of political representation. According to him, since the transposition of such a heuristic onto the question of the canon conflates political representation with literary representation, the canon wars were bound to result in reductive and misleading ideas of the relationship between social identities and literary and cultural valuation.[19] A transparent, one-to-one correspondence between a writer's social identity and the value of her work was assumed for many arguments on the inclusion of minority writers in the university curriculum. Likewise, a similarly transparent, one-to-one correspondence between "canonical texts" and the values of Western civilization, never quite defined but often rhetorically called on to shore up the myth of unity, was assumed among conservative critics.[20] The frame of reference for representation and value used by those engaged in the canon wars lodge cultural difference squarely in the social identity of the writer, largely irrespective of her writings. An effect of the model of inclusion and exclusion used in the canon wars not foregrounded in Guillory's analysis is the centrality of the nation-state in setting the horizon for inclusion and exclusion. This is largely due to modeling the issue of literary representation on political representation. While the emphasis on citizenship is an effective method of seeking substantial meanings of democracy in politics, if such representational politics is the sole basis for thinking about cultural difference in literary curriculum, then the multiculturalist mandate for inclusion naturally stops at literature by domestic minority writers.

If one parameter of cultural difference in higher education's multicultural curriculum was the central role of the nation-state in adjudicating cultural differences, another important parameter was the role given to literary studies in producing citizen-subjects who are amenable to corporate multiculturalism. Melamed's discussion of institutional multiculturalism's understanding of culture as a static object evacuated of politics and domesticated to align with multinational corporations' uses of culture as a marketing tool shows this well. According to Melamed, students who are interpellated as multicultural subjects through universities, and particularly through literary studies, come to assent to a set of "normative requirements, including the recognition of diversity as an asset to new economic orders and the endorsement of permissible articulations of racialized histories, racial consciousness, and how to live and put forward one's African Americanness, Asian Americanness, and so forth."[21] The engagement with cultural difference as is reflected in higher education's pedagogy of multiculturalism, then, is essentially a consumerist model of cultural difference. As such, it is not equipped to actively engage with, or even imagine, cultural difference that emerges in the stages of cultural production and circulation and entails a politics of difference. To put it slightly differently, US universities' pedagogy of multiculturalism may teach students how to consume cultural difference as long as it does not disrupt a neoliberal rationality, which subjects racial and cultural difference to market principles, but it falls short when it comes to teaching students how to interrogate the assumptions of such neoliberal rationality or to understand the political operations of categories of difference.

If multiculturalism in higher education is bound by a nation-state focus, then it is also bound by a consumerist focus that naturalizes the boundaries of African American, Asian American, or Latino as these identities have been produced by a management rationale of trafficking in consumable units of difference. Neither makes institutional multiculturalism conducive to recognizing the trade imbalance in literary translations as a problem. Both, rather, concede to the hegemony of global English. Viewed through the institutionalization of multiculturalism that Guillory and Melamed discuss, the two fields of World Literature in English and multicultural literature may not be so disparate as they initially seemed. Rather, the colonization of postcolonial studies by World Literature in English that Raley discusses may well be another facet of the operational logic of monolingual multiculturalism that Sollors laments.

Julia Alvarez and Ha Jin, two millennial bilingual writers, bring a certain attitude and style of cosmopolitanism to the national culture of American literature by fluidly crisscrossing national boundaries in their writings. They are of a handful of bilingual brokers who blur the line of national and world literature in the new millennium. In the rest of the chapter, I examine Alvarez's and Ha Jin's works with an eye to the cultural politics of circulation in their works that could be classified as World Literature in English and as US multicultural literature respectively. The cultural politics of circulation in their works is underscored by the institutional context of neoliberal multiculturalism that embraces, and even indulges in, cultural difference in so far as they do not challenge a liberal order that values individual freedom and rights over collective social action or group rights.

## WRITING FREEDOM IN ENGLISH: FROM A CULTURAL POLITICS OF LOCATION TO A CULTURAL POLITICS OF CIRCULATION

In Julia Alvarez's ¡Yo!, Lucinda, who lives in the Dominican Republic, turns a skeptical eye to her American cousin Yolanda's progressive politics and liberal mindedness, which she gets to experience during the summers when the American relatives visit. "They'd talk and talk about the unfairness of poverty, about the bad schools, the terrible treatment of the maids," she says. "Then, once they had us feeling like creeps, they'd leave for their shopping malls and their colleges, their sit-ins and their dope cigarettes and their boyfriends in rags with trust funds in the bank."[22] Lucinda bluntly points out that talking about justice and equality, hallmarks of US liberalism, does not amount to much when there are no political stakes to such talk. She also shows that the social position of the visitor does not make for the most effective or persuasive critiques when they are not accompanied by commitments to action. Through the eyes of a young, upper-class Dominicana, a "Latin American Barbie doll," who herself has spent some time at the same school as Yo in the United States, Alvarez portrays a popular strand of thought in discussions of authenticity in the works of writers identified as "ethnic."[23] What I call a cultural politics of location, this strand of thought often assumes that a community of color has a unified essence that suffers from misrepresentation by mainstream media, that authenticity in literary representation means revealing this essence, and that a writer needs to be located in the community to offer "true" stories of the community. Understandably, a distinct kind of moralism that is rooted in a historical understanding of the community and the view that political representation and literary representation are interrelated prevail in such cultural politics. So far the writings of Alvarez and Ha Jin that are set in their countries of origin have been embroiled in such a cultural politics of location. However, when we consider these works as World Literature in English, it is not really a cultural politics of location that makes them significant but a cultural politics of circulation that foregrounds the distance between the writer's subject and her location that makes these works significant.

The cultural politics of circulation locates Alvarez's and Ha Jin's works within the millennial context of accelerated exchanges of ideas and cross-border flows of people. The cultural work that a literary text performs in this context is dependent on factors external to the text such as what pedagogical function the text is asked to serve, and Alvarez's and Ha Jin's fictions set abroad frequently bear the burden of teaching American readers about unfamiliar cultures and places in the multicultural curriculum of higher education. In other words, they make up for the deficit in literary translations by providing stories in English that serve the purpose of education in cultural difference. Ellen McCracken's assessment of Alvarez's *In the Time of the Butterflies* (1994) as a text that prods American readers to learn the history of the Dominican Republic illustrates this kind of approach.[24] McCracken sees an important history lesson in Alvarez's historical fiction about the Mirabal sisters, lionized in Dominican history due to their resistance to the Trujillo dictatorship. "Now," she says, "American readers must remedy the myopic narratives of history taught in many US schools and become interested in an important history of a small Latin American country many can scarcely locate on a map."[25]

The sentiment of a belated arrival of long-due recognition McCracken conveys is premised on the distance between the United States and the Dominican Republic, both geographical and in terms of their political and economic power. To borrow the terms of the center and the periphery in Immanuel Wallerstein's world-systems analysis, whose initial architecture Wallerstein attributes to scholarship from the Third World and particularly the dependency theorists, the United States occupies the center in the world system and the Dominican Republic the periphery.[26] McCracken lauds Alvarez's text as a potential mediator of the center and the periphery. What is more important than acknowledging the role of Alvarez's text to mediate the center and the periphery, though, is the question of how this mediation takes place, what values become the common ground in mediating the center and the periphery, and why. As Wallerstein suggests, "core-periphery is a *relational* concept, not a pair of terms that are reified, that is, have separate essential meanings."[27] What kind of relation, then, is created between the United States and the Dominican Republic, the center and the periphery, through *In the Time of the Butterflies?*

Before I move on to answer this question, it is worth taking a detour through the cultural politics of location regarding *In the Time of the Butterflies.* In an otherwise sympathetic review of *In the Time of the Butterflies* in the *New York Times Book Review,* critic Roberto González Echevarría mentions that Alvarez's novel does not connect "links between individual destiny and pivotal political events" as "serious historical fiction" should and ends up turning the story of the Mirabal sisters into a melodrama and hagiography.[28] He suggests that it is Alvarez's outsider status that makes her susceptible to such melodramatization and monumentalization: she left the Dominican Republic when she was ten years old; "her English is sometimes marred by Hispanisms" (which he attributes to her confusion as to whether the Mirabal sisters should have accents in English or not); and she tries to emulate a Latin American tradition of writing exemplified by Gabriel García Márquez and his "disciple" Isabel Allende.[29] The writer Miguel Aquino-García not only notes the historical inaccuracies in English-language representations of the Mirabal sisters but is so bothered by them that he sets out to deliver a factually correct history of the Mirabal sisters. In the introduction to *Tres heroínas y un tirano: la historia verídica de las Hermanos Mirabal y su asesinato por Rafael Trujillo,* published one year after *In the Time of the Butterflies,* Aquino-García says that the purpose of his writing is to "recoger la esencia de los hechos verídicos que dieron forma a esta extraordinaria historia [de las hermanos Mirabal] (gather the true events that shaped this extraordinary history [of the Mirabal sisters])."[30] While he does not name Alvarez's novel, it seems plausible that Alvarez's novel is one of the texts contributing to the mythologization of the Mirabal sisters given the closeness in publication dates of the two books.

The idea that being removed from the Dominican Republic creates a problem in authentic fictional representation underscores both

Echevarría's and Aquino-García's interpretations of Alvarez's novel. The same idea also underscores the polarized views on Dominican Americans' representation of the Dominican Republic that Marta Caminero-Santangelo discusses. At one end, she says, is the view that "Dominican Americans should not try to represent Dominicans. At the other end stands an equally problematic assumption: Dominican Americans are 'essentially' connected to Dominicans."[31] While not as extreme as either pole, Echevarría's and Aquino-García's takes on *In the Time of the Butterflies* still conform to expectations of unity between national identity and the subject of writing. Under such expectations, however, authenticity in representation becomes a matter of contesting authorial intentions and splitting hairs over who knows the subject matter best. The irony of viewing Aquino-García's representation of the Mirabal sisters as an alternative to Alvarez's, for example, is that Aquino-García wrote his book in the United States in exile, as the critic Fernando Valerio Holgúin points out.[32] This is just one instance of the impasse that a cultural politics of location runs into when it comes to the writings of someone like Alvarez who defies expectations of fixed national identity and embraces a diasporic scope in her writings.

A tension between the cultural politics of location and the cultural politics of circulation can also be seen in the critic Kwai-Cheung Lo's analysis of Ha Jin's English-language novels set in China. Lo's critique of an Orientalist lineage of English-language writings on China, what he acerbically calls the "industry of writing Red China in the West," shows what I identify as a cultural politics of location whereby writers who write about communist China without lived experience are suspect of conforming to stereotypical expectations readers may have on communist China and of offering false representations.[33] A moral outcry against the false spokesperson is integral to the cultural politics of location since one of its key assumptions is that speaking on behalf of a group is only viable when speaking from the same location as that group. Even if they may temporarily acquire moral authority—especially when there is increasing awareness of the egregiousness of the stereotypes to which these critiques respond—critiques based on a cultural politics of location are ever burdened with having to show true representations against which false ones are defined. Yet Lo's main argument is not built on a cultural politics of location. Rather it gestures to a cultural politics of circulation. Having started with the question of where Ha Jin's writings fit in the spectrum of national and world literatures, Lo uses Jin's linguistic crossover as the occasion to probe the boundaries of Chinese literature in the global age. "The vague and fluid idea of nation as represented by Ha Jin," Lo argues, "no longer stops at a fixed frontier but rather designates a kind of mobility that can shift, but not transcend, from one frontier to another, no matter whether a geographical or linguistic one."[34] Because the "new subject" in Jin's English-language works still "speak[s] in the history of Chinese cultural nationalism," Lo views Jin's works as well suited to expose "the incompleteness and inconsistency of the being and identity of modern Chinese literature" and to "offe[r] new freedom to seek to redefine continuously the sense of Chineseness in the changing world."[35] Where Lo ends up in his analysis, I think, points to a cultural politics of circulation. If his earlier critique of the "industry of writing Red China" is based on the idea that geographical and linguistic distance between the subject of representation and the writer makes for misleading and untruthful representations, his identification of the schisms in the notion of Chineseness opened up by representations that play with such distance show a critic that is attuned to the significance of circulation.[36]

From the Asian American side, Steven Yao examines Ha Jin's poetry in the context of US liberal multiculturalism, and delivers a staunch critique of what he views as Ha Jin's "assimilationist cultural politics."[37] Both from the perspective of Ha Jin's aesthetic style and that of the reading practices he encourages, Yao views the writer as supporting an ideological agenda of American exceptionalism wherein the United States becomes the land of freedom and opportunities, defined against communist China. According to Yao, Ha Jin's "aesthetic conservatism" is both a sign of "his efforts at complete assimilation to prevailing norms of poetic expression in English" and a result of the way he uses English "in a thoroughly transparent way to depict specifically named Chinese historical settings and subjectivities, including his own, in a lyric testimonial fashion."[38] The reading practice that Yao sees Ha Jin as encouraging through his aesthetics assumes a reader who will be sympathetic to Chinese suffering depicted on the pages (perhaps even acquire cathartic pleasure) but who will not be moved to interrogate the systemic production of such suffering.[39] In short, Ha Jin's writings, as Yao reads them, are directed at an American audience complacent with the kind of weak pluralism offered by liberal and neoliberal multiculturalism. While he explicitly disavows an engagement with authenticity, Yao's critique is nonetheless situated in a politics of location wherein the disjunction between Ha Jin's language of writing and the language of his subject matter is a point of critical suspicion.

Arguably, the cultural politics of circulation that Alvarez and Ha Jin engage in is necessarily embracing of the linguistic fluidity and flexibility that Yao is skeptical of. It may not be a stretch to say that the cultural politics of circulation takes as a given the political and cultural economy of English dominance wherein the disparity of literary and cultural capital between English and other languages is hard to miss. A decreasing identification with the category of "exile" and an increasing identification with that of "migrant" that Carine Mardorossian observes among contemporary writers suggests that the cultural politics of circulation as shown in Alvarez and Ha Jin may be part of an epochal shift in the cultural politics of bilingual brokering in literature. Mardorossian astutely asserts that the shift from one category to the other is reflective of the "change from an epoch of revolutionary nationalism and militant anticommunism which produced exiles to an epoch of capitalist triumphalism which makes various migrant experiences possible."[40] The displacement of strong political ideologies such as "revolutionary nationalism" and "militant anticommunism" with capitalist concerns such as profit-making or developing markets in the paradigmatic transition from "exile" to "migrant" literature resonates with the transmutation of postcolonial studies into World Literature in English that Raley speaks of and with Melamed's view of neoliberal multiculturalism. If the epoch of strong ideologies saw the bilingual writer as struggling to mediate between sometimes clashing ideologies of her two languages, the new epoch of global capital encourages the bilingual writer to use the language of dominant literary capital.

Reading Alvarez's *In the Time of the Butterflies* and Ha Jin's *War Trash* with an eye to the idea of freedom that emerges in their critiques of political oppression overseas shows a new terrain of cultural politics that may not be based on strong ideologies but that engage in persuasion through an abnegation of moral authority and an emphasis on flexible alliances. Despite their differences in terms of the subject matter and the writer's background, *In the Time of the Butterflies* and *War Trash* both employ the trope of translation to project a cultural politics of circulation as a continuous process of negotiation with the readers, the ultimate effect of which is the creation of "a transnationally translatable monoculture" that valorizes individual rights and freedom.[41]

In contrast to Aquino-Garcia, who says that his account of the Mirabal sisters is for future generations of Dominicans and who writes in Spanish for this intended audience, Alvarez envisions a readership that is not bound by the dictates of the nation-state.[42] In the postscript to the novel, she identifies the readers she has in mind through her language of writing. "I would hope," she says, "that through this fictionalized story I will bring acquaintance of these famous sisters to English-speaking readers."[43] "To Dominicans separated by language from the world I have created," she continues a few sentences later, "I hope this book deepens North Americans' understanding of the nightmare you endured and the heavy losses you suffered—of which this story tells only a few."[44] It is noteworthy that she identifies her imagined readers through language (i.e., English) rather than a nation-state (i.e., the United States) while acknowledging that the victims of the dictatorship she indicts in the novel are citizens of a nation-state who suffered during the Trujillo regime (1930–61). In the author's note to *Before We Were Free* (2002), a young-adult fiction that also portrays the lack of freedom under Trujillo's regime, although this time from the perspective of a young girl whose family participates in a scheme to assassinate Trujillo, Alvarez expresses the universalism of her authorial aspiration more directly, saying that "this story could have taken place in any of the many dictatorships in Nicaragua, Cuba, Chile, Haiti, Argentina, Guatemala, El Salvador, or Honduras—a sad but not uncommon occurrence in the southern half of our America not too long ago."[45] Alvarez's envisioning of a coalition of English-speaking readers from various countries who care about individual freedom parallels her move to create connections among the Latin American countries with different national histories and cultures. Such attempts to emphasize affinities and connections, of course, diminish the particularities of the individual readers and the countries being hailed. English, as the language of potentially sympathetic readers, implicitly becomes the language associated with a set of liberal values that uphold individual freedom and rights over nationalism or decolonization.

This does not mean, however, that Alvarez discards the importance of groups. She constructs bonds of affinities that relate the individual to groups that are suited to upholding the values of individual freedom and rights. In *In the Time of the Butterflies*, female heroism becomes the basis for imagining a collectivity imbued with social meaning and, possibly, political power, as historical memory is produced, safeguarded, and disseminated by women. The narrative perspectives rotate among the four sisters, Dedé, Minerva, María Teresa, and Patria. The sole surviving sister, Dedé, maintains the museum that is dedicated to the Mirabal sisters and that brings in "delegations from as far away as Peru and Paraguay."[46] She is also the custodian of the narrative, as her chapters bookmark her sisters' chapters. Temporally, she is the one sister who can move back and forth between the past and the present in her narrative. Within this sisterhood, Alvarez inserts another female character, the *gringa dominicana*, who stands for the writer herself. The *gringa dominicana* appears in Dedé's narratives, and her curiosity about the Mirabals instigates Dedé's recollections. Obviously an outsider to both the family and the nation, the *gringa dominicana*'s relationship with Dedé tests the boundaries of the sisterhood, the strong bond of solidarity that enabled the heroic acts of standing up against Trujillo. If the *gringa dominicana* can be incorporated into the sisterhood, if not by blood then by spirit, then other outsiders who might be even more removed from the time and place of the Mirabal sisters may still be able to understand and be inspired by the sisters. In the narrative, the writer's alter ego actually models the reader while the narrative authority is given to the sisters.

Such desire for universalism that would bring together readers of different backgrounds, however, is prone to erase important lines of division and distinction in its presentation of a universal model of identification. A notable ambivalence, for example, exists in the criticism of *In the Time of the Butterflies* regarding Alvarez's treatment of class and race. Caminero-Santangelo notes that the novel is primarily narrated from an upper-middle-class perspective with few working-class people in the narrative, even as she gives Alvarez credit for not having the Mirabal sisters speak for the working class, a sign that there is "an increased attention to the difficulties of bridging class division."[47] The erasure of class as a sign of difference in the novel is related to Alvarez's silence on the issue of race. Considering that the domestics and the peasants (or *campesinos*) are often made up of indigenous people (*Tainos*) or people of Haitian origin in her fictions, Alvarez's inattention to class also translates into her inattention to race as a marker of division. Pointing to Minerva Mirabal's effort to "exhume the Tainos as the original and thus truest Dominicans," Shara McCallum suggests that such a symbolic approach to the Tainos come dangerously close to that adopted in the *indianista* novels that idealize the Indian at the expense of African Dominicans in order to stabilize the political power of the middle-class Domini-cans.[48] The Haitian massacre, a national tragedy during the Trujillo regime, is only mentioned once in passing in *In the Time of the Butterflies*, despite the fact that many scholars view race as a formative element of Dominican national identity.[49] On the other side of Alvarez's foregrounding of women's solidarity and female heroism as a point of identification, the specters of race and class show the schisms of Alvarez's universalism.[50]

I think Alvarez is well aware of the schisms in her representation of the Dominican Republic. In fact, her trope of translation, which can be seen through the figure of the *gringa dominicana* as the transla-tor, seems to indicate that her aspiration to universal female heroism is neither fixed nor static but risks ceaseless misunderstandings and, therefore, is in need of perpetual translation. The *gringa dominicana* is well aware of her outsider status to the struggle for democracy that the Mirabal sisters—and by extension, the Dominicans—waged, but she makes up for what distance she recognizes with sincerity and ear-nestness. In fact, her Spanish, which Dedé characterizes as speckled with "imported nonsense" and whose imperfection is rendered in the narrative through syntactically awkward English, corroborates her sincerity and earnestness:[51]

> She is originally from here but has lived many years in the States, for which she is sorry since her Spanish is not so good. The Mirabal sis-ters are not known there, for which she is also sorry for it is a crime that they should be forgotten, these unsung heroines of the under-ground, et cetra.[52]

The supposed transcription of the *gringa dominicana*'s speech indicates that her Spanish is in fact a translation of her dominant language, English. It is worth turning here to Lawrence Venuti's dis-cussion of the two methods of translation, first commented on by the nineteenth-century German philosopher Friedrich Schleiermacher, to examine Alvarez's foreignizing of English. According to Venuti, it is the "domesticating method," "an ethnocentric reduction of the for-eign text to target-language cultural values, bringing the author back home," that prevails in postwar US translation industry.[53] Against this, he argues that we should actively employ a "foreignizing method," which is about putting "an ethnodeviant pressure on [target-language cultural] values to register the linguistic and cultural difference of the foreign text, sending the reader abroad."[54] Alvarez's presentation of the *gringa dominicana*'s speech in awkward English is interesting as the readers are expected to take it as a sign of awkward Spanish in comparison to the fluent Spanish of Dedé that Alvarez indexes through fluent English. Alvarez's foreignizing of English, then, entails quite a few layers of translation for the reader. Instead of focusing on the content of what the *gringa dominicana* says, the reader is asked to look past the imperfections of speech and empathize with the returning diasporic subject's desire to learn more about these heroines with whom she shares a heritage. Heritage, in this case, is not something one is simply born into but something that one actively constructs even if that means humbling oneself by being marked as a foreigner.

Alvarez models a reading practice that is well suited to the era of global English. The humility the *gringa dominicana* exhibits in her approach to the story of the Mirabal sisters, as well as the readiness of an apology for not knowing the Dominican Republic as well as she would like, are key elements of the reading practice that would guide the reader to consume stories of peripheral countries and learn a thing or two about individual heroism for a healthy democracy. Rather than focus on how English came to be the language to represent individual freedom, the language that is associated with promoting liberal values, Alvarez chooses to focus on exposing the wrongs of totalitarianism as the mission of her writing.

In this regard, it might be instructive to briefly compare *In The Time of the Butterflies* with *Before We Were Free*, Alvarez's portrayal of the oppression of the Dominicans under Trujillo for a young-adult readership. *Before We Were Free* is an obvious echo of the paradigmatic Holocaust story, Anne Frank's *The Diary of a Young Girl*, in its employment of a young girl's perspective, of the motif of hiding out, and of the use of the diary form.[55] In their analysis of the postwar popularity of life narratives in the field of human rights, Kay Schaffer and Sidonie Smith suggest that the Holocaust has come to be the "emblematic limit case of human rights abuse in the twentieth century" and Holocaust life narratives "exemplary of the literature of traumatic remembering in the West."[56] In her formal emulation of a notable text of the Holocaust, Alvarez not only places the atrocities of the Trujillo dictatorship in a continuum with the genocide that for many defines the post–World War II era, but also defends the universalism of a conception of freedom that actually works within the parameters of the dominant industry of English-language publishing. As Schaffer and Smith point out, "life narratives have become salable properties in today's markets" and "telling life stories in print or through media by and large depends on a Western-based publishing industry, media, and readership."[57] If the conception of freedom becomes limited by the parameters of postwar liberalism and the publishing industry, this seems to be a limitation that Alvarez seems willing to accept.

This limited notion of freedom, however, is what enables the grouping of Alvarez's *In the Time of the Butterflies* and Ha Jin's *War Trash* together under the category of World Literature in English, despite the fact that they treat very different places with disparate histories in their works. The differences between the Dominican Republic and the People's Republic of China, between the Third World and the Second World, fade into the background as the attainment of individual freedom becomes the locus of narrative desire in the consumption of these works of fiction. In his use of English as the language for representing individual freedom in *War Trash* (2004), Ha Jin is much more explicit about the ideological function of World Literature in English than Alvarez, for whom English more or less coincidentally becomes the language of individual freedom. A novel that marks a point of transition in Ha Jin's creative writing career from writing on mainland China to writing on the United States, *War Trash* takes the form of a memoir by a former Chinese soldier, Yuan Yu, who fought in the Korean War and who was imprisoned in a POW camp in Korea. Almost half a century after the war, Yuan chronicles his and his fellow POW's experiences when he visits his son's family in Atlanta, Georgia.

The location of writing is noticeably at odds with the location where the experiences being chronicled took place and also with the narrator's permanent residence. His language of choice for writing—English, a language he first learns through a missionary in his hometown—is arbitrary enough that it needs to be explained:

> I'm going to do it [writing] in English, a language I started learning at the age of fourteen, and I'm going to tell my story in a documentary manner so as to preserve historical accuracy. I hope that someday Candie and Bobby and their parents will read these pages so that they can feel the full weight of the tattoo on my belly. I regard this memoir as the only gift a poor man like me can bequeath his American grandchildren.[58]

Yuan's readership is limited to his immediate family whose "first" language Yuan indicates is different from his due to immigration, especially for the American-born grandchildren. As Yuan's metaphor of the gift implies, the projective function of the memoir seems two-fold: to teach his grandchildren about their heritage and to instill in them an appreciation of the value of individual freedom, something that was always a luxury for their Chinese grandfather. Given Ha Jin's often-commented-on status as a Chinese writer who writes in English, this intratextual reflection on the meaning of writing in English can also be viewed in relation to Ha Jin's authorial practice of writing in English. If Yuan's memoir is his gift to his grandchildren to affirm their individual freedom, what kind of gift is *War Trash* to US readers? A gift that possibly guides them to renew their belief in the good life of US liberalism and be reassured of being on the right side of the Cold War?

The dual temporality in the narrative also highlights the cultural work of recollecting the Cold War from the vantage point of the post–Cold War. The historical and geographical settings of the Korean War and the Korean peninsula as the dramatic theater for Yuan's deliberations on which side to choose as a POW illustrate the global geopolitics of the Cold War, wherein a young Chinese soldier ends up in a camp in a foreign country, witnessing the ideological stand-off between the so-called free world and Communism. While Yuan's chronicles vividly convey the moment of the Cold War conflict, the framing narrative of the seventy-three-year-old Yuan looking back on this moment adds another temporality to the time of the Cold War. The time gap between when Yuan makes the hard decision to return to China instead of repatriating to Taiwan and when he visits his son's family in the Atlanta suburb contains seismic social changes in the People's Republic of China that go unmentioned or are only mentioned in passing in the novel: the Cultural Revolution, the Democracy Wall movement, the economic reforms started by Deng Xiaping, and the Tiananmen Square uprising.

At the same time, the passage of time is clearly indexed in the life that Yuan's son makes for himself in the United States. As someone who comes over to the United States for graduate studies in engineering and ends up staying as a professional, Yuan's son illustrates a way of life that is quite different from Yuan's. If Yuan's encounter with a world that is bigger than his place of birth is propelled by Cold-War militarism, the globalism of his son is made possible by the gradual receding of the Cold War climate. From the US side, the liberal immigration reform of 1965 is what enables the wave of professional immigrants like Yuan's son who fill the US economy's need for skilled labor.[59] If English was a language of survival for the father, who was able to communicate with the US medical team and soldiers using the language, serving as an interpreter for the Chinese POWs at times, it is for the son a language of transnational opportunities.[60] The changed role of the language over the course of one generation seems to imply a resignation to the idea that future prosperity lies with English, the language of his grandchildren.

Similar to what Alvarez does in *In the Time of the Butterflies*, Ha Jin also employs the trope of translation to engage in a cultural politics of circulation that valorizes flexibility over fixity and affiliations based on choice over affiliations that one is born into. However, the affect that is associated with the dominance of the English language is quite different in the two texts. Whereas Alvarez's *gringa dominicana* is apologetic for having English as her dominant language, the translator Yuan in *War Trash* is apprehensive that English is not his dominant language, that it is a language that dominates him despite the fact that he chooses it as the language appropriate for his memoir. His obsession with the English-language tattoo on his abdomen epitomizes his linguistic apprehension. Inscribed on his body against his will in the POW camp, the tattoo is a sign of how Yuan, as an individual, has no control over his own fate. At the camp, which was divided into pro-Nationalists and Communists, with each trying to recruit more prisoners to its side, the pro-Nationalists come up with the strategy of tattooing anti-Communist slogans on those whom they wish either to repatriate to Taiwan or to sabotage. Because he is identified as someone who will be helpful if taken to Taiwan, the pro-Nationalists tattoo an incendiary anti-Communist phrase on Yuan's abdomen after knocking him out cold: "FUCK COMMUNISM."[61]

The pro-Nationalists' strategy of word tattoos actually is a superb illustration of what the philosopher John L. Austin called the performative power of language.[62] The two English words do not mean much in themselves. They express defiance; they suggest vulgarity for some. But there is not much meaning in the two words when they are viewed as a constative statement. From this perspective, the response of the US general, Matthew Bell, to Yuan's tattoo registers the triviality of the two words in the context of the English-speaking everyday. When the Chinese and Korean prisoners take Bell hostage to negotiate better treatment of the POWs, Yuan shows the general the tattoo on his stomach when his turn comes to report on the unchecked abuses in the camp. "To my surprise," Yuan says, "General Bell chuckled. He immediately checked himself, yet his large nose still gave out a snuffling sound."[63] Such response is dramatically opposed to Yuan's response to the tattoo when he first discovers it, which Ha Jin describes as unadulterated terror: "The tattoo terrified me [Yuan]. With these words on me, how could I return to China? Tear gushed out of my eyes, though I squeezed my lids to force them back. As if stabbed in the heart, I blacked out again."[64]

The terror Yuan feels in the English words, a stark contrast to the humor General Bell notes in the same words, can only be explained by the different contexts in which these words take on meaning as speech acts. Ha Jin delivers a strong critique of Communism through his depiction of the performative power of Yuan's tattoo in the Communist world. In this world, the presumption that that there is a one-to-one correspondence between the sign and the intention of the speaker (the bearer of the sign, in this case) burdens language with a transparency of meaning that has not only been challenged in modern language philosophies but also falls short of the lived experiences of linguistic beings. At the same time that he turns a critical eye to the Communists' reductive use of language, Ha Jin also hints at the symbolic power of English. Observing General Bell's response to his tattoo and realizing that these words can be used with levity, Yuan comes to see that even though he knows English through his hard-earned learning, he still cannot afford to use the language with the same sense of play, comfort, and leisure as Bell. Yuan can only imagine the material conditions of the English-language speakers that enable such affects and gestures.

After Yuan chooses to return to the People's Republic of China, the doctor at the Repatriates Center changes his tattoo from "FUCK COMMUNISM" to "FUCK . . . U . . . S . . ." (341). Such resignifying of the original tattoo is a joke to the clinic's doctor, who "knew English and would play with the alphabet," yet it works like a "charm" that protects Yuan against accusations of ideological lapses during turbulent times.[65] When he enters the borders of the United States to visit his son, however, Yuan worries once again that his tattoo will cause trouble. "Sometimes when I walk along the streets here," says Yuan in Atlanta, "a sudden consternation will overtake me, as though an invisible hand might grip the front of my shirt and pull it out of my belt to reveal my secret to passersby."[66] For all his fluency in English, Yuan still cannot enjoy the comfort of English that seems to come so easily to its American speakers. Yuan's discomfort in English in the United States is particularly worth noting since his visit to the United States is a belated tryout of the path that he did not choose at the POW camp. Yuan's return to his native land proves to be a disappointment: His mother is already dead; his fiancée has left; he is viewed as ideologically suspect for having been taken as a prisoner, a stigma that continuously keeps him on the margins of society. Finally, his visit to the United States seems to be a moment for Yuan to regret his bad choice. Yet even as he admits that his family's future lies in the English-speaking United States, Yuan remains ambivalent about his choice.

The affect of ambivalence that Yuan displays has come to have a strange extratextual correlative in the reception of *War Trash* in the Chinese-speaking world, with allegations of plagiarism against Ha Jin marring the integrity of the writer and the text. In her study of English-Chinese bilingual writers, Jing Tsu details the development of accusations against Ha Jin for plagiarizing the Chinese writer Zhang Zeshi's *Personal Records from the American Prison Camps*, a memoir of Zhang's time as a POW during the Korean War that is well known in China.[67] In terms of legal accountability, the debates involved whether Ha Jin's use of Zhang's memoir is use of historical material or of a literary artifact. Tsu, however, reads the plagiarism debates as demonstrative of the slipperiness of translation between languages as the word-for-word sameness that Ha Jin's accusers claim they see between *War Trash* and Zhang's memoir is hardly there in the loop of translation between English and Chinese. What Tsu sees as the infelicity of translation in *War Trash* is worth heeding:

> The treatment of Chinese POWs appropriately touched on the sensitive nerve of the then stirring controversy in the United States over the detainees at Guantanamo Bay. In this way, the novel brought the question of historical accountability to bear on its English context as well. The novel made one historical experience into an allegory for another by using one language to speak for another. That *War Trash* was, in the process, caught in the question of abusing the power of bilingualism makes it a thought-provoking case to test the theoretical limits of languages and translation.[68]

The abuse of the power of bilingualism Tsu refers to may well be a hazard of bilingual brokering in the millennium. Yet there is another infelicity of bilingual brokering that goes unmentioned in Tsu's discussion, that of (literary) capital. The fact that the dispute regarding *War Trash* was not about ideological differences but about plagiarism—an

English-language writer "stealing" literary capital from a Chinese-language writer—and that it took the course of litigation and settlement says something about the stakes of bilingual brokering in the new millennium. The "ethnic *ressentiment*" that Rey Chow sees in the native's response to the bilingual broker is more about capital than about ideologies in this instance.[69]

I think Ha Jin is well aware of such a trait of bilingual brokering. The abject status of Yuan as translator toward the end of his life, in particular, seems to speak to Ha Jin's ambivalence on the efficacy of translation. While the figure of the translator in *In the Time of the Butterflies* models a reading practice that Alvarez views as effective for the transmission of liberal values, the figure of the translator in *War Trash* seems to imply that one can be fucked despite incessant translation to the point where one's discernment is suspended. Between the two signs of "FUCK COMMUNISM" and "FUCK . . . U . . . S . . ." it is unclear which sign has the moral upper hand.

It is clear, though, which sign is economically superior. In the post–Cold War world order, it is material comfort and consumer culture that rule the day. In the suburban home of his son, Yuan decides to finally have his tattoo removed while watching an episode of *The Simpsons* where Bart Simpson gets a tattoo removed from his arm. Ha Jin constructs an unexpected intertextuality between his historical fiction and a popular US cartoon with this reference to *The Simpsons*. According to Tsu, Ha Jin's use of Yuan's tattoos is a detail that is taken from Zhang's memoir, so the introduction of Bart Simpson actually creates a multilayered relation among Zhang's memoir, Ha Jin's historical fiction, and a popular US cartoon.[70] The episode Yuan mentions is the first episode of the first season of *The Simpsons*, "Simpsons Roasting on an Open Fire," which aired on 17 December 1989, a little more than a month after the fall of the Berlin Wall on 9 November 1989. In this episode, Bart decides to get a tattoo as a Christmas gift to himself. He sees a design of a red heart shape with the word "MOTHER" written across toward the bottom, a design he is sure his mother would appreciate too. Marge Simpson, however, catches Bart in the middle of the act, and he is dragged out of the tattoo parlor two letters short of the tattoo's completion. "MOTHER" becomes "MOTH."

But the relationship between *The Simpsons* episode and *War Trash* goes beyond the similarity of word play with tattoos. Read as a meta-commentary on his own use of the motif of the tattoo in Zhang's memoir, Ha Jin's use of the cartoon episode is both a preemptive self-explanation for being too close to Zhang's published text—word plays involving tattoos are common enough to be found even in a cartoon episode—and a commentary on Ha Jin's views on a postmodern leveling of differences. A deliberate juxtaposition of the trivial with the serious is what makes Bart's failed attempt at getting a tattoo funny. MOTHER, a word that implies nurture and nobility and inspires affection—all the reasons Bart decided that Marge would accept this tattoo as his Christmas gift to her—becomes MOTH, an insect known for its short life span. Such deliberate juxtaposition of two incongruous objects can be seen in Ha Jin's pairing of Bart with Yuan and of *The Simpsons* episode with a historical novel that deals with the Cold War. With the fall of the Berlin Wall as the symbolic demise of the Cold War, Ha Jin seems to suggest that the consumer-driven popular culture that *The Simpsons* represents is what we are left with. In this postmodern leveling of the distinction between the trivial and the serious, the high and the low, it is unclear which side of the two signs of "FUCK COMMUNISM" AND "FUCK . . . U . . . S . . ." is trivial and which serious. What is clear, though, is that both are in English, and this is the condition that Ha Jin seems to point to as the condition for millennial bilingual brokering.

Reading Alvarez and Ha Jin as bilingual writers of millennial capitalism whose English-language writings set in their countries of origin become absorbed into World Literature in English shows these writers as participating in a cultural politics of circulation, perhaps regardless of their intention. The discrepancy between the language of writing and the language of the place where the novel is set succinctly points to a new kind of cultural politics wherein fidelity to the nation-state is no longer the anchor of individual freedom. What then, takes the place of the nation-state in the cultural politics of circulation? Or does it need an alternative for the nation-state at all? I address these questions in the next section through Alvarez's and Ha Jin's attachment to language as a potential alternative to the nation-state.

## LANGUAGE IS THE ONLY HOMELAND?

The statement that "language is the only homeland," often attributed to the Nobel-prize winning poet, Czeslaw Milosz, initially seems to capture well the worldviews of Alvarez and Ha Jin.[71] In an interview, Alvarez discusses her response to Milosz's statement at length.

> I think what Milosz meant was that the ability to create a place and feel like you belong in the human family happens through language. Coming to the United States, I was suddenly thrust into a new country, and everything I knew was left behind. Not being understood was like being in the tower of Babel, and I realized that language was going to be how I connected with these babblers! And so language became the bond I trusted; no longer did I want to sink my soul in a piece of land, a national culture, because I had seen how quickly that could go. Language was a portable homeland, so I became interested in words in a really international way, as I hadn't been with my native language, because I learned it as a baby.[72]

A narrative of overcoming underscores Alvarez's empathetic identification with Milosz's statement. Her own experience of dislocation sends her into the "tower of Babel," the ultimate metaphor of linguistic confusion and alienation. Yet she overcomes the negative condition of multilingualism through learning the new language. Not only does she develop new bonds of trust with this new language but also develops a sense of internationalism by withdrawing her affective investment from "a piece of land, a national culture" and reinvesting her affection in language. Rita Raley also mentions a similar sense of internationalism attendant on global English, although this is not exactly a desirable phenomenon according to her:

> Instead of the euphemistic British Commonwealth, what we are left with, in part, is a spatial formation even beyond the wildest imaginings of empire: a kind of English-speaking diaspora, a group of people for whom there is no need of a homeland and who are universally linked, not really by syntax, idiom, orthography, or orthoëpy, but by a basic vocabulary.[73]

Whether one agrees with Raley that the "English-speaking diaspora" is an emergent imperial formation or with Alvarez (and Milosz) that it is a reflection of the realities and experiences of increased migration, one has to admit that this new idea of a "basic vocabulary" as the basis of a group identity challenges the dominant paradigm of national literature. The limitation of the paradigm of national literature, to which Alvarez alludes above, can succinctly be seen in a heated exchange between the main character Nan and a Chinese foreign student, Hong, in Ha Jin's *A Free Life*. Hong accuses Nan of being a traitor for writing in English. *"A madman is what you are,"* Hong shouts at Nan, *"You always despise China and our language. That's why you've been writing in English and dreaming of becoming another Conrad or Nabokov!"*[74] Such unadulterated nationalism is at a far remove from the sentiment that "language is the only homeland." According to Hong, "despis[ing] China" is tantamount to despising "our language," and writing in another language equals betrayal of the nation. As a Chinese who chooses to identify with other expatriate writers who wrote in English, Nan is so outside Hong's nationalist frame of reference that he can only be a "madman."

In his 2008 collection of essays, *The Writer as Migrant*, Ha Jin reflects at length on the significance of the motif of betrayal for bilingual expatriate writers, Conrad and Nabokov being his primary examples.[75] Interestingly though, his essay, which is supposedly on "The Language of Betrayal," is not solely about betrayal but also about triumph. After the first few pages, the topic that Ha Jin delves into is how these writers "turn their 'handicaps' to their advantage."[76] The essay, perhaps unsurprisingly, ends with a reminder that a writer "must be loyal only to his art."[77] Despite the fact that the vocabulary of betrayal seems to bespeak a cultural politics of location, I think that Ha Jin's essay is actually informed by a cultural politics of circulation that allows him to move fluidly between betrayal and loyalty, between handicap and advantage.

However, such fluid movements entail as many mistranslations as translations. If Alvarez's and Ha Jin's works that lend themselves to the category of World Literature in English rely on the trope of translation, their works that fall under the rubric of multicultural literature actively engage with the trope of mistranslation. Viewed as a counterpart to the trope of translation, the trope of mistranslation shows another side of the cultural politics of circulation that is about the anxieties and uncertainties about finding one's place in and through language. Freed from the dictates of national language, the writer who proclaims that language is her homeland now has to find a way of anchoring the insecurities of her tongue in the face of too many possible yet unstable affiliations. In their works that are classified as multicultural literature, Ha Jin and Alvarez implode the idea that there is a unifying idea of national literature or language through their tropes of mistranslation but also shows that the abnegation of such comes at a great cost.

The lukewarm and unenthusiastic reviews of Ha Jin's *A Free Life*, published in 2007, are a noticeable contrast to the reviews of his earlier works that were full of praise and admiration for his craft and insights into the communist world. Writing for *SF Gate*, reviewer Charles May draws a line between Ha Jin's previous works and his new novel in terms of the marketability of the subject matter. "At almost 700 pages," May writes, "this chronicle of Nan Wu, a Chinese immigrant who wants to be a poet but is caught up pursuing 'the American dream, a house, two cars,' does not have the cachet of revealing a hidden cultural world that 'Waiting' did."[78] While other reviewers are not as blunt as May in attributing Ha Jin's literary repute to the subject matter of his writing, they still read *A Free Life* as a big flop. The reviews seem to agree that *A Free Life* is "a relatively lumpy and uncomfortable work" even as they admit that the genre of immigrant literature may inherently be limited by the prosaic and predictable qualities of assimilation.[79] As Walter Kirn says, a story of immigration is "hard to reinvent, mostly because reinvention is its theme."[80]

The quality and style of Ha Jin's prose also take center stage in these reviews but not for their virtues, as was the case for his other works, but for their foreignness. John Updike, for example, says that "Ha Jin's English in 'A Free Life' shows more small solecisms than in his Chinese novels."[81] The clumsiness of prose that the reviewers are put off by, though, may have to do with Ha Jin's attempt to index multilingualism in English-language prose. In the same review where he mentions Ha Jin's solecisms, Updike also notices his experiment, calling Ha Jin's use of italics to signal what is thought or spoken in Mandarin "a striking typographical device" that "conveys the inside and outside of the linguistic problem."[82] In addition to the italics, Ha Jin employs a direct phonetic transcription of Nan's speech when he represents his dialogues, textually rendering Nan's imperfections in English through nonstandard English. The reviewers' dislike of Ha Jin's prose in *A Free Life* suggests that, ironically, this novel may be a text that requires more work of translation for the American reader despite the fact that the subject matter may be much more familiar.

The novel as a whole, however, seems skeptical of the idea that translation works, something that appears in Nan's prolonged indecision about where he belongs in the literary world, if he belongs at all. While it is seemingly about Nan's struggles to assimilate into American life, *A Free Life*'s central dilemma is whether Nan can be a poet and, if so, what language he should write in. In this sense, the novel is as much a *Künstlerroman* as a novel of immigration. Here I read Nan's literary struggle as symptomatic of the unmooring effected by the turn to language as a homeland, a move that for Nan is motivated by a profound disaffection with the Communist Party in the People's

Republic of China after the Tiananmen Square uprising. Repeatedly, Nan avows individualism in his vision of the writer: He believes that a poet should be a "complete individual"; he wonders how any poet can belong to a clique when that to him seems to go against the ideal of being "a self-sufficient individual"; when attacked for writing in English by Chinese patriots, Nan defends it as part of his choice to be a "real individual."[83] Such individualism is what allows him to finally make the decision to write in English at the end of the novel for it frees him from the dictates of Chinese nationalism and the attendant mandate that a Chinese writer should write in Chinese. The problem, though, is that no literary tradition is really built on such extreme individualism as Nan understands it.

Throughout the novel, Nan adheres to a purist view of literature, which maintains that literature is autonomous from its social context. For example, when he attends a memorial held to commemorate the first anniversary of the Tiananmen Square uprising at the Harvard-Yenching Institute, Nan becomes frustrated with a speech by a well-known Taiwanese poet, Yong Chu, because he detects an overtly propagandist drive in Chu's speech. Interestingly, it is not Chu's political position that Nan disagrees with, for Chu extols Wei-lin Wang, otherwise known as the Tank Man after the image of his stepping in front of a long line of marching tanks in protest during the Tiananmen Square uprising went viral in the Western media. As someone who decided to stay in the United States after the Tiananmen Square uprising, Nan most likely sides with Chu in his political support of the protesters. His frustration seems to be with Chu's overt appropriation of nationalism and the rhetoric of comparative diminishment he employs to valorize the heroism of the protesters over his own poetry. "I declare," says Chu, "that the whole body of my poetry isn't even worth one drop of the blood shed by the martyrs in Tiananmen Square."[84] In judgment Nan "wonder[s] why Mr. Chu had let national pride supersede the value of his poetry, as though patriotism and literary arts should be judged by the same criteria" when "as an accomplished poet, he should see that the function of his poetry was to transcend history and to outlast politics and that a poet should be responsible mainly for the language he use[s]."[85] The idea that poetry "transcend[s] history" and "outlast[s] politics" is key to Nan's purist view of literature.

While Nan never acknowledges that his purism may have a social and literary context, his adherence to literary purism resonates with the aesthetics of a group of writers commonly identified as the Misty Poets and associated with the literary magazine *Jian Tian* (今天 *Today*), which ran for two years from 1978 before it was banned by the Chinese government.[86] As Bei Dao, the most well known of this group of writers, mentions in a brief 2008 statement for *World Literature Today*, the abjuring of overt political rhetoric and the emphasis on the literariness of language in the Misty Poets' aesthetic credo was a reaction to the desiccation of the arts and culture they saw during the Cultural Revolution: "The 'misty' or 'obscure' poetry—a pejorative term applied by the authorities—that appeared in *Today* was able to challenge the dominance of the official social discourse, by opening a new space and possibilities for the modern Chinese language."[87] The distaste Nan shows for examining any intersection between the political and the literary seems possibly to be in line with such an aesthetic credo that is a reaction to the regulation of the arts and letters by the state. When *New Lines*, a New York-based Chinese-language literary magazine of which Nan is the managing editor, encounters financial difficulty, the chief editor Bao suggests that the magazine "include articles on current events and social issues, and even a few advertisements" to increase its circulation.[88] This proposition, however, is voted down by the rest of the editors, including Nan, who believe that the magazine "should remain strictly literary" even if that means forgoing the chance to expand the reach of the journal and bring in revenue.[89] The aversion to mixing the literary with the political that the editors of the magazine express seems to suggest that their views have been shaped by mainland Chinese cultural politics of the 1980s. As Nan comes to see repeatedly, though, such an aesthetic credo does not translate well into the US literary scene in the 1990s.

Nan gets to look into the lives of mainstream American poets through three poets he meets: Sam Fisher, a poet whose fame makes Bao invite him to be on the board of *New Lines* and who is interested enough in Chinese literature and culture to accept that invitation; Dick Harrison, a friend of Sam who befriends Nan when he gets a teaching post at Emory University close to Nan's Chinese restaurant; and the MacArthur fellowship recipient Edward Neary whom Dick invites for a poetry reading at Emory.[90] As an outsider looking in, Nan is repeatedly shocked by how much the insider culture of poets is dependent on institutional networks created by MFA programs, literary awards, and publishers, and to what extent American poets are mindful of such an institutional structure. Through the eyes of an immigrant who loves literature but is wary of institutions, Ha Jin reveals the workings of what Mark McGurl called the "Program Era" in US literature, if with an emphasis on poetry, an area of literature untouched by McGurl.[91] Dick, in particular, functions as Nan's guide to the American literary polysystem. By inviting Nan to Neary's reading, Dick reveals to Nan a world of professional networking among poets underscored by its own economy of favors asked and granted. "The network," Dick informs Nan, "is essential" for poets whose fate and fame are based on the anthologies they are included in, the prizes they win, the publishers they publish with, and the places they are invited to for readings.[92] Nan watches Dick undergo a career crisis when the publishing deal for his new collection of poems, *Unexpected Gifts*, falls through, only to be luckily picked up by a New York publisher on the recommendation of his late friend, Sam.[93] Ha Jin's inclusion of such details brings into high relief the foreignness of the American literary polysystem to an outsider such as Nan who views the literary cliques as "territorial and xenophobic."[94] While he seemingly only worries about the producer (or addresser, writer) and repertoire (or code) among the six elements of Even-Zohar's literary polysystem when he deliberates on what language to write in, it is equally his unfamiliarity with the remaining four elements of institution (context), consumer (addressee or reader), market (contact/channel), and product (message) that holds him back from being part of the new literary polysystem.

Literary translations of Chinese into English are never mentioned in *A Free Life*, perhaps a sign of the paucity of literary translations in the postwar US publishing industry. But Ha Jin acknowledges two hybrid forms of literary traditions that exist at the interstices of dominant literary cultures: Chinese American literature, which Nan reflects on when he visits the Museum of Chinese Immigrant Culture in New York, and "overseas student literature," in which his friend Danning Meng becomes well known.[95] Nan is dissatisfied with both. Along with the other artifacts of Chinese American culture that are represented in the museum, he dismisses Chinese American literature, represented in the novel by "a handful of books, by contemporary authors such as Maxine Hong Kingston, Amy Tan, and Gish Jen," as falling far short of the achievements of Western culture, of "Picasso or Faulkner or Mozart."[96] On the one hand, his dissatisfaction with Chinese American culture (which he apparently thinks he has grasped after one brief trip to the museum) registers Nan's understanding of the relationship between the material conditions of existence and cultural flourishing. "How could it be possible," Nan asks, "for an unfettered genius to rise from a tribe of coolies who were frightened, exhausted, mistreated, wretched, and possessed by the instinct for survival? Without leisure, how can art thrive?"[97] On the other hand, Nan never stops to question his own assumptions about what constitutes beauty and cultural greatness.

If he dismisses Chinese American literature as insignificant, Nan is also critical of the opportunism he detects in "overseas student literature," which "pande[rs] too much to the Chinese readers' taste and depen[d] too heavily on exotic details and nationalistic sentiments."[98] Danning's stories of Chinese workers who suffer from hard labor and racism in an Alaskan cannery, *Winds and Clouds at an Alaskan Seafood Cannery,* and of the racist treatment of Chinese employees by American employers, *Good-bye, My American Boss,* exemplify the general spirit of this genre of literature as Nan perceives it.[99] These stories fail to move Nan due to their documentary aesthetic and use of hyperbole. Nan defines the literature he wants to write against such literature that he views as inconsequential. What he wants to produce, in other words, may be Literature. Yet it becomes more and more unclear throughout the narrative what this Literature that Nan craves really is.

For the expatriate Chinese artists, translation can be used to their advantage, as Nan observes through the case of Bao, the chief editor of *New Lines* who reinvents himself as a painter of minor acclaim. Bao, whose fluency in English is limited, asks Nan to translate an English-language article that one of his students wrote on him in a local art magazine. Within a couple of months, Nan observes an altered version of his Chinese translation appear in a Chinese-language newspaper and then, again, in a high profile Chinese-language art magazine. None of the reprints credit him as translator at any point. Nan soon realizes that Bao was using the Chinese-speaking readers' lack of knowledge on the American art scene to repackage a relatively minor article on him as something that is substantial. "In short," Nan muses, "the whole misleading process helped to raise Bao's image to a higher level to the Chinese audience."[100] The Chinese expatriate artist's self-promotion is much more involved than what Nan observes in the American poet, Dick, perhaps a sign that some newcomers to the US cultural institutions learn to play the game too well, to the point of having no codes of ethical conduct. A moralistic purist, Nan decries the opportunism he sees in expatriate artists like Bao. Bao's translations, which are not even his own but procured from Nan without credit, are not so much a way of creating art but "fraudulence" or "clever chicanery."[101]

Distancing himself from such facile and potentially unethical translations, Nan has no other option but to keep trying to publish his English-language poems as he stoically pursues his line of aesthetics. At the end of the novel, we see Nan relinquishing the pursuit of financial prosperity, selling the Chinese restaurant after his wife Ping-ping's miscarriage and health issues, working at a motel, and turning to writing poetry, the passion of his life. "To be a free individual," Ha Jin writes, Nan "had to go his own way, had to endure loneliness and isolation, and had to give up the illusion of success in order to accept his diminished state as a new immigrant and as a learner of this alphabet."[102] The impact of such heroic and noble resolution, however, is mitigated by what Ha Jin includes in the Epilogue, "Extracts From Nan Wu's Poetry Journal" and "Poems by Nan Wu." The entries in the journal show a record of Nan's submissions to and rejections from poetry magazines, and while there is an encouraging note now and then from editors, what stands out the most is no doubt the nativist prejudice and condescension of the editor Gail Upchurch, who writes to Nan to inform him that "for a native speaker like myself, [the way Nan use English] almost amounts to an insult."[103] The rhetorical question that Upchurch poses Nan—"Can you imagine your work becoming part of our language?"—still lingers at the end of the novel, not so much because of an individual editor's narrow-mindedness but because Nan's abnegation of coteries, networks, traditions and his belief in individualism seem extreme.[104] As the reader matches the poems appended to the novel to the episodes in Nan's narrative, one cannot but wonder if the poems are Literature that will ultimately be discovered and made a part the US literary polysystem or whether they are literature in a limbo outside any orbit of cultural circulation.

The main character, Yo, in Julia Alvarez's ¡Yo!, does not have to go through the same agonies as Nan in deciding what language to write in as her childhood immigration to the United States allows her to have a close relationship to English while growing up in it. While it is emphasized in the novel that Yo's first language is Spanish, her bilingualism is presented as an advantage rather than a disadvantage. What Yo's college professor notes about Yo's languages in the reference letter he writes on her behalf for her Fulbright application to study in Chile shows this succinctly. "Her first language, Spanish," he writes in the letter, "would be indispensable to her in understanding the original texts. . . . Yes, her English was flawless. Though still sporting a slight accent—that had indeed been his unfortunate verb, *sporting*—she had a native's intuitive grasp of the language of Milton and Chaucer and Shakespeare."[105] Garfield's comments highlight the advantages Yo has in her fellowship application. Side by side with the lauding of her superb English, the professor's mention that Spanish is Yo's home language creates the impression that her Spanish fluency is well beyond that of a foreign language learned solely in school. A consequence of this advantageous bilingualism in the novel is that the stakes of mistranslations are relatively low. If Ha Jin focuses on the cultural politics of literary institutions with his trope of mistranslation, Alvarez universalizes the trope to examine mistranslations as an integral part of writing and human relations, as what happens because of the nature of language itself. In doing so, the specificity of the bilingual writer as someone caught between two languages also dissipates, and the bilingualism of the writer becomes more or less a metaphor for the precariousness of connecting through language in general.

A brief exchange between Yo and her third husband Doug illustrates the misunderstanding that results from the slipperiness of language. Doug has a hard time differentiating among the Spanish-speaking people and makes the mistake of calling Yo "Spanish."[106] Yo's response to this mistake is marked by the spirit of political correctness in that it emphasizes the point of the view of the victim (or the oppressed) and the history of oppression that produced victimization: "I'm not *Spanish*! I'm from the D. R.," Yo exclaims, "People in Spain would probably think of me as a . . . a savage."[107] Alvarez shows a markedly post-1960s ethos of cultural difference in such passages whereby cultural difference is not something to be ashamed of but something that should be expressed if not asserted. What she says in interviews and essays about the influence of multicultural literature on her development as a writer seems to corroborate this view. While she has formerly believed that "writing of your own ethnic experience was writing sociology," Alvarez says that reading Maxine Hong Kingston has made her change her mind.[108] In addition to Kingston, Alvarez also cites as her literary influence the emergence of literature by Latina writers, which empowered her to view ethnic literature as legitimate.[109] Such literary influences can be seen in Alvarez's characterization of Yo as the bilingual writer of color who embraces her heritage, gender, and languages and tries to explain these differences to others who are not familiar with them. The pedagogical imperative of Alvarez's multiculturalism can clearly be seen in Yo's chiding of Doug. For Yo, the distinction between a Spanish speaker from Spain and a Spanish speaker from the Dominican Republic is not something that can be dismissed.

Yet the question of whether Yo is Spanish or not and the implications of calling her Spanish are never fully explored in the bedroom tiff between Yo and Doug. The tension dissipates rapidly when Doug, out of exasperation, "grabs the sunrise saucer, and dumps it over [Yo's] head."[110] Being a quirky writer, Yo is charmed by "such a wonderfully spontaneous and unusual move for him" and Doug's spontaneity wins out over his ignorance in Yo's estimation of him.[111] In the familiar and endearing dynamic between the interracial, heterosexual couple, foreignness is domesticated, if I may borrow the terms of Venuti's classification of translation methods. The more uncomfortable topic of colonialism as something that underscores the production of the Spanish-speaking peoples and cultural imperialism is brushed to the side as the more familiar and less serious subject of marital conflict resolution takes center stage. This may well be the predicament of monolingual multiculturalism discussed above where the imperative to engage with cultural difference bypasses any substantial engagement with cultural barriers that are difficult to negotiate—such as language—and settles with superficial traits of cultural difference that are easier to manage.

This is not do dismiss the significance of Alvarez's multiculturalism. One cannot deny that the domesticated foreignness in Alvarez's multiculturalism prods the reader to think about cultural difference. Compared to Nan's blind pursuit of Literature, Yo's attunement and openness to various kinds of literatures that stem from different perspectives and ways of life reveal an egalitarian approach to literature at odds with Nan's moralistic purism. Yet the mistranslations that proliferate among speakers of the same language in the novel, be it Spanish or English, belie the idealism Alvarez expresses with the statement that language is the only homeland. Instead of security or stability, language, as a metaphorical homeland for the bilingual writer, seems to add anxiety and confusion to the acts of brokering that millennial bilingual writers such as Ha Jin and Alvarez engage in.

In his review of *A Free Life*, John Updike places Ha Jin among other bilingual writers of note: Ha Jin's "prize-winning command of English has a few precedents, notably Conrad and Nabokov," he says, "but neither made the leap out of a language as remote from the Indo-European group in grammar and vocabulary, in scriptural practice and literary tradition, as Mandarin."[112] Updike's observation has several implications for thinking about millennial bilingual writers. As the examples of Conrad and Nabokov show, writers who leave their mother tongue to write in what Ha Jin calls a "stepmother tongue" are not exactly new.[113] Yet Updike marvels at Ha Jin's English-language writing because his understanding of the foreignness of some languages over others is based on an idea of language family whose origin goes back to nineteenth-century European ethnology. Ha Jin's example ruptures a common complacency in our views of what languages go together well and what do not, what languages are more foreign and what less. The fact that Ha Jin can be placed alongside Conrad and Nabokov in Updike's appraisal shows that the flows of people and cultures in the millennium defy the categories of knowledge we inherited as part of our knowledge on modernity. It is likely that there will be more category-defying bilingual writers like Ha Jin in the years to come.

Yet the admiration that Ha Jin deserves for bending the paradigm of national literature to a degree that seems unprecedented for many readers needs to be contextualized within a longer history of cultural imperialism that has created English into a language of value. Recounting how she realized that English is a privileged language from an early age, Alvarez uses the metaphor of border crossing to allude to the political economy that underscores the valorization of English: "I grew insecure about Spanish. My native tongue was not quite as good as English, as if words like *columpio* were illegal immigrants trying to cross a border into another language. But Teacher's discerning grammar-and-vocabulary patrol ears could tell and send them back."[114] Through the perspective of a child in school, Alvarez poignantly illustrates that behind a few individuals' ability to cross borders and to defy existing categories, there actually may be many more unaccounted for and unsuccessful attempts at crossing and defying man-made borders and categories. It is also through these borders and categories that some places become First World and some Third, some languages become the language of cultural capital and some do not. In the present, though, the dominant literary system that accommodates those writers and readers who refuse to be bound by traditional paradigms of national language and literature unfortunately seems to be one that is defined by a cultural politics of circulation wherein a transnational monoculture and monolingual multiculturalism appear as two sides of the same coin.

# Epilogue

*The Future of Bilingual Brokering*

In the above chapters I have tried to show how Asian American and Latino writers have tried to create a home in literary English and how such efforts register the flexibility of language to either index exceptional belonging or suggest nonbelonging. In the climate of postwar capitalist developments within which immigration from Asia and Latin America took place, I have argued that English is not only a sign of cultural capital for immigrants and their children but that it becomes a core element of human capital in the racialization of new immigrants. Against the narrative of liberal progress that suggests a movement from exclusion to inclusion as the normative social belonging for people of color in the United States, the texts I have examined above show much more nuanced and multilayered views on belonging and point to exclusion and inclusion as not a one-time happening but a spectrum of social existence. As was the case with most of US history, English continues to be the proof of assimilation and belonging; yet I have focused on the unique cultural politics of bilingualism in postwar America to suggest that the postwar tides of cultural changes contain the social valorization of particular forms of bilingualism that accords with possessive individualism. Against the narratives of English dominance or heritage language celebration, I have tried to show that the significance of bilingual personhood actually lies in the capacity to reflect a regime of racialization where selective inclusion based on one's demonstrated human capital is pervasive. The literary representations of bilingual personhood I have examined above draw upon the structure of feeling of this regime of racialization.

David Henry Hwang's recent play, *Chinglish*, which was on Broadway in 2011, is a good text for thinking about the cultural politics of
bilingualism in the twenty-first century because the play queries the
meaning of bilingualism for a white American man, a representative
of middle America. *Chinglish* tells the story of Daniel Cavanaugh's
education in Chinese business practices. Owner of a small business
called Ohio Signage, Daniel hires a self-styled business consultant
and longtime resident of China, Peter Timms, to help him win the
bid for the signs for a new arts center in the small city of Guiyang in
China. Peter's connection to Cai, the cultural minister of Guiyang,
proves futile when Daniel and Peter find out that Cai had already
decided to give the job to his sister-in-law. Yet Daniel's business venture is saved when he gets entangled in the vice cultural minister's
intricate scheme to oust Cai from the office of the cultural minister.
Initially it seems like the Vice Cultural Minister, Xi Yan, is helping
Daniel out of a romantic interest as the affair between Daniel and
her heats up despite the language barrier. Yet the final turn in the
play reveals that Daniel's expectation of leaving his wife and getting
together with Xi has been entirely misguided as Xi was actually helping Daniel's business win the bid to ultimately advance her husband's
career and prospects. Most of the play's drama and humor evolve
around the mistranslations that take place in the process of Daniel's
pursuit of the job. In the play, mistranslation is dramatized at multiple
levels, from the mistranslation between languages, which makes for
many instances of humor in the play, to the mistranslation of cultural
cues and attitudes.

It is worth returning to Chapter 2's discussion of the congressional debates on the Bilingual Education Act in light of Hwang's play,
which thematically brings together American business interests and
bilingualism, a combination that piqued the interests of many participants of the congressional debates. Hwang's play shows a world
where the realization of bilingual education, at least in the idealized
ways in which it was imagined and discussed in Congress, was unsuccessful as Daniel faces the challenge of monolingualism in Guiyang
and almost fails to broker the business deal. While the primary constituency of bilingual education was certainly children from non-
English-speaking households, the appeal of bilingual education for
the participants of the discussion was that it was a form of cultural
capital for everyone, including white American students who would
grow up to face a global economy. The world of US-China relations in

*Chinglish* shows this global economy to be a current reality; the play seemingly suggests that the predictions of bilingualism's usefulness in the late 1960s did not miss the mark.

On a closer look, though, not really, for it is not the bilingual Peter but the monolingual Daniel that is held up as the model of intercultural interaction in Hwang's play. Peter and Daniel, as Hwang sets them up, represent two different phases of journey to the East by Westerners who seek opportunities there. Hwang describes Peter "as a composite of the many non-Chinese expats I'd met during my trips over there."[1] "In some ways," he says, "they are the reverse of my parents: immigrants who traveled from the West to Asia. They could also, however, be considered the descendants of Colonialists from earlier centuries who settled in the 'Orient' to rule and exploit it."[2] From this perspective, Hwang's confession that he did not like the character of Peter at one point in the rehearsals for the play's Broadway production is revealing of his thoughts on the ethics of intercultural exchanges. Confronted with the dramaturge's persistent questions about the scenes with Peter, Hwang says that he realized the problem was that he had come to dislike the character after cutting a scene where Peter did a good turn for another character. This moment reveals an important point about the playwright's views on how one should conduct oneself in intercultural settings. "Ever since [I cut the scene that shows Peter doing something nice]," Hwang says, "Peter doesn't do anything selfless in the play. He simply takes from China, without giving back."[3]

In a play that is about brokering a successful business deal, Hwang makes a point of upholding Daniel's lack of bilingualism over Peter's excellent bilingualism, overturning conventional expectations of language as symbolic capital. In the play it is the democratic model of intersubjectivity that becomes the facilitator of the business deal rather than the skill of bilingualism. The kind of equilibrium between giving and taking that Hwang has in mind is based on a principle of reciprocity that reverberates with the presumed parity between the two parties of the business contract and between the lovers in the affair. Daniel, according to Hwang, is much more suited to respecting and working with the other than Peter from this point of view. Daniel, for example, is not a CEO of a major corporation but a small business owner who is struggling to recover from the fall he took as an employee at Enron after the Enron scandal. Likewise, Guiyang is a small city, a perpetual underdog to more glamorous and glorious metropolises like Beijing or

Shanghai. The business partnership between Daniel and Guiyang is, in a way, a partnership between middle America and middle China. The relative parity between the two parties in the contractual relationship is captured in the examples of Chinglish that Daniel and Xi levy against each other to persuade the other party to consent to the contract. In response to Daniel's examples of the Chinglish signs that went up in Shanghai's Pudong Grand Theater—"Deformed Man's Toilet" for the "handicapped restrooms"—Xi makes fun of Westerners wearing t-shirts that say "I am pervert" in Chinese and academic journals in the West publishing "some ad of a girlie bar in Shanghai" as an example of "classic Chinese poetry."[4]

The lovers' conversations between Daniel and Xi are even more full of misunderstandings, halts, and pauses as there are no translators present for these. They actually contain personal attacks on and derisions of each other's limited English and Mandarin too as each person openly vents his or her frustration. She mutters "At least keep up with the English," when Daniel is slow in understanding her comment that "Cai disassemble."[5] He calls her an "idiot" when she uses a feminine pronoun to refer to his brother in a moment of rude awakening about the pitiful state of Daniel's company.[6] Yet these "broken" conversations, and not the official conversations, are what push the business deal through. Hwang's coupling of the economic transaction with an erotic one certainly puts a more human face to the business deal. More importantly, though, it suggests that the old practice of "guanxi," translated into English in the very first scene of the very first act as "the relationship" and suggestive of customs of (not always transparent) networking in China, may not work in the new century.[7] Old-timers like Peter are losing ground to newcomers like Daniel even when they are the ones with better command of Mandarin. In supplanting the guanxi between Peter and Cai with a more personal relationship between Daniel and Xi, Hwang seems to suggest that a new outlook on relationships is needed for the new era of US-China relations, a new era of Chinglish. In the last scene of the play, Daniel says to the audience that he has "sorta come to love the mistakes."[8] "Com[ing] to love the mistakes" may well be the central lesson of the play on interlingual communication.

Hwang's embrace of these mistakes in his play needs to be situated in the cultural context where popular cultural representations of languages spoken by Asians and Asian Americans are often negative.[9] Hwang himself acknowledges that the non- or limited-English-speaking

Asian characters have been poorly represented in American films and plays through versions of so-called broken English, and he sets up his artistic aim for the play directly against this convention. "I wanted to give the Chinese in this play the dignity of their own language," he says. "So I decided to write a bilingual play, where the characters who would be speaking Mandarin, do."[10] The literary and cultural sensibilities toward bilingualism that one sees in Hwang and his play seem decidedly postmulticultural in that the humor of interlingual play—the atmospheric lightness around broken English and broken Chinese—is preceded by mutual recognition of the other. *Chinglish*, which is on the surface about the pursuit of global opportunities, seems to suggest that an ethical relationship to the other may be more important than language skills in this pursuit.

Yet it is hard not to notice the irony of widening the purview of bilingual personhood so that it not only includes but celebrates interlingual lapses, irregularities, and mistakes through a play that is so carefully constructed bilingually in Mandarin and English. Hwang takes care to emphasize that the bilingualism of *Chinglish* is the result of collective and collaborative effort. Viewing his own Mandarin as insufficient to write the Mandarin parts of the play, Hwang says he sought a Mandarin-speaking collaborator, Candace Nui Ngam Chong, to participate in the writing of the play.[11] Revising and fine-tuning the dialogues was also a collaborative effort, according to Hwang. It typically involved not only Hwang and Chong but also one or both of the two Chinese cultural advisors Hwang had for the play, a software program that transliterates Mandarin into the English alphabet, and projecting surtitles on the stage.[12] Hwang's observation on the challenges of translation he confronted as a playwright captures well the appeal of the play to anyone who may have found herself caught between languages and cultures. "For instance," he says, "I wrote a line: 'It's a load of crap!' Translated literally into Chinese, that expression is nonsensical. Turns out, the equivalent Mandarin phrase is, 'It's dog fart!' Not only do these debates help me improve my own pathetic Chinese, it's fun that they play out one of the play's themes."[13]

What enables this successful, collaborative bilingualism of *Chinglish* deserves some thought. What conditions allowed the creation of Hwang's delightful bilingual play? In his production notes to *Chinglish*, Hwang provides some social contexts surrounding the making of the play. The Chinese state's interest and investment in having a Broadway show about China seem to have played a big role in the conception and production of *Chinglish*, as Hwang says it was the Chinese state's interest in "creat[ing] a homegrown musical which will end up on Broadway" which allowed him to be invited repeatedly to China as he was the "only even nominally-Chinese person who's ever written a Broadway show."[14] Contemporary US interest in China seems to have been an additional factor in the promotion of *Chinglish*. On the US side, the play's theme of a white American businessman navigating the treacherous waters of small-town Chinese politics and the emphasis on the humor of mistranslations made the play an ideal choice for cultural consumers interested in a new era of trans-Pacific, US-China commerce, the era of "the New China," as is referred to in Hwang's play.[15] Hwang's accounts on the reception of the play outside the narrow confines of theatergoers show this well. Three weeks into rehearsals for the Broadway production, Hwang notes that the *Chinglish* crew were invited to perform a scene from the play at the "Global China Summit," organized by *The Washington Post* and aimed at "bringing together diplomats, academics and experts from around the world to discuss the current state of China and its relationship to the rest of the world."[16] When the Bo Xilai scandal broke in 2012, Hwang recalls that he received emails and invitations from "journalists and China experts" who made connections between *Chinglish* and the scandal and who asked for his comments.[17]

Needless to say, the cultural work of *Chinglish*, including its intervention into the cultural politics of bilingualism, cannot be wholly accounted for by these external factors of the play's creation and reception. Yet these conditions of possibility for a bilingual play register a subtle shift in the ways in which language and racial difference relate, combine, and intersect in the twenty-first century compared to what I have examined in the previous chapters. The unique place of language difference in the postwar racialization of new immigrants shaped the contours of bilingual personhood in the mold of possessive individualism in Asian American and Latino literature I examined in the previous chapters. With new modes of racialization and new meanings of race in the twenty-first century, the cultural meaning of bilingual personhood and its significance may very well change. If *Chinglish* intimate such a change, then it is still worth recognizing that while bilingual personhood may recede from cultural significance as a site of examining the relationship between racial subjectivity and capital, bilingualism in cultural politics is still enmeshed in the flows of capital in this twenty-first century play.

ACKNOWLEDGMENTS

I have received a lot of support and incurred a lot of debts in the
completion of this book. Josephine Nock-hee Park was, and continues to be, an exemplary scholar, researcher, and teacher. Her scholarly integrity and generosity have been essential in my developing the
book to what it is now. I owe her an ongoing debt. With their typical
brilliance, David L. Eng, Amy Kaplan, and Heather Love challenged
my ideas and helped me think through complex questions. This book
has benefited a great deal from their input and support, and for that I
am grateful. More importantly, these scholars have provided me with
models of scholarship and scholarly life that I continue to work with
and aspire to. All the shortcomings of the current study, needless to
say, are my own.

The English department at the University of Pennsylvania gave me
the opportunity to learn with and from a talented group of peers
and faculty. The vibrant intellectual environment of Penn's English
department has shaped my views on research and teaching. Among
the faculty, I would like to thank Nancy Bentley, Jim English, David
Kazanjian, and Ania Loomba, in particular. My graduate cohort and
fellow members of the reading groups I participated in—American
Literature and Latitudes—will recognize themselves here, I am sure.
During my last year as a graduate student at Penn, I was able to participate in the Penn Program in Democracy, Citizenship, and Con-
stitutionalism, directed by Rogers Smith as a graduate fellow. It was
an intellectually memorable experience. He may not know this, but
Rogers Smith has really pushed me to reflect on and reexamine what
it means to do interdisciplinary work. I continue to benefit from his
example.

From the English department at Denison University, I have received generous support from colleagues who embody collegiality. I thank them all, but would especially like to acknowledge Linda Krumholz, David Baker, Ann Townsend, and Sandy Runzo for their stewardship of the department as chairs during my hiring and initial years. The English department, of course, would not function as well as it does without the help of Anneliese Davis. Outside the English department, John L. Jackson, Tony King, Veve Lele, Isis Nusair, Lina Yoo, Taku Suzuki, John Davis, and Christine Pae generously extended their time, support, and friendship to make Denison a professional home for me. I would also like to thank Brad Bateman, then provost at Denison, who made it possible for me to take a leave of absence from the college for personal reasons at a crucial time in the making of this book.

In the long making of this book and the even longer period of my intellectual formation, I have received generous support from many scholars and teachers. I would like to thank the planners and participants of the two workshops that have been important for me in testing out the idea of this book: the EoC junior faculty workshop planned by Tina Chen and Eric Hung and the AALAC workshop for Asian American studies organized by Joseph Jeon and Yoon Sun Lee. The dedication, commitments, and intellectual rigor brought to these events by scholars in Asian American studies, including Sue Kim, Judy Wu, and Warren Liu have been inspiring. Daniel Y. Kim, Yolanda Padilla, and Crystal Parikh are amazingly generous and brilliant scholars and colleagues. At various points, Allan Isaac, Jana Lipman, Jennifer Ho, Cathy Schlund-Vials, Bill Andrews, Jim Lee, Peter Paik, Anita Mannur, and Lili Hsieh have lent their time and support. Especially from my colleagues working in the field of Asian American studies, I have received so much generous help and support. I can only hope that one day I will be able to repay all the intellectual and professional debts. Gregory Steirer, Paul Lai, Lynn M. Itagaki, Fred Lee, and Michelle Har Kim read portions of this book in its multiple stages and offered vital feedback. It is a better book now because of these friends' care and attention. My initial interest in literature and criticism took shape in the English department at Seoul National University. I would like to acknowledge the wonderful teachers and peers from that school.

I was fortunate to work with Richard Morrison and the Fordham University Press family on this book. From beginning to finish, Richard shepherded this manuscript with care, professionalism, and experience that made the entire process of academic publishing, well, pleasurable. He was everything I could hope for in an editor.

I spent the last years of completing this book in Seoul. I would like to thank some longtime friends who have helped me during this time: Minjung Kim, Sungmin Park, and Eungwi Chung. I am grateful for their friendship. I was able to spend some time with my family after a period of absence when I was in Seoul. That opportunity provided me with an emotional energy I did not quite predict. My mom, Young-hye Sung, shared her home with me, and we were able to take advantage of her retirement and have lengthy conversations about a whole range of stuff, both serious and trivial. For that I am truly grateful. She has been an unwavering presence in my life; this book would not have been possible if not for her, and to her it is dedicated. Thank you, Jaewon Lim, Jeesoo Lim, Hyewon Lee, and Ilkwon Kim, for your love and support. But I thank my nieces and nephew more for the unadulterated love and joy they brought to my life—Ha-Eun, Suh-Eun, Minjae, and Minkyu, all between the ages of one and four. In particular, I would like to thank Ha-Eun for hanging out with me and for sharing her huge enthusiasm for life. I learned a lot from her. The Davis family graciously welcomed me into the fold. My mother-in-law, Joan Davis, has been a wonderful friend and supporter. Lastly, my partner, Charles L. Davis II, has seen this book from the very beginning through its various iterations unto the final manuscript. This book has benefited tremendously from our conversations and his scrupulous readings and comments. Through highs and lows, he has been a part of this book and my life. His creativity, intellectual passion, and dedication are a source of ongoing inspiration. I am a better scholar and a better person because we are together.

INTRODUCTION: BILINGUAL PERSONHOOD AND THE
CULTURAL POLITICS OF ASIAN AMERICAN AND LATINO
LITERATURE

1. Francois Grosjean, *Bilingual: Life and Reality* (Cambridge, Mass.:
Harvard University Press, 2010), 15–16.

2. Ibid., 15.

3. Ibid.

4. Ibid.

5. Ibid., 16.

6. Ibid.

7 The 1965 Hart-Celler Act, also known as the 1965 Immigration and
Nationality Act, abolished the 1924 Johnson-Reed Immigration Act's
national origin quotas, which had virtually suppressed immigration from
non-European countries. For how the immigration restriction worked
between 1924 and 1965, see Mae M. Ngai, *Impossible Subjects: Illegal
Aliens and the Making of Modern America* (Princeton, N.J.: Princeton University Press, 2004).

8. Marc Shell, "Babel in America; or, the Politics of Language Diversity
in the United States," *Critical Inquiry* 20, no. 1 (1993): 103–27; "Language
Wars," *CR: The Centennial Review* 1, no. 2 (2001): 1–17; Werner Sollors,
ed. *Multilingual America: Transnationalism, Ethnicity, and the Languages
of American Literature* (New York: New York University Press, 1998); Doris
Sommer, ed. *Bilingual Games: Some Literary Investigations* (New York: Palgrave Macmillan, 2003); Doris Sommer, *Bilingual Aesthetics: A New Sentimental Education* (Durham, N.C.: Duke University Press, 2004).

9. See the following for the most representative works. Rosaura Sán-
chez, *Chicano Discourse: Socio-Historical Perspectives* (Houston, Tex.:
Arte Público Press, 1987); Juan Bruce-Novoa, *Retrospace: Collected Essays
on Chicano Literature* (Houston, Tex.: Arte Público Press, 1990); Frances
Aparicio, "On Sub-Versive Signifiers: Tropicalizing English in the United
States," in *Language Ideologies: Critical Perspectives on the Official English
Movement*, vol 1., ed. Roseann Dueñas González and Ildikó Melis (Mah-
wah, Mass.: Lawrence Erlbaum Associates, Inc., 2000): 248–75; Gustavo

Pérez-Firmat, *Tongue Ties: Logo-Eroticism in Anglo-Hispanic Literature* (New York: Palgrave Macmillan, 2003); Kirsten Silva Gruesz, "Translation: A Key (Word) into the Language of America(Nists)," *American Literary History* 16, no. 1 (2004): 85–92.

10. Joshua Miller's recent book, *Accented America*, for example, is a study of multilingualism in American modernism yet his introduction squarely points to the English Only movement to argue for the political and cultural relevance of his project. Joshua L. Miller, *Accented America: The Cultural Politics of Multilingual Modernism* (Oxford: Oxford University Press, 2011).

11. Ana Celia Zentella, "Puerto Ricans in the United States: Confronting the Linguistic Repercussions of Colonialism," in *New Immigrants in the United States*, ed. Sandra Lee McKay and Sau-ling Cynthia Wang (Cambridge: Cambridge University Press, 2000), 156.

12. Epifanio Fernández-Vanga, quoted in Negrón-Muntaner, "English Only Jamás but Spanish Only Cuidado: Language and Nationalism in Contemporary Puerto Rico," in *Puerto Rican Jam: Rethinking Colonialism and Nationalism*, ed. Frances Negrón-Muntaner and Ramón Grosfoguel (Minneapolis: University of Minnesota Press, 1997): 267.

13. Ibid. See also Juan Bruce-Novoa's discussion of Fernández-Vanga's linguistic purism. Bruce-Novoa, *Retrospace*, 36.

14. Gustavo Pérez-Firmat, *Life on the Hyphen: The Cuban-American Way*, 2nd ed. (Austin: University of Texas Press, 2012), 43.

15. Einar Haugen, "The Stigmata of Bilingualism," in *The Ecology of Language: Essays*, selected and introduced by Anwar S. Dil (Stanford, Calif.: Stanford University Press), 308.

16. Eileen O'Brien, *The Racial Middle: Latinos and Asian Americans Living beyond the Racial Divide* (New York: New York University Press, 2008). The thesis of racial triangulation, offered by Claire J. Kim, also is based on a similar triad of black, white, and Asian. Claire Jean Kim, "The Racial Triangulation of Asian Americans," *Politics & Society* 27, no. 1 (1999): 105–38.

17. O'Brien, *The Racial Middle*, 12–18.

18. Ibid., 14.

19. See especially Werner Sollors's introduction to *Multilingual America*.

20. I use the term flexibility here with the currency it has gained in discussions of late capitalism in mind. My use of the term has been influenced by not only David Harvey's discussion of flexible accumulation as a mode of post-Fordist capitalism but also by Aihwa Ong's coinage of the term flexible citizenship to refer to the transnational Chinese elite and by Viet Thanh Nguyen's discussion of the "flexible strategies between resistance and accommodation" in Asian American writers. David Harvey, *The Condition of Postmodernity: An Enquiry into the Origins of Cultural Change*, reprint (Cambridge: Blackwell Publishers, 1992); Aihwa Ong, *Flexible Citizenship: The Cultural Logics of Transnationality* (Durham, N.C.: Duke University Press, 1999); Viet Thanh Nguyen, *Race and Resistance: Literature and Politics in Asian America* (Oxford: Oxford University Press, 2002), 4.

21. Pierre Bourdieu, *Distinction: A Social Critique of the Judgment of Taste* (Cambridge, Mass.: Harvard University Press, 1984); *The Field of Cultural Production* (New York: Columbia University Press, 1993); *Language and Symbolic Power* (Cambridge, Mass.: Harvard University Press, 1991).

22. Pierre Bourdieu, "The Forms of Capital," in *Handbook of Theory and Research for the Sociology of Education*, ed. John G. Richardson (New York: Greenwood Press, 1986), 243.

23. Bourdieu, "The Forms of Capital," 243–44; Gary S. Becker, *Human Capital: A Theoretical and Empirical Analysis with Special Reference to Education*, 3rd ed. (Chicago: The University of Chicago Press, 1993).

24. Bourdieu, "The Forms of Capital," 243. Italics in the original.

25. Ibid., 244.

26. Michel Feher's argument that "the rise of human capital as a dominant subjective form is a defining feature of neoliberalism" is a noteworthy recent critical attempt to think about human capital in terms of subjectivity. Unlike Feher, who is interested in illustrating a paradigmatic shift from what he calls the liberal condition to the neoliberal condition, I am more interested in examining how what he views as the neoliberal propensities of subjectivity are embedded in liberal conceptualization of personhood. Michel Feher, "Self-Appreciation; or, the Aspirations of Human Capital," *Public Culture* 21, no. 1 (2009): 24.

27. Bourdieu, "The Forms of Capital," 244.

28. Ibid., 244.

29. Quoted in Crawford B. Macpherson, *The Political Theory of Possessive Individualism: Hobbes to Locke* (Oxford: Oxford University Press, 1962), 214.

30. Karl Marx, *Economic and Philosophic Manuscripts of 1844*, ed. Drik J. Struik, reprint (Moscow: Progress Publishers, 1964), 106.

31. Feher, "Self-Appreciation," 21.

32. Marx, *Economic and Philosophic Manuscripts of 1844*, 108.

33. Étienne Balibar, "The Reversal of Possessive Individualism," in *Equaliberty: Political Essays* (Durham, N.C.: Duke University Press, 2014): 77–78.

34. Bourdieu, "The Forms of Capital," 245.

35. Crawford B. Macpherson, ed., *Property: Mainstream and Critical Positions* (Toronto: University of Toronto Press, 1978), 3. Balibar offers an illuminating account of not only Macpherson's thesis of possessive individualism but also how it has been received in "The Reversal of Possessive Individualism."

36. Cheryl I. Harris, "Whiteness as Property," *Harvard Law Review* 106, no. 8 (1993): 1707–91.

37. Peter F. Drucker, *The Landmarks of Tomorrow*, reprint (New Brunswick, N.J.: Transaction Publishers, 1996); Randall Collins, *The Credential Society: An Historical Sociology of Education and Stratification* (New York: Academic Press, Inc., 1979); Barbara Ehrenreich and John Ehrenreich, "The Professional-Managerial Class," *Radical America* 11, no. 2 (1997): 7–31.

38. Maurizio Lazzarato, "Immaterial Labor," in *Radical Thought in Italy: A Potential Politics*, ed. Paulo Virno and Michael Hardt (Minneapolis: University of Minnesota Press, 1996), 133–47.

39. Maurizio Lazzarato, *The Making of the Indebted Man: An Essay on the Neoliberal Condition* (Los Angeles: Semiotext(e), 2012); Feher, "Self-Appreciation"; Wendy Brown, *Undoing the Demos: Neoliberalism's Stealth Revolution* (New York: Zone Books, 2015). Lazzarato's view of the relations between the realm of economics and other spheres of life exemplifies this approach. He characterizes his approach as "a non-economistic interpretation of the economy," the premises of which are that "economic production is inseparable from the production and control of subjectivity and its forms of existence" and that "money, before fulfilling the economic functions of measure, means of exchange, payment, and accumulation, manifests the power to command and distribute the places and tasks assigned to the governed." *The Making of the Indebted Man*, 72.

40. Lazzarato, *The Making of the Indebted Man*, 50.

41. Brown, *Undoing the Demos*, 31.

42. Ibid., 38, 84.

43. Ibid., 202.

44. Ibid., 43.

45. Ibid.

46. Sau-ling Cynthia Wong, *Reading Asian American Literature: From Necessity to Extravagance* (Princeton, N.J.: Princeton University Press, 1993), 13–14.

47. Maxine Hong Kingston, *The Woman Warrior: Memoirs of a Girlhood among Ghosts*, reprint (New York: Vintage International, 1989), 6.

48. Ibid.

49. Mae M. Ngai, *The Lucky Ones: One Family and the Extraordinary Invention of Chinese America* (New York: Houghton Mifflin Harcourt, 2010). Chinese exclusion took place through a series of laws over a number of years, but the era of exclusion generally refers to 1882, when the Chinese Exclusion Act was passed in Congress, to 1952 when prohibition of immigration from Asian countries was lifted. See Chapter 1 for more information on Asian exclusion.

50. Norma Alarcón, "Traddutora, Traditora: A Paradigmatic Figure of Chicana Feminism," *Cultural Critique* 13 (1989): 57–87.

51. Ngai, *The Lucky Ones*, 224–25.

52. Ngai, of course, is not alone in her critical attunement to the dynamic nature of inclusion or in her refusal to see Asian American history through monolithic terms of resistance or accommodation. Especially in Asian American Studies, there has been a consistent effort on the part of critics to reflect on the limitations of articulating an Asian American identity or culture solely in oppositional terms to hegemonic (i.e., white American) identity or culture. Though to varying degrees and with varying emphases, these critics have tuned into the question of value—be it in the form of the cultural capital that accompanies institutionalization or the symbolic capital of a politics of resistance or the function of the immigrant family as an economic unit in the desire for economic uplift—to illustrate Asian America as essentially a heterogeneous site of multiple, sometimes contradictory, desires, needs, and identities. See Mark Chiang, *The Cultural Capital of Asian American*

*Studies* (New York: New York University Press, 2009); Nguyen, *Race and Resistance*; Erin Khuê Ninh, *Ingratitude: The Debt-Bound Daughter in Asian American Literature* (New York: New York University Press, 2011).

53. Rey Chow, *The Protestant Ethnic and the Spirit of Capitalism* (New York: Columbia University Press, 2002), 23.

54. Houston A. Baker Jr., *Blues, Ideology, and Afro-American Literature: A Vernacular Theory* (Chicago: The University of Chicago Press, 1984); Henry Louis Gates Jr., *The Signifying Monkey: A Theory of African-American Literary Criticism*, reprint (New York: Oxford University Press, 2014).

55. Baker Jr., *Blues, Ideology, and Afro-American Literature*, 121.

56. Ibid., 9.

57. Daniel Y. Kim, *Writing Manhood in Black and Yellow: Ralph Ellison, Frank Chin, and the Literary Politics of Identity* (Stanford, Calif.: Stanford University Press, 2001).

58. See, for one example, Manuel M. Martín-Rodríguez's *Life In Search of Readers: Reading (in) Chicana/o Literature* (Albuquerque: University of New Mexico Press, 2003).

59. Gates, *The Signifying Monkey*, 50.

60. Crystal Parikh, *An Ethics of Betrayal: The Politics of Otherness in Emergent U.S. Literatures and Cultures* (New York: Fordham University Press, 2009), 21.

61. Yasemin Yildiz, *Beyond the Mother Tongue: The Postmonolingual Condition* (New York: Fordham University Press, 2012), 6.

62. Ibid., 7.

63. Ibid., 9.

64. See Daniel Kim's scrupulous analysis of Frank Chin's views on Asian American vernacular. *Writing Manhood*, 205–14.

65. Like Parikh, Tina Chen also views the history of Asian racialization as aliens as central to the cultural politics of Asian American literature and culture. Her notion of "double agency" focuses on how Asian American cultural actors generate agency from the conditions of negation and reevaluates the conventionally negative term of impersonation in doing so. A similar condition of impersonation, I would say, prevails for performances in English for Asian Americans and Latinos. Tina Chen, *Double Agency: Acts of Impersonation in Asian American Literature and Culture* (Stanford, Calif.: Stanford University Press, 2005).

66. The category of Asian American, in particular, has received ample critical attention on its impossibility from the standpoint of deconstruction. Susan Koshy, "The Fiction of Asian American Literature," *The Yale Journal of Criticism* 9, no. 2 (1996): 315–46; Kandice Chuh, *Imagine Otherwise: On Asian Americanist Critique* (Durham, N.C.: Duke University Press, 2003).

67. Yen Le Espiritu, *Asian American Panethnicity: Bridging Institutions and Identities* (Philadelphia: Temple University Press, 1992); Suzanne Oboler, *Ethnic Labels, Latino Lives: Identity and Politics of (Re)Presentation in the United States* (Minneapolis: University of Minnesota Press, 1995); Linda Martín Alcoff, "Is Latina/O Identity a Racial Identity?," in *Hispanics/*

*Latinos in the United States: Ethnicity, Race, Rights*, ed. Jorge J. E. Garcia and Pablo de Greiff (New York: Routledge, 2000), 23–44.

68. Michael Omi and Howard Winant, *Racial Formation in the United States: From the 1960s to the 1990s* (New York: Routledge, 1994), 82.

69. Ibid., 89.

70. Ibid.

71. Ibid., 56.

72. Ibid.

73. Ibid., 82.

74. Ralph Yarborough, senator of Texas and the primary sponsor of the bill for bilingual education, limited bilingual education to Spanish-speaking students saying that "if you spread this idea to every language it would fragment and destroy the bill." Yet while it may have been a part of the rationale of the bill for bilingual education, any mention of limiting the program to Spanish-speaking students was left out of the actual public laws on bilingual education. United States Congress, Special Subcommittee on Bilingual Education of the Committee on Labor and Public Welfare, *Bilingual Education, Hearings Part I*, 1st Sess., May 18, 19, 26, 29, 31, 1967, 37. The term used in the public laws is "children of limited English-speaking ability." "Bilingual Education Act of 1968," in *Pub. L. 90–247* (2 January 1968). Sec. 701. Diane Ravitch says that not limiting the beneficiaries to Spanish-speaking students was a "necessary political compromise in order to garner support for the bill in Congress." Diane Ravitch, *The Troubled Crusade: American Education, 1945–1980* (New York: Basic Books, 1983), 273.

75. Boston schools in the 1970s had bilingual programs in Spanish, Italian, French and Chinese. Adam Nelson, *The Elusive Ideal: Equal Educational Opportunity and the Federal Role in Boston's Public Schools, 1950–1985* (Chicago: The University of Chicago Press, 2005), 111. The change in the list of languages offered in bilingual education in Dade County, Florida also shows that it was impossible in reality to restrict bilingual education to Spanish-English bilingualism. Dade County, Florida, where a large number of Cuban refugees settled in the late 1950s, started developing programs in bilingual education with a grant from the Ford Foundation before 1968. Throughout the 1970s it remained a model case for successful bilingual education. From having just Spanish in the beginning, the list of languages grew to include Haitian-French, Vietnamese, Chinese, Italian, Hebrew, Portuguese, German, Arabic, Greek, and Korean by 1975. Kenji Hakuta, *The Mirror of Language: The Debate on Bilingualism* (New York: Basic Books, 1986), 194, 204.

76. L. Ling-chi Wang, "*Lau v. Nichols*: History of a Struggle for Equal and Quality Education," in *The Asian American Educational Experience*, ed. Don Nakanishi and Tina Nishida (New York: Routledge, 1995), 58–94.

77. Kim, *Writing Manhood*; Vijay Prashad, *Everybody Was Kung-Fu Fighting: Afro-Asian Connections and the Myth of Cultural Purity* (Boston: Beacon Press, 2002); Bill V. Mullen, *Afro-Orientalism* (Minneapolis: University of Minnesota Press, 2004); James Kyung-Jin Lee, *Urban Triage: Race and the Fictions of Multiculturalism* (Minneapolis: University of Minnesota

Press, 2004); Parikh, *An Ethics of Betrayal*; Helen H. Jun, *Race for Citizenship: Black Orientalism and Asian Uplift from Pre-Emancipation to Neoliberal America* (New York: New York University Press, 2011); Julia H. Lee, *Interracial Encounters: Reciprocal Representations in African and Asian American Literatures, 1896–1937* (New York: New York University Press, 2011); Leslie Bow, *Partly Colored: Asian Americans and Racial Anomaly in the Segregated South* (New York: New York University Press, 2010); Grace Kyungwon Hong and Roderick A. Ferguson, eds., *Strange Affinities: The Gender and Sexual Politics of Comparative Racialization* (Durham, N.C.: Duke University Press, 2011).

78. Shu-mei Shih, "Comparative Racialization: An Introduction," *PMLA* 123, no. 5 (2008), 1350.

79. Ibid. Grace Hong and Roderick Ferguson also offer an interesting genealogy of comparison—from comparison as it is constituted in Western modernity to poststructuralist models of comparison, comparative inquiries of US minority nationalisms, and women of color and queer of color critiques—in the introduction to their recent edited collection. *Strange Affinities*, 1–22.

80. Elizabeth Welles's 2004 report on student enrollments in foreign-language courses in US colleges and universities, based on a 2002 survey, can be viewed as a trigger for the round of conversations on foreign-language instruction. There are a few essays, such as Mary Louise Pratt's manifesto on changing public ideas about multilingualism, that predate the 2004 report. Elizabeth B. Welles, "Foreign Language Enrollments in United States Institutions of Higher Education, Fall 2002" *Profession* (2004): 128–53; Mary Louise Pratt, "Building a New Public Idea about Language," *Profession* (2003): 110–19.

81. Carlos J. Alonso, "Spanish: The Foreign National Language," *Profession* (2007), 222. One ramification might be that the linguistic diversity internal to Spanish will be even more ignored than now. As pointed out especially by educators who work with immigrants from demographically less represented areas of Latin America, there are various kinds of Spanishes used in Latino communities. An official recognition of Spanish as a second national language would mean that standardization would become more important in Spanish instruction and have more social and cultural meaning generally. John M. Lipski, "The Linguistic Situation of Central Americans," in *New Immigrants in the United States: Readings for Second Language Educators*, ed. Sandra Lee McKay and Sau-ling Cynthig Wong, 189–215.

82. Maxine Hong Kingston, *China Men*, reprint (New York: Vintage International, 1989), 299.

83. Ibid., 300.

84. Ibid.

85. Ibid., 300–301.

86. Miranda Joseph, *Debt to Society: Accounting for Life under Capitalism* (Minneapolis: University of Minnesota Press, 2014), 66.

## CHAPTER 1. CULTURAL BROKERS IN INTERWAR ORIENTALISM

1. In US immigration laws, Asian exclusion took place over several phases. The Chinese Exclusion Act passed in 1882 to prohibit Chinese immigration. In 1907 the United States entered an immigration treaty with Japan to regulate Japanese immigration. The Immigration Act of 1917 prohibited immigration from the "barred Asiatic zone," which included almost all countries stretching from Afghanistan to the Pacific. The Immigration Act of 1924 prohibited the immigration of all persons ineligible to citizenship, which meant that all Asians were banned from immigrating. I date the beginning of Asian exclusion to 1882 when Chinese exclusion began and see it as continuing until 1952 when the Immigration and Nationality Act of 1952 struck down the "barred Asiatic zone." See Mae M. Ngai, *Impossible Subjects: Illegal Aliens and the Making of Modern America* (Princeton, N.J.: Princeton University Press, 2004).

2. Ngai, *Impossible Subjects*, 37.

3. Susan Koshy, "Morphing Race into Ethnicity: Asian Americans and Critical Transformations of Whiteness." *boundary 2* 28, no. 1 (2001).

4. Sucheng Chan, ed. *Entry Denied: Exclusion and the Chinese Community in America, 1882–1943* (Philadelphia: Temple University Press, 1991); Lisa Lowe, *Immigrant Acts: On Asian American Cultural Politics* (Durham, N.C.: Duke University Press, 1996).

5. Fredric Jameson, *The Political Unconscious: Narrative as a Socially Symbolic Act* (Ithaca, N.Y.: Cornell University Press, 1981), 75.

6. Elaine H. Kim, *Asian American Literature: An Introduction to the Writings and Their Social Context* (Philadelphia: Temple University Press, 1984), 32.

7. Not all critics agree on Bulosan's desire for inclusion in America. E. San Juan Jr., most notably, is wary of reading Bulosan's romanticization of America in isolation from what he argues are Bulosan's overall literary sensibilities that reveal that contradictions of American democracy. "It is necessary," says San Juan, "to guard against the untenable opinion that Bulosan, like misguided Filipinos clamoring for statehood for the Philippines, sought the final reconciliation of colonizer and colonized in the capitalist United States. Nothing can be further from the truth." E. San Juan Jr., *From Exile to Diaspora: Versions of the Filipino Experience in the United States* (Boulder, Colo.: Westview Press, 1998), 111.

8. George Lipsitz, *The Possessive Investment in Whiteness: How White People Profit from Identity Politics* (Philadelphia: Temple University Press, 1998). See Mark Chiang, *The Cultural Capital of Asian American Studies* (New York: New York University Press, 2009), for how this investment in Asian American identity becomes inexorably tied to cultural capital with the institutionalization of Asian American Studies.

9. Ange-Marie Hancock, *Solidarity Politics for Millennials: A Guide to Ending the Oppression Olympics* (New York: Palgrave Macmillan, 2011), 111, 116.

10. Megan C. Thomas, *Orientalists, Propagandists, and Ilustrados: Filipino Scholarship and the End of Spanish Colonialism* (Minneapolis: University of Minnesota Press, 2012), 7.

11. Carlos Bulosan, *America Is in the Heart*, reprint (Seattle: University of Washington Press, 1973), 265.

12. Ibid.

13. I primarily rely on Sunyoung Lee's chronology included in the Kaya edition of *East Goes West* for the important dates in Kang's life. Sunyoung Lee, "The Unmaking of an Oriental Yankee / Chronology: The Life and Work of Younghill Kang," in *East Goes West: The Making of an Oriental Yankee* (New York: Kaya Press, 1997). David Strange mentions that in addition to introducing Kang to his own editor, Wolfe also wrote a glowing review of Kang's first novel, *The Grass Roof*, when it was published. Strange also argues that Wolfe's recommendation played a significant role in Kang's award of the prestigious Guggenheim fellowship. David Strange, "Thomas Wolfe's Korean Connection," *Thomas Wolfe Review* 18, no. 1 (1994): 36–41.

14. Uk-tong Kim's Korean-language monograph on Kang offers detailed information about Kang's involvement with the United States Army Military Government in Korea. Uk-tong Kim, *Younghill Kang: His Life and Literature [Kang Yong-hul: ku ui sam kwa munhak]* (Seoul: Seoul National University Press, 2004). All translations from Kim's book are my own.

15. Kang, "Younghill Kang," in *Twentieth-Century Authors*, ed. S. J. Kunitz (New York: The H. W. Wilson Company, 1965), 509.

16. Kim, *Asian American Literature*, 33–34.

17. Ibid., 33.

18. Lady Hosie, "A Voice from Korea," *The Saturday Review*, April 4, 1931, 707; John Carter, "A Vital Narrative from the Ireland of the Far East," *New York Times Book Review*, March 15, 1931, 4; Thomas Wolfe, "A Poetic Odyssey of Korea That Was Crushed," *New York Evening Post*, April 4, 1931.

19. Uk-tong Kim says that Kang had an agent who booked his lectures (Harold R. Pitt) and offers a list of Kang's lecture subjects as well as a separate list of courses Kang taught. His lecture subjects are both encyclopedic in scope and ambitious in their intellectual reach. They included "A Comparative Study: Psychology of the East and the West," "The Disappearance of Gods: A Comparative Study of Religion," "The Influence of the East on Western Art and Literature," "An Appeal to the God of Tyranny: The Political Situation in the East," and "The Shining Temple of Japan: The Rulers of the Japanese." Kim, *Younghill Kang*, 58. See also Henry Yu's discussion of Rose Hum Lee, the first Chinese American female sociologist in the United States. While their lectures are separated by approximately two decades in time, Lee's lecture topics on China, which included "Chinese Art and Symbolism" and "America as Seen through Chinese Eyes," echo Kang's in the sense that they assume the Asian speaker to be an expert on all things Asian. Henry Yu, *Thinking Orientals: Migration, Contact, and Exoticism in Modern America* (New York: Oxford University Press, 2011), 159.

20. Mark McGurl, *The Program Era: Postwar Fiction and the Rise of Creative Writing* (Cambridge, Mass.: Harvard University Press, 2009), 101.

21. Ibid.

22. Elaine Kim uses the phrase "ambassadors of goodwill" to characterize late nineteenth and early twentieth-century Asian American writers, most of whom were cultural elites and who in their writings tried "to bridge the gap between East and West and plead for tolerance by making usually highly euphemistic observations about the West on the one hand while explaining Asia in idealized terms on the other." *Asian American Literature*, 24.

23. While all the other characters are called by their first name in the novel, Kim is consistently referred to by his last name. This may have to do with the untranslatability of Kim's first name as I discuss later. Stephen Knadler views Chungpa as modeling cosmopolitanism in *East Goes West*. I agree with Knadler's interpretation that Kang emphasizes identities as continuously becoming rather than as final products and that he views the Asian American as affected but subsumed by the black-white racial binary. But I think concluding that Chungpa is cosmopolitan based on these traits downplays the institutional strictures on Chungpa's identity, which Kang takes care to highlight. Stephen P. Knadler, *The Fugitive Race: Minority Writers Resisting Whiteness* (Jackson: University Press of Mississippi, 2002), 85–111.

24. Younghill Kang, *East Goes West: The Making of an Oriental Yankee*, reprint (New York: Kaya Press, 1997), 218.

25. Lee, "The Unmaking of an Oriental Yankee," 405.

26. Kang, *East Goes West*, 218.

27. Raymond Williams, *Marxism and Literature*, reprint (Oxford: Oxford University Press, 2009), 121.

28. Ibid., 123, 126.

29. Ibid., 125.

30. Yoon Sun Lee, *Modern Minority: Asian American Literature and Everyday Life* (New York: Oxford University Press, 2013), 16.

31. Kang, *East Goes West*, 218.

32. Ibid., 157.

33. Historian Thomas Holt notes this metaphor of the family in the notion of language families, "like the branches on a family tree, with geneticlike nodes in which one linguistic pattern begets another." Language, according to him, starts as a sign of common culture in defining a nation and later comes to "define racial belonging and to ordain racial boundaries." Thomas C. Holt, *The Problem of Race in the Twenty-First Century* (Cambridge, Mass.: Harvard University Press, 2002), 45.

34. Ping Chen, *Modern Chinese: History and Sociolinguistics* (Cambridge: Cambridge University Press, 1999), 14.

35. Modeled after the Japanese language reform, the national language movement in China was based on the idea that "a modern standard Chinese" shared by everyone was "a necessary precondition for the unity of the country." Chen, *Modern Chinese*, 14.

36. Kang, *East Goes West*, 206.

37. In her reading of Younghill Kang and Carlos Bulosan as examples of Asian American realism, Yoon Lee suggests that "while Kang and Bulosan express nostalgia for their childhood worlds, they criticize anticolonial movements as regressive." *Modern Minority*, 33.

38. Kang, *East Goes West*, 206.

39. Ibid.

40. Frantz Fanon, *The Wretched of the Earth* (New York: Grove Press, 2004), 98, 100, 98.

41. Ibid., 100–101.

42. Kang, *East Goes West*, 295.

43. Ibid., 296.

44. Ibid., 299.

45. Ibid.

46. Ibid.

47. Karen Kuo, *East Is West and West Is East: Gender, Culture, and Interwar Encounters between Asia and America* (Philadelphia: Temple University Press, 2013), 67.

48. Kang, *East Goes West*, 257.

49. Ibid., 211.

50. Ibid., 256.

51. Ibid., 257.

52. Ibid.

53. Cynthia H. Tolentino, *America's Experts: Race and the Fictions of Sociology* (Minneapolis: University of Minnesota Press, 2009), 82–84.

54. Ibid., 83. Tolentino also explains the work of comparative racialization Park's "racial uniform" does. Whereas both African Americans and Asian Americans wear the racial uniform, "Park argues that only Asian Americans, if given the opportunity by whites, possess the capacity to assimilate." Ibid., 83. Tolentino reads such a view as prefiguring the notion of Asian Americans as the model minority.

55. Yu, *Thinking Orientals*, 86.

56. Kang, *East Goes West*, 363–64.

57. Ibid., 159.

58. Michael Denning, *The Cultural Front: The Laboring of American Culture in the Twentieth Century* (New York: Verso, 1997); Alan M. Wald, *American Night: The Literary Left in the Era of the Cold War* (Chapel Hill: University of North Carolina Press, 2012).

59. Caroline S. Hau, "'Patria é intereses': Reflections on the Origins and Changing Meanings of *Ilustrado*," Philippine Studies 59, no. 1 (2011), 11.

60. Ibid.

61. Ibid., 12.

62. Bulosan, *America Is in the Heart*, 71. I use "Carlos" to refer to the narrator of *America Is in the Heart* since I read this text as autobiographical fiction rather than autobiography.

63. Caroline S. Hau and Benedict Anderson, introduction to *All the Conspirators* by Carlos Bulosan (Seattle: University of Washington Press, 2005), xxi.

64. Martin J. Ponce, *Beyond the Nation: Diasporic Filipino Literature and Queer Reading* (New York: New York University Press, 2010), 17.

65. Ibid., 16. Ponce asserts that dismissing English as a language of Filipino literature is overly hasty because "many Filipinos in the early decades of the twentieth century actively sought to cultivate the new language [of English]."

66. In an essay he wrote on the literary contest sponsored by the Philippine Writer's League in 1942, Bulosan says that the languages represented in the contest were "English, Spanish, and Tagalog," "the three most important languages in the Philippines." Carlos Bulosan, *On Becoming Filipino: Selected Writings of Carlos Bulosan,* ed. E. San Juan Jr. (Philadelphia, Temple University Press, 1995), 135.

67. Thomas, *Orientalists, Propagandists, and Ilustrados,* 25. The salience of racial anthropology as a discourse of colonial rule also can be seen in the example of US colonialism in the Philippines. In his analysis of the mass media representation of the Philippines in the turn of the twentieth century, David Brody argues that "the mass media depicted the Philippines as a visually curious site where civilization did not exist and all that could be found was the taint of exoticized bodies, odd customs, and contaminated blood." Brody also points out that such relegation of the Philippines to the periphery of civilization did not prevent the United States from using the Philippines for commerce. David Brody, *Visualizing American Empire: Orientalism and Imperialism in the Philippines* (Chicago: The University of Chicago Press, 2010), 61.

68. Thomas, *Orientalists, Propagandists, and Ilustrados,* 34–35.

69. John Guillory, *Cultural Capital: The Problem of Literary Canon Formation* (Chicago: The University of Chicago Press, 1993), 18.

70. Ibid.

71. Oscar Campomanes and Todd S. Gernes, "Two Letters from America: Carlos Bulosan and the Act of Writing," *MELUS* 15, no. 3 (1988), 22.

72. Bulosan, *On Becoming Filipino,* 65.

73. San Juan Jr., *From Exile to Diaspora,* 102.

74. Bulosan, *On Becoming Filipino,* 66.

75. Ibid., 69.

76. Ibid., 69.

77. Ibid., 67, 71.

78. Ibid., 71.

79. Ibid., 109.

80. Ibid., 110.

81. Ibid., 113.

82. San Juan Jr., *From Exile to Diaspora,* 122.

83. Ibid., 106.

84. Ibid.

85. Ibid., 122.

86. Bulosan, *On Becoming Filipino,* 112.

87. Thomas, *Orientalists, Propagandists, and Ilustrados,* 31. See also Paul Kramer's discussion of how the *ilustrados* involved in the Propaganda

movement used folklore. Paul Kramer, *The Blood of Government: Race, Empire, and the United States and the Philippines* (Chapel Hill: The University of North Carolina Press, 2006), 64–66.

88. Bulosan, *On Becoming Filipino,* 113.

89. Ibid.

90. Jameson, *The Political Unconscious,* 29.

91. Ibid., 30.

92. Bulosan, *On Becoming Filipino,* 138.

93. Ibid., 140.

94. Ibid., 141, 142.

95. Ibid., 142.

96. Bulosan, *America Is in the Heart,* 172.

97. Ibid.

98. Augusto Fauni Espiritu, *Five Faces of Exile: The Nation and Filipino American Intellectuals* (Stanford, Calif.: Stanford University Press, 2005), 60.

99. Lee, "The Unmaking of an Oriental Yankee / Chronology," 408; Kim, *Younghill Kang,* 75–80; Hyung-ju Ahn, *Between Two Adversaries: Korean Interpreters at Japanese Alien Enemy Detention Centers during World War II* (Fullerton: California State University at Fullerton, 2002), 40.

100. Younghill Kang, foreword to *Korea: A History,* by Bong-Youn Choy (Rutland, Vt.: Charles E. Tuttle Company, 1971), i.


## CHAPTER 2. BILINGUAL PERSONHOOD AND THE AMERICAN DREAM

1. Carlo Bulosan, *America Is in the Heart,* reprint (Seattle: University of Washington Press, 1973), 14.

2. Ibid.

3. The lawsuit in question is *Guey Heung Lee v. Johnson* (1971). Hyung-Chan Kim, ed., *Asian Americans and the Supreme Court: A Documentary History* (New York: Greenwood Press, 1992), 904. See also Charles Wollenberg, *All Deliberate Speed: Segregation and Exclusion in California Schools, 1855–1975* (Berkeley: University of California Press, 1978), 46.

4. L. Ling-chi Wang, "*Lau v. Nichols*: History of a Struggle for Equal and Quality Education," in *The Asian American Educational Experience,* ed. Don Nakanishi and Tina Nishida (New York: Routledge, 1995).

5. It may also seem to go against the desire of an earlier generation of Asian immigrants who wanted access to white public schools. See Mae Ngai, "History as Law and Life: *Tape v. Hurley* and the Origins of the Chinese American Middle Class," in *Chinese Americans and the Politics of Race and Culture,* ed. Sucheng Chan and Madeline Y. Hsu (Philadelphia: Temple University Press, 2008), 62–90.

6 English Plus is the term advocates of public bilingualism used to counter the English Only slogan. See James Crawford, *At War with Diversity: US Language Policy in an Age of Anxiety* (New York: Multilingual Matters, 2000), 45–47.

7. Lydia H. Liu, *The Freudian Robot: Digital Media and the Future of the Unconscious* (Chicago: The University of Chicago Press, 2011), 88; Yunte Huang, "Basic English, Chinglish, and Translocal Dialect," in *English and Ethnicity*, ed. Janina Brutt-Griffler and Catherine Evans Davies (New York: Palgrave Macmillan, 2006), 77. Liu offers an interesting analysis of Basic English in relation to the mid-twentieth century scientific search for the language of universal communicability. Huang observes that institutions such as Voice of America used a variation of Basic English, Special English, in winning the minds of enemies during the Cold War. Both scholars point out the imperial ambition in the acronym of BASIC: "British, American, Scientific, International, and Commercial." Liu, *The Freudian Robot*, 89; Huang, "Basic English, Chinglish, and Translocal Dialect," 77.

8. Huang, "Basic English, Chinglish, and Translocal Dialect," 77.

9. Mrs. Earles's pedagogy of bilingual instruction precedes the Bilingual Education Act of 1968. The bilingual program at Nye Elementary School is one of the few bilingual programs that developed out of the lived experiences of bilingual communities in the southwest. See Ofelia García, *Bilingual Education in the 21st Century: A Global Perspective* (Chichester, U.K.: Wiley-Blackwell, 2009), 168.

10. National Education Association of the United States, "The Invisible Minority," Washington D.C.: National Education Association, 1966, 15. http://www.nea.org/home/46866.htm. Accessed January 13, 2015.

11. Ibid.

12. I use the second edition of *Language in Thought and Action*, as opposed to *Language in Action*, which was published in 1941, because the revised edition includes an anecdote that reflects the precarious situation of Japanese Americans in the United States after the bombing of Pearl Harbor. Oblique as it is, it is a rare published example of Hayakawa's thoughts on wartime American reaction to Japanese Americans, and I read it as significant in further understanding his views on assimilation and uplift. Samuel I. Hayakawa, *Language in Thought and Action*, 2nd ed. (New York: Harcourt, Brace and Company, 1949).

13. Jodi Melamed, *Represent and Destroy: Rationalizing Violence in the New Racial Capitalism* (Minneapolis: University of Minnesota Press, 2011), 8.

14. In the context of mid-twentieth century racial liberalism, Hayakawa's take on how to avoid and combat racism by using language correctly was well received by African American civic leaders. He was even invited to be a regular contributor to *The Chicago Defender* for a few years. Hayakawa, *Language in Thought and Action*, iv. Fred Turner places Hayakawa's *Language in Action* in the lineage of Alfred Korzybski's General Semantics movement, which was based on Korzybski's view that "much human unhappiness in both the psychological and social realms could be traced to our inability to separate the pictures in our heads and the communicative processes that put them there from material reality itself." Fred Turner, *The Democratic Surround: Multimedia and American Liberalism from World War II to the Psychedelic Sixties* (Chicago: The University of Chicago Press, 2013), 22–23.

15. See Chapter 2 of Daryl J. Maeda, *Chains of Babylon: The Rise of Asian America* (Minneapolis: University of Minnesota Press, 2009).

16. Hayakawa, *Language in Thought and Action*, 193.

17. Ibid., 189; emphasis in original.

18. Ibid., 193.

19. Ibid., 199.

20. Edna Bonacich, "A Theory of Middleman Minorities," *American Sociological Review* 38, no. 5 (1973): 583–94.

21. Hayakawa, *Language in Thought and Action* 199.

22. Ibid., 204.

23. Ibid., 200.

24. Ibid., 205.

25. Wendy Brown's discussion of the necessary distinction between political and economic liberalism in the climate of neoliberalism informs my thoughts on postwar liberalism. Wendy Brown, "Neoliberalism and the End of Liberal Democracy," in *Edgework: Critical Essays on Knowledge and Politics* (Princeton, N.J.: Princeton University Press, 2005), 37–59.

26. Crawford B. Macpherson, *The Political Theory of Possessive Individualism: Hobbes to Locke* (Oxford: Oxford University Press, 1962), 264.

27. Hayakawa, clarifies the location of this episode as Oshkosh, Wisconsin, in a reprint of the second edition published in 1964.

28. Hayakawa, *Language in Thought and Action*, 70, 71.

29. Ibid., 74.

30. Ibid., 73.

31. Ibid.

32. Ibid., 73–74.

33. Ibid., 74.

34. Quoted in James Crawford, ed. *Language Loyalties: A Source Book on the Official English Controversy* (Chicago: The University of Chicago Press, 1992), 19.

35. Adam Nelson, *The Elusive Ideal: Equal Educational Opportunity and the Federal Role in Boston's Public Schools, 1950–1985* (Chicago: The University of Chicago Press, 2005), 76.

36. *Brown v. Board of Education of Topeka* 347 U.S. 483, 1954.

37. Ibid. See Anne Cheng for a discussion of the ramifications of the Supreme Court's use of "psychological evidence" in the *Brown* decision. Anne Anlin Cheng, *The Melancholy of Race: Psychoanalysis, Race, and Hidden Grief* (New York: Oxford University Press, 2001), 3.

38. *Lau v. Nichols* was a class-action suit filed on behalf of approximately three-thousand Chinese-speaking students in the school district. Wang, "*Lau v. Nichols*," 58–59.

39. Wang, "*Lau v. Nichols*," 59.

40. Quoted in Wang, "*Lau v. Nichols*," 61.

41. *Brown v. Board of Education.* García, *Bilingual Education in the 21st Century*, 170. Many scholars point out that the *Lau* decision had more symbolic than practical significance. The Supreme Court did not specify what measures schools should take in redressing the situation of the

Chinese-speaking students and handed over the task to the Office of Civil Rights, which eventually developed a set of guidelines on bilingual education that met the standards of equal educational opportunities in the Civil Rights Act, later known as the Lau Remedies. Rachel F. Moran, "Undone by Law: The Uncertain Legacy of *Lau v. Nichols*," *Berkeley La Raza Law Journal* 16, no. 1 (2005); Philip T. Nash, "Asian Americans and Their Rights for Employment and Education," in *Asian Americans and the Supreme Court*, ed. Hyung-chan Kim (Westport, Conn.: Greenwood Press, 1992), 904.

42. Marc Shell, "Babel in America; or, the Politics of Language Diversity in the United States," *Critical Inquiry* 20, no. 1 (1993), 124.

43. Einar Haugen, "The Stigmata of Bilingualism," in *The Ecology of Language: Essays*, selected and introduced by Anwar S. Dil (Stanford, Calif.: Stanford University Press), 308.

44. Ibid.

45. Nelson, *The Elusive Ideal*, 31–60.

46. See Davies's discussion of possible political motives of Ralph Yarborough, Senator of Texas and sponsor of the bill on bilingual education. Gareth Davies, *See Government Grow: Education Politics from Johnson to Reagan* (Lawrence: University Press of Kansas, 2007), 142–43.

47. Haugen, "The Stigmata of Bilingualism," 307. Much of the effort of researchers in bilingual education in the 1960s was spent on showing that bilingualism did not have a negative effect on cognitive development. For an overview of the debates on bilingual education, see Kenji Hakuta, *The Mirror of Language: The Debate on Bilingualism* (New York: Basic Books, 1986). Wallace Lambert's work on English-French bilingual children in Canada is often viewed as the work that challenged the dominant view of bilingualism as detrimental to cognitive development. See Francesco Cordasco's edited volume for discussions of bilingualism and intelligence that were widespread in the 1960s and 70s. Wallace E. Lambert and G. Richard Tucker, *Bilingual Education of Children: The St. Lambert Experiment* (Rowley: Newbury House Publishers, 1972); Francesco Cordasco, ed. *The Bilingual-Bicultural Child and the Question of Intelligence* (New York: Arno Press, 1978).

48. Joshua A. Fishman, *Language Loyalty in the United States: The Maintenance and Perpetuation of Non-English Mother Tongues by American Ethnic and Religious Groups* (London: Mouton & Co., 1966), 18, 370.

49. United States Congress, Special Subcommittee on Bilingual Education of the Committee on Labor and Public Welfare, *Bilingual Education, Hearings Part I*, 123. Emphasis added.

50. This view of language as a resource can be commonly seen in current discussions of foreign language instruction in higher education. See Mary Louise Pratt, "Building a New Public Idea about Language," *Profession* (2003).

51. Pierre Bourdieu, "The Forms of Capital," in *Handbook of Theory and Research for the Sociology of Education*, ed. John G. Richardson (New York: Greenwood Press, 1986), 245.

52. *Bilingual Education, Hearings Part I*, 121.

53. Ibid.

54. Gary S. Becker, *Human Capital: A Theoretical and Empirical Analysis with Special Reference to Education*, 3rd ed. (Chicago: The University of Chicago Press, 1993).

55. Bourdieu, "The Forms of Capital." 244.

56. Heinz Kloss, *The American Bilingual Tradition* (Rowley, Mass.: Newbury House Publishers, Inc., 1977), 19–20.

57. Ibid., 20.

58. Ibid.

59. *Bilingual Education, Hearings Part I*, 432, 249.

60. Ibid., 225.

61. Ibid., 253.

62. The relationship between education and socioeconomic mobility is a well-researched topic in sociology. Stephen Steinberg, for example, says that "it is an article of faith in American society that education is the key to material success, and the key to eliminating social inequalities as well." Stephen Steinberg, *The Ethnic Myth: Race, Ethnicity, and Class in America* (Boston: Beacon Press, 2001), 129.

63. *Brown v. Board of Education*.

64. Fishman, *Language Loyalty in the United States*, 381, 400–402.

65. United States Congress, Subcommittee on the Constitution of the Committee on the Judiciary *The English Language Amendment*, 2nd Sess., June 12, 1984, 55.

66. While the idea of the melting pot, originating from Israel Zangwill's 1908 play, and Horace Kallen's idea of cultural pluralism, published as "Democracy Versus the Melting Pot" in *The Nation* (February 25, 1915), point to two opposing sides in the social debates about European immigration and assimilation, such historical dimension is lost in US English's haste to present English as the language that would unify the nation in the face of the impending curse of Babel and to contain what it views as the radical potential of minority movements. Stephen Steinberg discusses Zangwill and Kallen as "representing two opposing strands of modern Jewish thought." Stephen Steinberg, *Race Relations: A Critique* (Stanford, Calif.: Stanford University Press, 2007). Kindle edition. Location 1567 of 2712.

67. Samuel I. Hayakawa, "The Case for Official English (1985)," in *Language Loyalties: A Source Book on the Official English Controversy*, ed. James Crawford (Chicago: The University of Chicago Press, 1992), 100.

68. Fishman, *Language Loyalty in the United States*, 120.

69. Ibid., 402.

70. Ibid., 121–22.

71. Ibid., 22–23, 405.

72. See Michael Omi and Howard Winant's discussion of the influence of the Civil Rights movement on liberal reform. Michael Omi and Howard Winant, *Racial Formation in the United States: From the 1960s to the 1990s* (New York: Routledge, 1994), 95–112. See Steinberg and Jacobson for the social interest and cultural investment in ethnicity in the 1960s and 70s. Steinberg, *The Ethnic Myth*; Matthew Frye Jacobson, *Roots Too: White*

*Ethnic Revival in Post-Civil Rights America* (Cambridge, Mass.: Harvard University Press, 2006).

73. *Bilingual Education, Hearings Part I*, 22.

74. Mary L. Dudziak, *Cold War Civil Rights: Race and the Image of American Democracy* (Princeton, N.J.: Princeton University Press, 2000).

75. While it does not specifically discuss bilingual education, Ellen Wu's study of Japanese American and Chinese American communities' endeavors to present themselves as upstanding and loyal Americans during the Cold War also shows how racial minorities saw an opportunity for inclusion in the climate of heightened concerns about national security. Wu shows, however, that these endeavors were often not unified but riddled with schisms internal to the communities. Ellen D. Wu, *The Color of Success: Asian Americans and the Origins of the Model Minority* (Princeton, N.J.: Princeton University Press, 2014).

76. The National Defense Education Act was mentioned as a provision of the Bilingual Education Act and referred to throughout the Hearings by the legislators and expert witnesses. See *Bilingual Education, Hearings Part I*, 18.

77. Diane Ravitch, "Politicization and the Schools: The Case of Bilingual Education," *Proceedings of the American Philosophical Society* 129, no. 2 (1985), 126.

78. Ibid.

79. Ibid., 124. See also Diane Ravitch, *The Troubled Crusade: American Education, 1945–1980* (New York: Basic Books, 1983), 271–80.

80. Omi and Winant, *Racial Formation in the United States*, 113–36.

81. "U.S. English," http://www.us-english.org/.

82. Crawford, *At War with Diversity*; Roseann Dueñas González with Melis, ed. *Language Ideologies: Critical Perspectives on the Official English Movement, Vol. 2: History, Theory, and Policy* (New York: Routledge, 2001); Dennis E. Baron, *The English-Only Question: An Official Language for Americans?* (New Haven, Conn.: Yale University Press, 1992); Deborah J. Schildkraut, *Press One for English: Language Policy, Public Opinion, and American Identity* (Princeton, N.J.: Princeton University Press, 2005).

83. Stephen Steinberg, "Human Capital: A Critique," *The Review of Black Political Economy* 14, no. 1 (1985), 68.

84. Ibid.

85. Ibid., 68–70.

86. William Petersen, "Success Story, Japanese-American Style," *New York Times*, January 9, 1966.

87. Ibid.

88. Ibid.

89. Thomas Sowell, *Race and Culture: A World View* (New York: Basic Books, 1994), 16.

90. Ibid.

91. One may wonder about the policy implications of such naturalization of ethnic differences. It does not seem that Sowell thinks his thesis should have any policy implications, something that is in accord with his free market

capitalism. He suggests that the free market is the best solution to problems of racism, something that comes up in his discussion of discrimination and employment. Sowell, *Race and Culture*, 100.

92. See the Oakland Resolution on Ebonics for how it drew on the principles of bilingual education. http://linguistlist.org/topics/ebonics/ebonics-res1.html. Accessed May 19, 2014.

93. David Dante Troutt, "Defining Who We Are in Society," *Los Angeles Times*, January 12, 1997.

94. Crawford B. Macpherson, *The Political Theory of Possessive Individualism: Hobbes to Locke* (Oxford: Oxford University Press, 1962), 263.

95. Pierre Bourdieu, "The Forms of Capital," in *Handbook of Theory and Research for the Sociology of Education*, ed. John G. Richardson (New York: Greenwood Press, 1986), 243–46.

96. Pierre Bourdieu, *Language and Symbolic Power* (Cambridge, Mass.: Harvard: University Press, 1991), 50.

97. Ibid., 55.

98. Haugen, "The Stigmata of Bilingualism," 307.

99. Ibid., 307, 308.

100. Cheryl Harris places the institution of slavery at the heart of US legal history that has produced property value in whiteness. Cheryl I. Harris, "Whiteness as Property," *Harvard Law Review* 106, no. 8 (1993).

101. Quoted in Melamed, *Represent and Destroy*, 57.

102. One example of the confusion around racialized victimhood can be seen in the classification of African American students as "Anglos" to meet racial imbalance laws in certain school districts with the implementation of bilingual education. Adam Nelson says that in 1971 Boston schools "counted black English speakers as 'Anglos' to satisfy the quotient of forty percent 'Anglo' students in bilingual classes," which would allow the schools to have racially integrated bilingual classes and, hence, eligible for federal funding. The absurdity of an African American student, herself the victim of segregated education in the *Brown* decision occupying the position of the normative English speaker against which the language minority student's aberration is measured, is hard to miss. Adam Nelson, *The Elusive Ideal: Equal Educational Opportunity and the Federal Role in Boston's Public Schools, 1950–1985* (Chicago: The University of Chicago Press, 2005), 284n70.

103. Richard Rodriguez, "Bilingualism, Con: Outdated and Unrealistic." *New York Times*, November 10, 1985.

104. Ibid.

105. Ibid.

106. Richard Rodriguez, "Beyond the Minority Myth," *Change* 10, no. 8 (September, 1978): 28–34.

107. Ibid., 34.

108. David D. Cooper, "Interview with Richard Rodriguez," *Fourth Genre: Explorations in Nonfiction* 5, no. 2 (2003), 108–9.

109. Richard Rodriguez, *Days of Obligation: An Argument with My Mexican Father* (New York: Viking, 1992), 177–79. The different value of Spanish for himself and for Faherty that Rodriguez notices can be explained

by Frances Aparicio's notion of "differential bilingualism." Aparicio uses the term to refer to how Spanish is a valued foreign language to white American students whereas it is associated with disadvantage for Latino/a students. Frances Aparicio, "Of Spanish Dispossessed," in *Language Ideologies: Critical Perspectives on the Official English Movement*, vol. 1, ed. Rosean Dueñas and Ildikó Melis (Mahwah, Mass.: Lawrence Erlbaum Associates, Inc., 2000), 254–55.

## CHAPTER 3. SCHOOLING BILINGUALS IN AND AGAINST MULTICULTURALISM

1. United States Congress, Special Subcommittee on Bilingual Education of the Committee on Labor and Public Welfare. *Bilingual Education, Hearings Part II*, 1st Sess., June 24 and July 21, 1967, 553.

2. Charles Taylor, "The Politics of Recognition," in *Multiculturalism: Examining the Politics of Recognition*, ed. Amy Gutmann (Princeton, N.J.: Princeton University Press, 1994), 25.

3. *Bilingual Education, Hearings Part II*, 557.

4. Nancy Fraser, "Rethinking Recognition," *New Left Review* 3 (2000): 107–20.

5. Taylor, "The Politics of Recognition," 25.

6. Ramón Saldívar, *The Borderlands of Culture: Américo Paredes and the Transnational Imaginary* (Durham, N.C.: Duke University Press, 2006), 53, 92.

7. Ibid., 149.

8. Recovering the U.S. Hispanic Literary Heritage Project at Arte Público Press is one such recovery project. https://artepublicopress.com/recovery-project/. Accessed November 2, 2015.

9. Américo Paredes, *George Washington Gómez: A Mexicotexan Novel* (Houston, Tex.: Arte Público Press, 1990), 16.

10. Ibid., 284.

11. Ibid., 36.

12. Ibid., 45.

13. Ibid., 46.

14. Ibid., 16.

15. Ibid., 138.

16. Ibid.

17. Ibid.

18. For a book-length study of El Plan de San Diego, see Benjamin Heber Johnson, *Revolution in Texas: How a Forgotten Rebellion and Its Bloody Suppression Turned Mexicans into Americans* (New Haven, Conn.: Yale University Press, 2003).

19. Paredes, *George Washington Gómez*, 19.

20. Ibid., 19, 27.

21. Ibid., 19.

22. María Josefina Saldaña-Portillo, "'Wavering on the Horizon of Social Being': The Treaty of Guadalupe-Hidalgo and the Legacy of Its Racial

Character in Américo Paredes's *George Washington Gómez*," *Radical History Review* 89 (2004), 152, 153.

23. Paredes, *George Washington Gómez*, 16.

24. Saldaña-Portillo, "'Wavering on the Horizon of Social Being,'" 154.

25. Ibid., 154.

26. Paredes, *George Washington Gómez*, 16, 17, 19.

27. Ibid., 116.

28. Ibid., 116–17.

29. Mary Seliger examines the limits of rule by law in Paredes's novel by showing that the assumptions of contract law, such as the abstract free subject as the agent of contractual relations or parity between parties entering into a contract, are exposed as myths in Paredes's emphasis on the "invisible social and economic relations of exploitation." Mary A. Seliger, "Colonialism, Contract and Community in Américo Paredes's *George Washington Gómez* and . . . *And the Earth Did Not Devour Him* by Tomás Rivera," *Latino Studies* 7, no. 4 (2009), 440.

30. Paredes, *George Washington Gómez*, 147, 148.

31. Ibid., 147, 148.

32. Saldívar, *The Borderlands of Culture*, 165.

33. Ibid.

34. Ibid., 166.

35. Paredes, *George Washington Gómez*, 148.

36. Ibid.

37. Parikh offers a slightly different way of looking at the discrepancy between the family's expectation of schooling for Guálinto and Guálinto's response to it. She says that "while those in his family and community recognize that Guálinto/George must attain the symbolic and cultural capital that will legitimize him as a 'leader of his people,' the process by which he will secure these privileges, which are in turn meant to be reinvested into the community, also gives birth to the traitorous Anglo-American George." Crystal Parikh, *An Ethics of Betrayal: The Politics of Otherness in Emergent U.S. Literatures and Cultures* (New York: Fordham University Press, 2009), 108. At the same time that I agree with Parikh's assessment of the school's influence on Guálinto's Americanization, I suggest that it also plays a role in the production of a resistant identity.

38. Paredes, *George Washington Gómez*, 110.

39. Ibid., 137.

40. Ibid., 149.

41. My reading of Althusser is informed by Rey Chow's discussion of the "interpellation of the ethnic subject." Rey Chow, *The Protestant Ethnic and the Spirit of Capitalism* (New York: Columbia University Press, 2002), 108.

42. Louis Althusser, "Ideology and Ideological State Apparatuses," in *Lenin and Philosophy and Other Essays* (New York: Monthly Review Press, 1971), 174.

43. Ibid.

44. Wendy Brown, "Injury, Identity, Politics," in *Mapping Multicultural-ism*, ed. Avery F. Gordon and Christopher Newfield (Minneapolis: University of Minnesota Press, 1996), 155.

45. Paredes, *George Washington Gómez*, 173; Brown, "Injury, Identity, Politics," 157.

46. Brown, "Injury, Identity, Politics," 162.

47. Ibid.

48. Paredes, *George Washington Gómez*, 148.

49. Ibid., 149.

50. Erving Goffman, *Stigma: Notes on the Management of Spoiled Identity* (New York: Simon & Schuster, 1963).

51. A note on my use of the phrase "cultural nationalist" may be in order here. *George Washington Gomez* predates the Civil Rights movement and El Movimiento, the Chicano movement of cultural nationalism, so my use of the term "cultural nationalism" is not strictly historical but a reference to the ethos of Mexican nationalism among the Spanish-speaking residents of the United States–Mexican border that Paredes shows most prominently through the Seditionists.

52. Paredes, *George Washington Gómez*, 292.

53. See Paredes's interview with Ramón Saldívar. Paredes mentions that he "tried to represent through Guálinto how members of this new middle class were trying hard to assimilate, to pass as 'white,' to bring up their children as monolingual English speakers." He also refers to the League of Latin American Citizens (LULAC) as an organization that promoted assimilationism: "They counseled their members not to speak Spanish at all to their children, to bring them up as American citizens and nothing else." Paredes situates Guálinto's character in this general climate of assimilationism. Saldívar, *The Borderlands of Culture*, 124, 125. Seliger likewise reads Guálinto as conforming to the dominant ethos of assimilationism. Seliger, "Colonialism, Contract and Community," 447.

54. Many critics have commented on the politics of cultural nationalism in the literary anthology *Aiiiieeeee*'s editors' condemnation of Kingston and *The Woman Warrior*. Sau-ling Wong's essay offers an incisive interpretation of the controversy within the field concerns of Asian American Studies. See King-Kok Cheung's "The Woman Warrior versus the Chinaman Pacific" for an analysis of the controversy with a focus on gender politics. Sau-ling Cynthia Wong, "Autobiography as Guided Chinatown Tour? Maxine Hong Kingston's *The Woman Warrior* and the Chinese American Autobiography Controversy," in *Maxine Hong Kingston's "The Woman Warrior": A Casebook*, ed. Sau-ling Cynthia Wong, 29–53; King-Kok Cheung, "The Woman Warrior Versus the Chinaman Pacific: Must a Chinese American Critic Choose between Feminism and Heroism?" in *Maxine Hong Kingston's "The Woman Warrior": A Casebook*, ed. Sau-ling Cynthia Wong, 113–33.

55. King-Kok Cheung, *Articulate Silences: Hisaye Yamamoto, Maxine Hong Kingston, Joy Kogawa* (Ithaca, N.Y.: Cornell University Press, 1993), 77.

56. Frank Chin and Benjamin R. Tong are known for their critiques of "dual personality." Attributing the term to the Japanese American writer

Daniel Okimoto, Chin says that Okimoto used the phrase "to denote what had always been called the 'identity crisis'" and that Okimoto used it to blame Japanese culture for the lack of organized resistance among American-born Japanese against Internment. Frank Chin, "Come All Ye Asian American Writers," in *The Big Aiiieeeee! An Anthology of Chinese American and Japanese*, ed. Frank Chin, Jeffery Paul Chan, Lawson Fusao Inada, and Shawn Wong (New York: Meridican, 1991), 51. Tong, a trained clinical psychologist, criticized white American psychologist such as Vita Sommers and Chinese American psychologists such as Stanley and Derald Sue, for characterizing the psychological troubles of the Chinese Americans that are caused by racism as problems of deficiency in their cultural heritage. The following quote succinctly shows that Tong objected to viewing "Chinese" and "American" as discrete cultural entities: "Fundamental to [the Sues'] perspective is the assumption that Chinese America as a unique, vital, self-generating way of life does not exist. We are either sinological museum pieces or foreigners living only to be white." Benjamin R. Tong, "On the Confusion of Psychopathology with Culture," in *The Iatrogenics Handbook: A Critical Look at Research and Practice in the Helping Professions*, ed. Robert F. Morgan (Toronto: IPI Publishing Limited, 1983), 358. See also Benjamin R. Tong "The Ghetto of the Mind," *Amerasia* 1, no. 3 (1971): 1031.

57. Taylor, "The Politics of Recognition," 25.

58. Ibid.

59. Chin, "Come All Ye Asian American Writers," 3.

60. Cheung, *Articulate Silences*, 78.

61. Chin, "Come All Ye Asian American Writers," 3.

62. Ibid.

63. Maxine Hong Kingston, *The Woman Warrior: Memoirs of a Girlhood among Ghosts*, reprint (New York: Vintage International, 1989), 34.

64. Ibid., 35.

65. Ibid., 45, 46.

66. Ibid., 46.

67. Anne Cheng offers a similar interpretation of the narrator's China stories. The point, she says, is not whether "the narrator is making up stories about how her family treats her but rather that she is clearly invested in rehearsing a historical origin, true or not, for the difficulties she has in 'fitting in.' This search for explanation . . . in turn cauterizes the pain of social adversities." Anne Anlin Cheng, *The Melancholy of Race: Psychoanalysis, Race, and Hidden Grief* (New York: Oxford University Press, 2001), 82.

68. Kingston, *The Woman Warrior*, 5.

69. Ibid., 87.

70. Ibid., 48.

71. Ibid., 165.

72. Ibid., 53.

73. Brown, "Injury, Identity, Politics," 157.

74. I would like to thank Lynn Itagaki for this insight.

75. Kingston, *The Woman Warrior*, 180.

76. Several critics have examined the exchange between the narrator and her classmate, pointing out that the silent classmate functions as a double of the narrator and that the narrator's violence reflects her confused reproduction of the racial hierarchy and norms she learns. Sau-ling Cynthia Wong, *Reading Asian American Literature: From Necessity to Extravagance* (Princeton, N.J.: Princeton University Press, 1993), 77–117; Cheng, *The Melancholy of Race*, 78.

77. Kingston, *The Woman Warrior*, 180.

78. Ibid., 167.

79. Chicago Cultural Studies Group, "Critical Multiculturalism," *Critical Inquiry* 18, no. 3 (1992): 530–32; Jodi Melamed, *Represent and Destroy: Rationalizing Violence in the New Racial Capitalism* (Minneapolis: University of Minnesota Press, 2011), 34.

80. Kingston, *The Woman Warrior*, 106.

81. Ibid., 107.

82. Will Kymlicka, *Multicultural Citizenship: A Liberal Theory of Minority Rights* (Oxford: Oxford University Press, 1995), 6. See Patricia Chu's discussion of how the "immigrant analogy" has been used to misrepresent the racial formation of certain groups in the United States. Patricia P. Chu, *Assimilating Asians: Gendered Strategies of Authorship in Asian America* (Durham, N.C.: Duke University Press, 2000), 7.

83. Michael Omi and Howard Winant, *Racial Formation in the United States: From the 1960s to the 1990s* (New York: Routledge, 1994).

84. Cheng, *The Melancholy of Race*, 93.

85. Kingston, *The Woman Warrior*, 182.

86. Ibid.

87. Grace Kyungwon Hong, "Existentially Surplus: Women of Color Feminism and the New Crisis of Capitalism," *GLQ: A Journal of Lesbian and Gay Studies* 18, no. 1 (2012), 92.

88. Kingston, *The Woman Warrior*, 163.

89. Feminist critics, in particular, have highlighted the relationship between the body and language and between the mother and the daughter in their readings of the narrator's tongue cutting. Sidonie Smith, one of the earliest critics to comment on this passage, says that Kingston's relationship to language "originates in the memory of her mother's literally cutting the voice out of her." Sidonie Smith, *A Poetics of Women's Autobiography: Marginality and the Fictions of Self-Representation* (Bloomington: Indiana University Press, 1987), 168. Deborah L. Madsen, "(Dis)Figuration: The Body as Icon in the Writings of Maxine Hong Kingston," *Yearbook of English Studies* 24 (1994): 247–50; Lisa Plummer Crafton, "'We Are Going to Carve Revenge on Your Back': Language, Culture, and the Female Body in Kingston's *The Woman Warrior*," in *Women as Sites of Culture: Women's Roles in Cultural Formation from the Renaissance to the Twentieth Century*, ed. Susan Shifrin (Aldershot: Ashgate, 2002); Lee Quinby, "The Subject of Memoirs: *The Woman Warrior*'s Technology of Ideographic Selfhood," in *De/Colonizing the Subject: The Politics of Gender in Women's Autobiography*, ed. Sidonie Smith and Julia Watson (Minneapolis: University of Minnesota Press, 1992).

90. Kingston, *The Woman Warrior*, 164.

91. Jeehyun Lim, "Cutting the Tongue: Language and Body in Kingston's *The Woman Warrior*," *MELUS* 31, no. 3 (2010): 49–65.

92. Kingston, *The Woman Warrior*, 172.

93. Ibid., 168.

94. Ibid., 169.

95. Erin Khuê Ninh, *Ingratitude: The Debt-Bound Daughter in Asian American Literature* (New York: New York University Press, 2011), 66.

96. Kingston, *The Woman Warrior*, 196.

97. Ibid., 170.

98. Ibid., 190.

99. Ibid., 192.

100. Ibid., 186.

101. Ibid., 190.

102. Ibid., 195.

103. Ibid., 201.

104. Ibid.

105. Ibid., 202.

106. Chin, "Come All Ye Asian American Writers," 3.

107. Ibid.

108. Paredes, *George Washington Gómez*, 281.

109. Ibid., 282.

110. Ibid.


## CHPATER 4. DORMANT BILINGUALISM IN NEOLIBERAL AMERICA

1. Kenji Yoshino, *Covering: The Hidden Assault on Our Civil Rights* (New York: Random House, 2006), 120.

2. Yoshino draws from Erving Goffman's 1963 sociological study, *Stigma*, to establish his concept of covering.

3. See also his law review article, published in 2001 of the same title as the later memoir. While his ideas on covering appear in both his memoir and his law review essay, I mostly use the law review essay when I discuss his idea of covering since the legal analysis appears a bit more pointedly there. Kenji Yoshino, "Covering," *The Yale Law Journal* 111 (2001): 769–939.

4. François Grosjean, *Life with Two Languages: An Introduction to Bilingualism* (Cambridge, Mass.: Harvard University Press, 1982), 239.

5. David L. Eng delivers a trenchant critique of analogy in the production of knowledge on racialized identities, especially in the realm of law, drawing on works by scholars such as Janet Halley and Miranda Joseph. Eng sees the logical and cultural work of analogy as being opposed to the critical objectives of intersectional analysis. While I agree with Eng on the limits of analogy in legal reasoning, I make a distinction between analogy as it is employed in law and in politics or cultural representations. Colleen Lye's discussion of the "Afro-Asian analogy," for example, shows that at a certain

time in Asian American Studies analogy was employed to conceptualize and to politicize Asian American identities vis-à-vis African American identities. While Lye clearly shows that this was a provisional strategy at best, she also shows the influence this analogy has had on scholarly interests in Black-Asian relations. In fact, a strict distinction between analogy and intersection does not always seem to be productive in the uses of analogy in politics and cultural representations. David L. Eng, *The Feeling of Kinship: Queer Liberalism and the Racialization of Intimacy* (Durham, N.C.: Duke University Press, 2010), 40–41; Colleen Lye, "The Afro-Asian Analogy," *PMLA* 123, no. 5 (2008), 1732–36.

6. Cristina M. Rodríguez, "Language and Diversity in the Workplace," *Northwestern University School of Law* 100, no. 4 (2006), 1728.

7. Cristina Rodríguez, "Language and Participation," *California Law Review* 94, no. 3 (2006): 687–767; Mark Colón, "Line Drawing, Code Switching, and Spanish as Second-Hand Smoke: English-Only Workplace Rules and Bilingual Employees," *Yale Law & Policy Review* 20, no. 1 (2002): 227–61; Alfredo Mirandé, "'En la tierra del ciego, el tuerto es rey' ('In the Land of the Blind, the One-Eyed Person Is King'): Bilingualism as Disability," *New Mexico Law Review* 75 (1996): 25–105; Edward M. Chen, "'Symposium: Labor and Immigration: Examining the Intersection' Speech, Labor Law and Language Discrimination," *Asian Law Journal* 6 (1999): 223–30; Mari J. Matsuda, "Voices of America: Accent, Antidiscrimination Law, and a Jurisprudence for the Last Reconstruction," *The Yale Law Journal* 100, no. 5 (1991): 1329–407.

8. United States Equal Employment Opportunity Commission, "Laws Enforced by EEOC" http://www.eeoc.gov/laws/statutes/index.cfm. Accessed December 1, 2014.

9. The argument that language is like race can be seen in several defenses delivered on behalf of bilingual plaintiffs. The specific quote of "like-race" I take from Roberto J. Gonzalez, "Cultural Rights and the Immutability Requirement in Disparate Impact Doctrine," *Stanford Law Review* 55, no. 6 (2003): 2195–227.

10. Bonnie Urciuoli, "Skills and Selves in the New Workplace," *American Ethnologist* 35, no. 2 (2008), 211.

11. The case brief identifies "75% of the population in [Gloor Lumber's] business area" as being "of Hispanic background." 618 F. 2d 264 (5th Cir. 1980). http://www.leagle.com/decision/1980882618F2d264_1831.xml/GARCIA%20v.%20GLOOR Accessed November 1, 2014.

12. The case brief uses the term "Hispanic" to refer to the currently more academically accepted term of "Latino." I use the term Hispanic when it is used in the legal briefs to describe the background of people involved in the lawsuits or the demographics of a region.

13. 618 F. 2d 264 (5th Cir. 1980).

14. Yoshino, "Covering," 892.

15. 998 F. 2d 1480 (9th Cir. 1993). http://www.leagle.com/decision/199 32478998F2d1480_12256.xml/GARCIA%20v.%20SPUN%20STEAK%20 CO. Accessed November 1, 2014.

16. 618 F. 2d 264 (5th Cir. 1980).

17. After *Garcia v. Gloor* the primary argument on behalf of bilinguals relied on a slightly different analogy of language as a proxy of national origin. Mark Colón suggest that this is probably due to the Equal Employment Opportunity Commission's response to the *Gloor* court's decision. Colón, "Line Drawing, Code Switching, and Spanish as Second-Hand Smoke," 239. While it is an important legal distinction, I do not differentiate between race and national origin in my discussion of the "like-race" analogy in the legal defense of bilingual plaintiffs in workplace language disputes.

18. Yoshino mentions that "the American legal antidiscrimination paradigm has been dominated by the cases of race, and, to a lesser extent, sex. The solicitude directed toward racial minorities and women has been justified in part by the fact that they are marked by 'immutable' and 'visible' characteristics—that is, that such groups cannot assimilate into mainstream society because they are marked as different." "Covering," 771.

19. Marc Shell, "Language Wars," *CR: The Centennial Review* 1, no. 2 (2001): 1–17.

20. 29 CFR 1606. 7. When English-only rules "are applied only at certain times," the EEOC guidelines indicate that the employer needs to show that "the rule is justified by business necessity."

21. 618 F. 2d 264 (5th Cir. 1980).

22. Ibid.

23. 618 F. 2d 264 (5th Cir. 1980).

24. 998 F. 2d 1480 (9th Cir. 1993).

25. 618 F. 2d 264 (5th Cir. 1980).

26. 998 F. 2d 1480 (9th Cir. 1993).

27. 618 F. 2d 264 (5th Cir. 1980).

28. Ibid.

29. Urciuoli, "Skills and Selves in the New Workplace," 211.

30. Ibid.

31. Monica Heller, "Globalization, the New Economy, and the Commodification of Language and Identity," *Journal of Sociolinguistics* 7, no. 4 (2003), 474. Heller examines the French-speaking in Canada as her example.

32. Urciuoli, "Skills and Selves in the New Workplace," 220.

33. See Tomás Rivera, Ramón Saldívar, Rosaura Sanchez, and Norma Alarcón for the first position; Nidesh Lawtoo for the second; and Randy Rodriguez and David William Foster for the last. Tomás Rivera, "Richard Rodriguez's *Hunger of Memory* as Humanistic Antithesis," *MELUS* 11, no. 4 (1984): 5–13; Ramón Saldívar, "Ideologies of the Self: Chicano Autobiography," *Diacritics: A Review of Contemporary Criticism* 15, no. 3 (1985): 25–34; Rosaura Sánchez, "Calculated Musings: Richard Rodriguez's Metaphysics of Difference," in *The Ethnic Canon: Histories, Institutions, and Interventions*, ed. David Palumbo-Liu (Minneapolis: University of Minnesota Press, 1995), 153–73; Norma Alarcón, "Tropology of Hunger: The 'Miseducation' of Richard Rodriguez," in *The Ethnic Canon: Histories, Institutions, and Interventions*, ed. David Palumbo-Liu (Minneapolis: University of Minnesota Press, 1995), 140–52; Nidesh Lawtoo, "Dissonant

Voices in Richard Rodriguez's *Hunger of Memory* and Luce Irigaray's *The Sex Which Is Not One*," *Texas Studies in Literature and Language* 8, no. 3 (2006), 220–49; Randy A. Rodríguez, "Richard Rodriguez Reconsidered: Queering the Sissy (Ethnic) Subject," *Texas Studies in Literature and Language* 40, no. 4 (1998), 396–423; David William Foster, *El ambiente nuestro: Chicano/Latino Homoerotic Writing* (Tempe, Ariz.: Bilingual Press/Editorial Bilingüe, 2006).

34. Several critics have noted the prominence of a paradigm of liberal personhood in Rodriguez's first memoir. Norma Alarcón, notably, offers an illuminating account of the complexity of Rodriguez's liberal project, his "miseducation," in *Hunger of Memory* and its ultimate effect of constitutively denying the subaltern, the "(im)migrant laborer or Indian," a place in the public sphere. "Tropology of Hunger," 140, 151.

35. Wen Jin offers a concise overview of the term before she embarks on a comparative analysis of US and Chinese multiculturalisms. Wen Jin, *Pluralist Universalism: An Asian Americanist Critique of U.S. and Chinese Multiculturalism* (Columbus: The Ohio State University Press, 2012), 4.

36. According to Rachel Adams, the idea of North America, as opposed to a hemispheric understanding of the Americas, emerged in the second half of the twentieth century. She calls the North American Free Trade Agreement a "watershed moment in the invention of North America" "which brought the continent into being as an economic entity and was hailed by some as a harbinger of a newfound continental sensibility." She also makes it clear that North America is "a concept that is more the invention of politicians and economists than the product of its inhabitants' collective imagination." Rachel Adams, *Continental Divides: Remapping the Cultures of North America* (Chicago: The University of Chicago Press, 2014), 14, 17.

37. Richard Rodriguez, *Brown: The Last Discovery of America* (New York: Penguin, 2002), 162–63.

38. Ibid., 162.

39. Ibid., 163.

40. Ibid., 161.

41. Ibid., 131–32.

42. Richard Rodriguez himself prefers the term Hispanic to Latino to refer to people of Latin American descent in the United States. He states that while those who refuse the term Hispanic do so because it "places Latin America (once more) under the rubric of Spain," "Latino commits Latin America to Iberian memory as surely as does Hispanic." *Brown*, 109. I use the term Latino when I refer to people of Latin American descent in the United States as is the common practice in American studies and ethnic studies today. I retain the term Hispanic when I cite Rodriguez.

43. Rodriguez, *Brown*, 163.

44. Ibid., 164.

45. Ibid.

46. Richard Rodriguez, *Hunger of Memory: The Education of Richard Rodriguez* (New York: Bantam, 1982), 200.

47. David D. Cooper, "Interview with Richard Rodriguez," *Fourth Genre: Explorations in Nonfiction* 5, no. 2 (2003), 106, 107.

48. Ibid., 107–8.

49. Ibid., 108.

50. Rodriguez, *Hunger of Memory*, 34.

51. Rodriguez, *Brown*, 111.

52. Ibid., 127.

53. Stephen Steinberg, *The Ethnic Myth: Race, Ethnicity, and Class in America* (Boston: Beacon Press, 2001), 270. On the opposite end of the political spectrum of this black analogy Rodriguez mentions is the solidarity with African Americans that a writer like Hisaye Yamamoto expressed in her writings. See James Lee's discussion of Yamamoto in James Kyung-Jin Lee, *Urban Triage: Race and the Fictions of Multiculturalism* (Minneapolis: University of Minnesota Press, 2004).

54. Rodriguez, *Brown*, xi.

55. Rodriguez, *Brown* 30, 126–27; Jennifer Lee and Frank D. Bean, *The Diversity Paradox: Immigration and the Color Line in 21st Century America* (New York: Russell Sage Foundation, 2010), 29–33. Jared Sexton's discussion of multiracialism's morphing into antiblackness is a trenchant critique of the kind of hybridity that Richard Rodriguez extols. Jared Sexton, *Amalgamation Schemes: Antiblackness and the Critique of Multiracialism* (Minneapolis: University of Minnesota Press, 2008), 1–10.

56. Rodriguez, *Brown*, xi.

57. Rodriguez, *Hunger of Memory*, 34, 157.

58. Rodriguez, *Brown*, 128.

59. Ibid., 52.

60. Ibid., 53.

61. Ibid., 134.

62. Ibid., 135, 134.

63. See Alarcón for a discussion of how Chicana feminism can interpret the figure of La Malinche. Norma Alarcón, "Traddutora, Traditora: A Paradigmatic Figure of Chicana Feminism," *Cultural Critique* 13 (1989).

64. Claudia M. Milian Arias, "Brown Is the Color of Philosophy: An Interview with Richard Rodriguez," *Nepantla: Views from South* 4, no. 2 (2003), 278. In pointing out the masculinist bias of Chicano criticism on *Hunger of Memory*, Randy Rodriguez suggests that Richard Rodriguez has figuratively become La Malinche, the symbol of the race traitor: "Like La Malinche, the traitor of the Mexican people (because she consorted with Cortés and facilitated the Spanish colonization of the Aztec empire in the early 1500s), Rodriguez is el chingada (the fucked or violated one) because he consorts with the Anglo-American colonizer." "Richard Rodriguez Reconsidered," 403.

65. Jeehyun Lim, "'I Was Never at War with My Tongue': The Third Language and the Performance of Bilingualism in Richard Rodriguez," *Biography: An Interdisciplinary Quarterly* 33, no. 3 (2010): 518–42.

66. Homi Bhabha, *The Location of Culture* (New York: Routledge, 1994).

67. David Theo Goldberg, *The Racial State* (Oxford: Blackwell Publishers, 2002), 28, 29.

68. Ibid., 32.

69. Rodriguez, *Hunger of Memory*, 14.

70. Ibid.

71. See Alicia Camacho for a critique of Rodriguez's liberalism based on an analysis of his notion of privacy. Alicia Schmidt Camacho, *Migrant Imaginaries: Latino Cultural Politics in the U.S.-Mexico Borderlands* (New York: New York University Press, 2008).

72. Rodriguez, *Brown*, 114.

73. Ibid., 115.

74. Ibid.

75. Ibid., 120.

76. Ibid. I would like to thank Paul Lai for pointing out Rodriguez's paradoxical assertion of Hispanic Spanish as simultaneously hybrid and uniform.

77. Ibid.

78. Ibid., 18.

79. Ibid., 31.

80. Rodriguez, *Hunger of Memory*, 34.

81. Rodriguez, *Brown*, 127.

82. Ibid.

83. Hector A. Torres, "'I Don't Think I Exist': Interview with Richard Rodriguez," *MELUS* 28, no. 2 (2003), 172.

84. Rodriguez, *Brown*, 140.

85. "subtext, n," OED Online. September 2014. Oxford University Press. http://o-www.oed.com.dewey2.library.denison.edu/view/Entry/193161?redirectedFrom=subtext. Accessed December 1, 2014.

86. Several critics have examined Henry's profession as an undercover agent in relation to his racial difference as an American-born Asian and have noted the theme of linguistic difference in the text. Crystal Parikh, *An Ethics of Betrayal: The Politics of Otherness in Emergent U.S. Literatures and Cultures* (New York: Fordham University Press, 2009), 110–12; Tina Chen, *Double Agency: Acts of Impersonation in Asian American Literature and Culture* (Stanford, Calif.: Stanford University Press, 2005), 152–53.

87. Chang-rae Lee, "The Faintest Echo of Our Language," *New England Review* 15, no. 3 (1993), 87.

88. Ibid.

89. Ibid., 88.

90. Ibid., 89.

91. Ibid., 91.

92. Ibid.

93. In her reading of *Native Speaker*, Betsy Huang directs attention to the correlation between "the absence of Asian Americans in American political systems" and "in literary representations of Asian immigrant and Asian American experiences." This representational lacuna is noted in several works of criticism, including Huang's. Huang looks at the issue of representation through ethnic citizenship; Rachel Lee examines the practice of reading and

racialized and gendered citizenship; Daniel Kim and Min Hyoung Song focus on intergroup relations between black and Korean Americans in the novel. Betsy Huang, "Citizen Kwang: Chang-rae Lee's *Native Speaker* and the Politics of Consent," *Journal of Asian American Studies* 9, no. 3 (2006), 244; Rachel C. Lee, "Reading Contests and Contesting Reading: Chang-rae Lee's *Native Speaker* and Ethnic New York," *MELUS* 29, no. 3/4 (2004): 341–52; Daniel Y. Kim, "Do I, Too, Sing America? Vernacular Representaitons and Chang-rae Lee's *Native Speaker*," *Journal of Asian American Studies* 6, no. 3 (2003): 231–60; Min Hyoung Song, *Strange Future: Pessimism and the 1992 Los Angeles Riots* (Durham, N.C.: Duke University Press, 2005).

94. Kim, "Do I, Too, Sing America?," 243.

95. Chang-rae Lee, *Native Speaker* (New York: Riverhead Books, 1995), 218.

96. Ibid., 49.

97. Ibid., 183.

98. Ibid., 50. If the origin of *ggeh* lies in agrarian Korean culture, its function as ethnic capital in the United States can hardly be explained through cultural essentialism. As Min Song astutely points out, in the text, "*Ggeh* is not the seamless continuation of a Korean cultural practice these immigrants have brought with them, but is a brought-over cultural practice that has been cleverly refashioned [just as consummate *bricoleurs* did, in Claude Levi-Strauss's sense of the term] to meet the needs of their new situations." *Strange Future*, 187.

99. Lee, *Native Speaker*, 187.

100. Ibid., 334.

101. Ibid., 53.

102. Ibid.

103. Ibid., 12.

104. Ibid.

105. Ibid., 11.

106. See Yasemin Yildiz's discussion of the German philosopher Johann Gottfried Herder for the rise of the idea that "each language is conceived as distinct and separate and as belonging to just one equally distinct and separate people." "What this position cannot abide," Yildiz says, "is the notion of blurred boundaries, crossed loyalties, and unrooted languages." Yasemin Yildiz, *Beyond the Mother Tongue: The Postmonolingual Condition* (New York: Fordham University Press, 2012), 7, 7–8.

107. Lee, *Native Speaker*, 11.

108. Ibid., 119.

109. Ibid., 121.

110. Ibid., 173.

111. Stephen Steinberg, "Human Capital: A Critique," *The Review of Black Political Economy* 14, no. 1 (1985), 69.

112. Ibid.

113. Lee, *Native Speaker*, 127.

114. Ibid., 205, 206.

115. Ibid., 170.

116. Ibid.
117. Ibid., 202.
118. Ibid., 328.
119. Ibid., 182–83, 183.
120. Ibid., 139.
121. Ibid., 23.
122. Ibid., 139.
123. Ibid., 146.
124. Ibid., 138.
125. Ibid., 179.
126. Ibid., 234.
127. Ibid., 297.
128. Ibid., 302.
129. Ibid., 133.
130. Ibid., 69. It is no wonder that since You-me Park and Gayle Wald turned their attention to the character of Ahjumma "who leads her entire life within a highly claustrophobic domestic sphere" many essays on *Native Speaker* end with a reflection on the inarticulate Korean women in the text as the sign of the subaltern for these women are the most vulnerable group in the text. You-me Park and Gayle Wald, "Native Daughters in the Promised Land: Gender, Race, and the Question of Separate Spheres," *American Literature* 70, no. 3 (1998), 622. See Parikh, *An Ethics of Betrayal*, 127; James Kyung-Jin Lee, "Where the Talented Tenth Meets the Model Minority: The Price of Privilege in Wideman's *Philadelphia Fire* and Lee's *Native Speaker*," *Novel* (2002 Spring/Summer), 252.
131. Lee, *Native Speaker*, 145, 262.
132. Ibid., 237.

## CHAPTER 5. GLOBAL ENGLISH AND THE PREDICAMENT OF MONOLINGUAL MULTICULTURALISM

1. Rita Raley, "On Global English and the Transmutation of Postcolonial Studies into 'Literature in English,'" *Diaspora: A Journal of Transnational Studies* 8, no. 1 (1999), 52.
2. Werner Sollors, ed. *Multilingual America: Transnationalism, Ethnicity, and the Languages of American Literature* (New York: New York University Press, 1998), 4.
3. Ibid.
4. Sarah Fay, "Ha Jin, the Art of Fiction No. 202," *The Paris Review* Winter 2009. http://www.theparisreview.org/interviews/5991/the-art-of-fiction-no-202–ha-jin.
5. Bulosan's *America Is in the Heart* recounts Carlos's life both in the Philippines and in the United States, and Kang demonstrates his binational scope by portraying his boyhood in Korea in *Grass Roof* and the experiences of an "Oriental Yankee" in *East Goes West*. Carlo Bulosan, *America Is in the Heart*, reprint (Seattle: University of Washington Press, 1973). *The Grass*

*Roof.* New York: C. Scribner's Sons, 1931. Younghill Kang, *The Grass Roof,* New York: C. Scribner's Sons (1931); *East Goes West: The Making of an Oriental Yankee,* Reprint (New York: Kaya Press, 1997).

6. Jodi Melamed, *Represent and Destroy: Rationalizing Violence in the New Racial Capitalism* (Minneapolis: University of Minnesota Press, 2011), xv.

7. Ibid., 41.

8. Emily Apter, *The Translation Zone: A New Comparative Literature* (Princeton, N.J.: Princeton University Press, 2006), 99.

9. Lawrence Venuti, *The Translator's Invisibility: A History of Translation* (London: Routledge, 2004), 14.

10. Ibid., 12–13.

11. Apter, *The Translation Zone,* 101.

12. Ibid., 267–68n16.

13. Itamar Even-Zohar, "Polysystem Studies," *Poetics Today* 11, no. 1 (1990), 37.

14. Ibid., 46.

15. Ibid., 47.

16. Edwin Gentzler's study of the mid-twentieth century US literary culture is one application of Even-Zohar's theory to the US literary polysystem. Edwin Gentzler, "Translation, Counter-Culture, and the Fifties in the USA," in *Translation, Power, Subversion,* ed. Román Álavrez and M. Carmen-África Vidal (Clevedon, U.K.: Multilingual Matters, 1996), 116–37.

17. Melamed, *Represent and Destroy,* 2–3, 32–34; Guillory, *Cultural Capital,* 3–82.

18. Melamed, *Represent and Destroy,* 33, 33–34.

19. John Guillory, *Cultural Capital: The Problem of Literary Canon Formation* (Chicago: The University of Chicago Press, 1993), 6–8.

20. Guillory presents the following three propositions as shared by both critics from both camps of the canon wars: (1) "Canonical texts are the repositories of cultural values"; (2) "The selection of texts is the selection of values"; (3) "Value must be either intrinsic or extrinsic to the work." *Cultural Capital,* 25–26.

21. Melamed, *Represent and Destroy,* 38.

22. Julia Alvarez *¡Yo!* (Chapel Hill: Algonquin Books, 1997), 36.

23. Ibid.

24. See also Elizabeth Coonrod Martínez, "Teaching Spanish Caribbean History through *In the Time of the Butterflies*: The Novel and the Showtime Film," *Journal of Hispanic Higher Education* 5, no. 2 (2006): 107–26.

25. Ellen McCracken, *New Latina Narratives: The Feminine Space of Postmodern Ethnicity* (Tucson: The University of Arizona Press, 1999), 83–84.

26. Immanuel Wallerstein, *World-Systems Analysis: An Introduction* (Durham, N.C.: Duke University Press, 2004), 11–12.

27. Ibid., 17.

28. Roberto González Echevarría, "Sisters in Death," *New York Times,* December 18, 1994.

29. Ibid.

30. Miguel Aquino-García, *Tres heroínas y un tirano: la historia verídica de las hermanas Mirabal y su asesinato por Rafael Leónidas Trujillo* (Santo Domingo, Dominican Republic: Corripio, 1996), xiv. My translation.

31. Marta Caminero-Santangelo, *On Latinidad: U.S. Latino Literature and the Construction of Ethnicity* (Gainesville: University Press of Florida, 2007), 76.

32. Fernando Valerio Holguin, "*En el tiempo de las mariposas* de Julia Alvarez: Una reinterpretacio de la historia," *Chasqui: revista de literatura latinoamericana* 27, no. 1 (1998): 92–102.

33. Kwai Cheung Lo, "The Myth of 'Chinese' Literature: Ha Jin and the Globalization of 'National' Literary Writing," *Journal of Modern Literature in Chinese* 6, no. 2 / 7, no. 1 (2005), 67.

34. Ibid., 74.

35. Ibid., 74.

36. It seems pertinent to mention that Lo's analysis was published before Jin started writing works that are set outside the People's Republic of China in the Korean peninsula (*War Trash*) and in the United States (*A Free Life, A Good Fall*). As Jin moves to perhaps what could be his second phase in writing and publishing that actively involves fiction set in the United States, the porousness of the boundaries among Chinese, American, and world literature is bound to become more pronounced.

37. Steven G. Yao, *Foreign Accents: Chinese American Verse from Exclusion to Postethnicity* (Oxford: Oxford University Press, 2010), 138.

38. Ibid., 129, 115.

39. Ibid., 119–21.

40. Carine M. Mardorossian, "From Literature of Exile to Migrant Literature," *Modern Language Studies* 32, no. 2 (2002), 16, 17–18.

41. Apter, *The Translation Zone*, 99.

42. Aquino-García, *Tres heroínas y un tirano*, xiii.

43. Julia Alvarez, *In the Time of the Butterflies* (Chapel Hill, N.C.: Algonquin Books, 1998), 324.

44. Ibid.

45. Julia Alvarez, *Before We Were Free* (New York: Laurel Leaf, 2002), 166.

46. Alvarez, *In the Time of the Butterflies*, 3.

47. Caminero-Santangelo, *On Latinidad*, 81.

48. Shara McCallum, "Reclaiming Julia Alvarez: *In the Time of the Butterflies*," *Women's Studies: An Interdisciplinary Journal* 29, no. 1 (2009), 101, 102–3.

49. Caminero-Santangelo, *On Latinidad*, 81–83; Ramón A. Figueroa, "Fantasmas ultramarines: La Dominicadad en Julia Alvarez y Junot Diaz," *Revista Iberoamericana* 71, no. 212 (2005), 731–33; Stephen P. Knadler, "'Blanca from the Block': Whiteness and the Transnational Latina Body," *Genders* 41 (2005); Lucía M. Suárez, "Julia Alvarez and the Anxiety of Latina Representation," *Meridians: Feminism, Race, Transnationalism* 5, no. 1 (2004), 117–45.

50. Julia Alvarez's recent nonfiction, *A Wedding in Haiti*, may be read as the writer's response to such criticisms on her relative silence on issues of race and class. These issues are at the center of this narrative that chronicles her two trips to Haiti, one before the earthquake of 2010 and one after. Julia Alvarez, *A Wedding in Haiti* (Chapel Hill, N.C.: Algonquin Books, 2012). Kindle Edition.

51. Alvarez, *In the Time of the Butterflies*, 4.

52. Ibid., 3.

53. Venuti, *The Translator's Invisibility*, 20.

54. Ibid., 20.

55. The diary form also appears in *In the Time of the Butterflies* in María Teresa's chapters. Alvarez's use of the diary form also accords with her own statement that she writes in the tradition of the Latin American "testimonio." Alvarez, *Before We Were Free*, 166.

56. Kay Schaffer and Sidonie Smith, "Conjunctions: Life Narratives in the Field of Human Rights," *Biography: An Interdisciplinary Quarterly* 27, no. 1 (2004), 7.

57. Ibid., 11.

58. Ha Jin, *War Trash*, reprint (New York: Vintage International, 2005), 5.

59. See John M. Liu, "The Contours of Asian Professional, Technical and Kindred Work Immigration, 1965–1988," *Sociological Perspectives* 35, no. 4 (1992): 673–704.

60. Jin, *War Trash*, 47, 154.

61. Ibid., 97.

62. J. L. Austin, *How to Do Things with Words*, 2nd ed. (Cambridge, Mass.: Harvard University Press, 1975), 6.

63. Jin, *War Trash*, 178.

64. Ibid., 98.

65. Ibid., 341, 3.

66. Ibid., 3.

67. Jing Tsu, *Sound and Script in the Chinese Diaspora* (Cambridge, Mass.: Harvard University Press, 2010), 107–10.

68. Ibid., 110.

69. Rey Chow, *The Protestant Ethnic and the Spirit of Capitalism* (New York: Columbia University Press, 2002), 189.

70. Tsu, *Sound and Script*, 110.

71. Czeslaw Milosz, Poetry Reading at the MLA Convention, 1998, quoted in Luz Maria Umpierre, "Unscrambling Allende's 'Dos palabras': The Self, the Immigrant/Writer, and Social Justice," *MELUS* 27, no. 4 (2002), 135.

72. Bonnie Lyons and Bill Oliver, "Julia Alvarez: 'A Clean Windshield,'" in *Passion and Craft: Conversations with Notable Writers* (Urbana: University of Illinois Press, 1998), 134–35. Ha Jin also references Milosz in a poem, "To Ah Shu," although in a different context than Alvarez. In his poem, Milosz is an example of a poet who is fetishized in China due to the fact that he is well received in the West. Ha Jin, *Facing Shadows* (New York: Hanging Loose Press, 1996), 67.

73. Raley, "On Global English," 59.

74. Ha Jin, *A Free Life* (New York: Pantheon Books, 2007), 498. Italics in the original.

75. Ha Jin, *The Writer as Migrant* (Chicago: The University of Chicago Press, 2008), 31–60.

76. Ibid., 48.

77. Ibid., 60.

78. Charles May, "Review: Ha Jin's 'A Free Life,'" *SF Gate*, November 14, 2007.

79. John Updike, "Nan, American Man," *New Yorker*, December 3, 2007.

80. Walter Kirn, "Pleased to Be Here," *New York Times*, November 25, 2007.

81. Updike, "Nan, American Man."

82. Ibid.

83. Jin, *A Free Life*, 153, 306, 496.

84. Ibid., 95.

85. Ibid.

86. "Bei Dao," *World Literature Today* 82, no. 6 (2008), 20. Ha Jin seems well aware of this journal. Lo mentions that Jin published an essay on modern Chinese in the journal. Lo, "The Myth of 'Chinese' Literature," 67.

87. Bei Dao, "Out of the Cradle, Endlessly Sleepwalking," *World Literature Today* 82, no. 6 (2008), 22. There is a significant critical conversation on whether Bei Dao's modernism conforms to Anglo American ideas of modernism or not. Steven Owen's 1990 article "What Is World Poetry" first criticized Bei Dao's modernism for being derivative and imitative of Western modernism, which immediately evoked a flurry of discussion on the topic. Rey Chow's rebuke of Owen's interpretation is the most widely cited opposition. Rey Chow, *Writing Diaspora: Tactics of Intervention in Contemporary Cultural Studies* (Bloomington: Indiana University Press, 1993), 3–5. David Damrosch revisits this controversy in *What Is World Literature* (Princeton, N.J.: Princeton University Press, 2003), 19–22.

88. Jin, *A Free Life*, 121.

89. Ibid.

90. Ruth Franklin observes that Sam Fisher is "obviously modeled on Allen Ginsberg." Ruth Franklin, "Portrait of the Artist as an Immigrant," *Slate*, November 19, 2007.

91. Mark McGurl, *The Program Era: Postwar Fiction and the Rise of Creative Writing* (Cambridge, Mass.: Harvard University Press, 2009).

92. Jin, *A Free Life*, 306.

93. Ibid., 437, 445.

94. Ibid., 306.

95. Ibid., 108–9, 473.

96. Ibid., 108.

97. Ibid., 109.

98. Ibid., 473.

99. Ibid., 247, 472.

100. Ibid., 459.

101. Ibid.

102. Ibid., 619.

103. Ibid., 626.

104. Ibid., 628.

105. Alvarez, ¡Yo!, 74.

106. Ibid., 262.

107. Ibid., 262.

108. Ben Jacques, "Julia Alvarez: Real Flights of Imagination," *Américas* 53, no. 1 (2001), 25; Julia Alvarez, *Something to Declare* (Chapel Hill, N.C.: Algonquin Books, 1994), 168.

109. Alvarez, *Something to Declare*, 169, Lyons and Oliver, "Julia Alvarez: 'A Clean Windshield,'" 135.

110. Alvarez, ¡Yo!, 262.

111. Ibid.

112. Updike, "Nan, American Man."

113. *A Free Life*, 263.

114. Alvarez, *Something to Declare*, 24.

## EPILOGUE: THE FUTURE OF BILINGUAL BROKERING

1. David Henry Hwang, "The 'Chinglish' Broadway Journal: Week 3 (Oct. 3, 2011)." http://youoffendmeyouoffendmyfamily.com/the-chinglish-broadway-journal-week-3-oct-3–2011/ Accessed October 2, 2014.

2. Ibid.

3. Ibid.

4. David Henry Hwang, *Chinglish: A Play* (New York: Theatre Communications Group, 2012), 24, 29, 31, 30.

5. Ibid., 43.

6. Ibid., 81.

7. Ibid., 10.

8. Hwang, *Chinglish*, 123.

9. As Elaine Kim says, "Asian English," in popular culture is "a 'dialect' characterized by thin, sing-song tones, pseudo-Confucian aphorisms, omission of articles (and, in some cases, of all auxiliary verbs), confused l's and r's, and accompanied by downcast eyes, sheepish buck-toothed grins, and a series of very respectful bows." Elaine Kim, "Yellow English," *Asian American Review* 2 (1975), 44.

10. Ibid. The cultural politics of bilingualism Hwang discusses briefly is reminiscent of the skewed representations of Asian Americans in books published by mainstream publishing houses and in Hollywood movies that the editors of *Aiiieeeee!* criticized in 1974. It is ironic that Hwang, one of the Asian American writers Frank Chin vehemently attacked in the later expanded edition of the original anthology of Asian American writers and in his essay, "Come All Ye Asian American Writers of the Real and the Fake," expresses an artistic principle of self-determination that echoes Chin's sentiments when he speaks of representing the Chinese by using their own

language. Frank Chin, "Come All Ye Asian American Writers," in *Aiiieeeee! An Anthology of Asian-American Writers*, ed. Jeffery Paul Chan, Frank Chin, Lawson Fusao Inada, and Shawn Hsu Wong (Washington, DC: Howard University Press, 1974).

11. Hwang, "The 'Chinglish' Journal: Week 1 (May 23, 2011)." http://youoffendmeyouoffendmyfamily.com/the-chinglish-journal-week-1-may-23–2011/. Accessed October 2, 2014.

12. Hwang, "The 'Chinglish' Journal: Week 3 (June 6, 2011)." http://youoffendmeyouoffendmyfamily.com/the-chinglish-journal-week-3-june-6–2011/. Accessed October 2, 2014.

13. Ibid.

14. Hwang, "The 'Chinglish' Journal: Week 1 (May 23, 2011)." http://youoffendmeyouoffendmyfamily.com/the-chinglish-journal-week-1-may-23–2011/. Accessed October 2, 2014.

15. Hwang, *Chinglish,* 122.

16. Hwang, "The 'Chinglish' Broadway Journal: Week 3 (Oct. 3, 2011)." http://youoffendmeyouoffendmyfamily.com/the-chinglish-broadway-journal-week-3-oct-3–2011/. Accessed October 2, 2014. Hwang's honest reflections on what it means for him to participate in a forum of this kind as a Chinese American in the same blog-journal entry reveal the complexity of negotiating a hyphenated identity for Asian Americans when one of the stock racist assumptions about the group is that they are foreign and not "really" American.

17. Hwang, "The 'Chinglish' Journal: A New Chapter." http://youoffendmeyouoffendmyfamily.com/the-chinglish-journal-a-new-chapter/. Accessed October 2, 2014. The Bo Xilai scandal, which played out in the media throughout 2012 and which centered on Bo Xilai's wife's murder of Neil Heywood, a British citizen who had been acting as the Bo family's middleman in their dealings with Western companies, exposed how a politically elite family engaged in abusing their power.

# BIBLIOGRAPHY

Adams, Rachel. *Continental Divides: Remapping the Cultures of North America*. Chicago: The University of Chicago Press, 2014.

Ahn, Hyung-ju. *Between Two Adversaries: Korean Interpreters at Japanese Alien Enemy Detention Centers during World War II*. Oral History Program, California State University, Fullerton, 2002.

Alarcón, Norma. "Tropology of Hunger: The 'Miseducation' of Richard Rodriguez." In *The Ethnic Canon: Histories, Institutions, and Interventions*, edited by David Palumbo-Liu, 140–52. Minneapolis: University of Minnesota Press, 1995.

———. "Traddutora, Traditora: A Paradigmatic Figure of Chicana Feminism." *Cultural Critique* 13 (1989): 57–87.

Alcoff, Linda Martín. "Is Latina/O Identity a Racial Identity?" In *Hispanics/Latinos in the United States: Ethnicity, Race, Rights*, edited by Jorge J. E. Garcia and Pablo de Greiff, 23–44. New York: Routledge, 2000.

Alonso, Carlos J. "Spanish: The Foreign National Language." *Profession* (2007): 218–28.

Althusser, Louis. "Ideology and Ideological State Apparatuses." In *Lenin and Philosophy and Other Essays*, 127–86. New York: Monthly Review Press, 1971.

Alvarez, Julia. *A Wedding in Haiti*. Chapel Hill, N.C.: Algonquin Books, 2012. Kindle Edition.

———. *Before We Were Free*. New York: Laurel Leaf, 2002.

———. *Something to Declare*. Chapel Hill, N.C.: Algonquin Books, 1998.

———. *¡Yo!* Chapel Hill, N.C.: Algonquin Books, 1997.

———. *In the Time of the Butterflies*. Chapel Hill, N.C.: Algonquin Books, 1994.

Aparicio, Frances. "Of Spanish Dispossessed." In *Language Ideologies: Critical Perspectives on the Official English Movement. Vol. 1*, edited by Roseann Dueñas González and Ildikó Melis, 248–75. Mahwah: Lawrence Erlbaum Associates, Inc., 2000.

———. "On Sub-Versive Signifiers: Tropicalizing Language in the United States." In *Tropicalizations: Transcultural Representations of Latinidad*, edited by Frances R. Aparicio and Susana Chávez-Silverman, 194–212. Hanover, N.H.: University Press of New England 1997.

Apter, Emily. *The Translation Zone: A New Comparative Literature*. Princeton, N.J.: Princeton University Press, 2006.

Aquino-García, Miguel. *Tres heroínas y un tirano: la historia verídica de las hermanas Mirabal y su asesinato por Rafael Leónidas Trujillo*. Santo Domingo, Dominican Republic: Corripio, 1996.

Austin, J. L. *How to Do Things with Words*. 2nd ed. Cambridge, Mass.: Harvard University Press, 1975.

Baker, Houston A., Jr. *Blues, Ideology, and Afro-American Literature: A Vernacular Theory*. Chicago: The University of Chicago Press, 1984.

Balibar, Étienne. "The Reversal of Possessive Individualism." In *Equaliberty: Political Essays*, translated by James Ingram, 67–98. Durham, N.C.: Duke University Press, 2014.

Baron, Dennis E. *The English-Only Question: An Official Language for Americans?* New Haven, Conn.: Yale University Press, 1992.

Becker, Gary S. *Human Capital: A Theoretical and Empirical Analysis with Special Reference to Education*. 3rd ed. Chicago: The University of Chicago Press, 1993.

"Bei Dao." *World Literature Today* 82, no. 6 (2008): 20–21.

Bhabha, Homi. *The Location of Culture*. New York: Routledge, 1994.

"Bilingual Education Act of 1968." In *Pub. L.* 90–247. January 2, 1968.

Bonacich, Edna. "A Theory of Middleman Minorities." *American Sociological Review* 38, no. 5 (1973): 583–94.

Bourdieu, Pierre. *The Field of Cultural Production*. New York: Columbia University Press, 1993.

———. *Language and Symbolic Power*. Cambridge, Mass.: Harvard: University Press, 1991.

———. "The Forms of Capital." In *Handbook of Theory and Research for the Sociology of Education*, edited by John G. Richardson, 241–58. New York: Greenwood Press, 1986.

———. *Distinction: A Social Critique of the Judgment of Taste*. Translated by Richard Nice. Cambridge, Mass.: Harvard University Press, 1984.

Bow, Leslie. *Partly Colored: Asian Americans and Racial Anomaly in the Segregated South*. New York: New York University Press, 2010.

Brody, David. *Visualizing American Empire: Orientalism and Imperialism in the Philippines.* Chicago: The University of Chicago Press, 2010.

Brown, Wendy. *Undoing the Demos: Neoliberalism's Stealth Revolution.* New York: Zone Books, 2015.

———. "Neoliberalism and the End of Liberal Democracy." In *Edgework: Critical Essays on Knowledge and Politics*, 37–59. Princeton, N.J.: Princeton University Press, 2005.

———. "Injury, Identity, Politics." In *Mapping Multiculturalism*, edited by Avery F. Gordon and Christopher Newfield, 149–66. Minneapolis: University of Minnesota Press, 1996.

Bruce-Novoa, Juan. *Retrospace: Collected Essays on Chicano Literature.* Houston: Arte Público Press, 1990.

Bulosan, Carlos. *America Is in the Heart.* 1943. Reprint, Seattle: University of Washington Press, 1973.

———. *On Becoming Filipino: Selected Writings of Carlos Bulosan.* Edited by E. San Juan Jr. Philadelphia: Temple University Press, 1995.

Camacho, Alicia Schmidt. *Migrant Imaginaries: Latino Cultural Politics in the U.S.-Mexico Borderlands.* New York: New York University Press, 2008.

Caminero-Santangelo, Marta. *On Latinidad: U.S. Latino Literature and the Construction of Ethnicity.* Gainsville: University Press of Florida, 2007.

Campomanes, Oscar, and Todd S. Gernes "Two Letters from America: Carlos Bulosan and the Act of Writing." *MELUS* 15, no. 3 (1988): 15–46.

Carter, John. "A Vital Narrative from the Ireland of the Far East," *New York Times Book Review*, March 15, 1931, 4.

Chan, Sucheng, ed. *Entry Denied: Exclusion and the Chinese Community in America, 1882–1943.* Philadelphia: Temple University Press, 1991.

Chen, Edward M. "Symposium: Labor and Immigration: Examining the Intersection 'Speech: Labor Law and Language Discrimination.'" *Asian Law Journal* 6 (1999): 223–30.

Chen, Ping. *Modern Chinese: History and Sociolinguistic.* Cambridge: Cambridge University Press, 1999.

Chen, Tina. *Double Agency: Acts of Impersonation in Asian American Literature and Culture.* Stanford, Calif.: Stanford University Press, 2005.

Cheng, Anne Anlin. *The Melancholy of Race: Psychoanalysis, Race, and Hidden Grief.* New York: Oxford University Press, 2001.

Cheung, King-Kok. "The Woman Warrior versus The Chinaman Pacific: Must a Chinese American Critic Choose between Feminism and Heroism?" In *Maxine Hong Kingston's "The Woman Warrior": A Casebook*, edited by Sau-ling Cynthia Wong, 113–33. New York: Oxford University Press, 1999.

———. *Articulate Silences: Hisaye Yamamoto, Maxine Hong Kingston, Joy Kogawa*. Ithaca, N.Y.: Cornell University Press, 1993.

Chiang, Mark. *The Cultural Capital of Asian American Studies*. New York: New York University Press, 2009.

Chicago Cultural Studies Group. "Critical Multiculturalism." *Critical Inquiry* 18, no. 3 (1992): 530–55.

Chin, Frank. "Come All Ye Asian American Writers of the Real and the Fake." In *The Big Aiiieeeee! An Anthology of Chinese American and Japanese American Literature*, edited by Frank Chin Jeffery Paul Chan, Lawson Fusao Inada, and Shawn Wong, 1–92. New York: Meridian, 1991.

Chin, Frank, and Jeffery Paul Chan, Lawson Fusao Inada, and Shawn Hsu Wong, eds. *Aiiieeeee! An Anthology of Asian-American Writers*. Washington, DC: Howard University Press, 1974.

Chow, Rey. *The Protestant Ethnic and the Spirit of Capitalism*. New York: Columbia University Press, 2002.

———. *Writing Diaspora: Tactics of Intervention in Contemporary Cultural Studies*. Bloomington: Indiana University Press, 1993.

Chu, Patricia P. *Assimilating Asians: Gendered Strategies of Authorship in Asian America* Durham, N.C.: Duke University Press, 2000.

Chuh, Kandice. *Imagine Otherwise: On Asian Americanist Critique*. Durham, N.C.: Duke University Press, 2003.

Collins, Randall. *The Credential Society: An Historical Sociology of Education and Stratification*. New York: Academic Press, Inc., 1979.

Colón, Mark. "Line Drawing, Code Switching, and Spanish as Second-Hand Smoke: English-Only Workplace Rules and Bilingual Employees." *Yale Law & Policy Review* 20, no. 1 (2002): 227–61.

Cooper, David D. "Interview with Richard Rodriguez." *Fourth Genre: Explorations in Nonfiction* 5, no. 2 (2003): 104–32.

Cordasco, Francesco, ed. *The Bilingual-Bicultural Child and the Question of Intelligence*. New York: Arno Press, 1978.

Corley, Liam. "'Just Another Ethnic Pol': Literary Citizenship in Chang-Rae Lee's *Native Speaker*." *Studies in the Literary Imagination* 37, no. 1 (2004): 61–81.

Crafton, Lisa Plummer. "'We Are Going to Carve Revenge on Your Back': Language, Cutlure, and the Female Body in Kingston's *The Woman Warrior*." In *Women as Sites of Culture: Women's Roles in Cultural Formation from the Renaissance to the Twentieth Century*, edited by Susan Shifrin, 51–63. Aldershot, U.K.: Ashgate, 2002.

Crawford, James. *At War with Diversity: US Language Policy in an Age of Anxiety*. New York: Multilingual Matters, 2000.

Crawford, James, ed. *Language Loyalties: A Source Book on the Official English Controversy.* Chicago: The University of Chicago Press, 1992.

Damrosch, David. *What Is World Literature.* Princeton, N.J.: Princeton University Press, 2003.

Dao, Bei. "Out of the Cradle, Endlessly Sleepwalking." *World Literature Today* 82, no. 6 (2008): 22.

Davies, Gareth. *See Government Grow: Education Politics from Johnson to Reagan.* Lawrence: University Press of Kansas, 2007.

Denning, Michael. *The Cultural Front: The Laboring of American Culture in the Twentieth Century.* New York: Verso, 1997.

Drucker, Peter F. *The Landmarks of Tomorrow.* 1957. Reprint, New Brunswick, N.J.: Transaction Publishers, 1996.

Dudziak, Mary L. *Cold War Civil Rights: Race and the Image of American Democracy.* Princeton, N.J.: Princeton University Press, 2000.

Echevarría, Roberto González. "Sisters in Death." *New York Times*, December 18, 1994.

Eng, David L. *The Feeling of Kinship: Queer Liberalism and the Racialization of Intimacy.* Durham, N.C.: Duke University Press, 2010.

Ehrenreich, Barbara, and John Ehrenreich. "The Professional-Managerial Class." *Radical America* 11, no. 2 (1997): 7–31.

Espiritu, Augusto Fauni. *Five Faces of Exile: The Nation and Filipino American Intellectuals.* Stanford, Calif.: Stanford University Press, 2005.

Espiritu, Yen Le. *Asian American Panethnicity: Bridging Institutions and Identities.* Philadelphia: Temple University Press, 1992.

Even-Zohar, Itamar. "Polysystem Studies." *Poetics Today* 11, no. 1 (1990): 1–268.

Fanon, Frantz. *The Wretched of the Earth.* Translated by Richard Philcox. New York: Grove Press, 2004.

Fay, Sarah. "Ha Jin, the Art of Fiction No. 202." *The Paris Review,* Winter 2009.

Feher, Michel. "Self-Appreciation; or, the Aspirations of Human Capital." *Public Culture* 21, no. 1 (2009): 21–41.

Figueroa, Ramón A. "Fantasmas Ultramarines: La Dominicadad en Julia Alvarez Y Junot Diaz," *Revista Iberoamericana* 71, no. 212 (2005): 731–44.

Fishman, Joshua A. *Language Loyalty in the United States: The Maintenance and Perpetuation of Non-English Mother Tongues by American Ethnic and Religious Groups.* London: Mouton & Co., 1966.

Foster, David William. *El ambiente nuestro: Chicano/Latino Homoerotic Writing* Tempe, Ariz.: Bilingual Press/Editorial Bilingue, 2006.

Franklin, Ruth. "Portrait of the Artist as an Immigrant." *Slate,* November 19, 2007.

Fraser, Nancy. "Rethinking Recognition." *New Left Review* 3 (2000): 107–20.

García, Ofelia. *Bilingual Education in the 21st Century: A Global Perspective.* Chichester, U.K.: Wiley-Blackwell, 2009.

Gates, Henry Louis, Jr. *The Signifying Monkey: A Theory of African-American Literary Criticism.* 1989. Reprint, New York: Oxford University Press, 2014.

Gentzler, Edwin. "Translation, Counter-Culture, and the Fifties in the USA." In *Translation, Power, Subversion,* edited by Román Álvarez and M. Carmen-África Vidal, 116–37. Clevedon, U.K.: Multilingual Matters, 1996.

Goffman, Erving. *Stigma: Notes on the Management of Spoiled Identity.* New York: Simon & Schuster, 1963.

Goldberg, David Theo. *The Racial State.* Oxford: Blackwell Publishers, 2002.

Gonzalez, Roberto J. "Cultural Rights and the Immutability Requirement in Disparate Impact Doctrine." *Stanford Law Review* 55, no. 6 (2003): 2195–227.

González, Roseann Dueñas, with Ildikó Melis, eds. *Language Ideologies: Critical Perspectives on the Official English Movement. Vol. 2: History, Theory, and Policy.* New York: Routledge, 2001.

Grosjean, François. *Bilingual: Life and Reality.* Cambridge, Mass.: Harvard University Press, 2010.

———. *Life with Two Languages: An Introduction to Bilingualism.* Cambridge, Mass.: Harvard Univesity Press, 1982.

Gruesz, Kirsten Silva. "Translation: A Key(Word) into the Language of America(Nists)." *American Literary History* 16, no. 1 (2004): 85–92.

Guillory, John. *Cultural Capital: The Problem of Literary Canon Formation.* Chicago: The University of Chicago Press, 1993.

Hakuta, Kenji. *The Mirror of Language: The Debate on Bilingualism.* New York: Basic Books, 1986.

Hancock, Ange-Marie. *Solidarity Politics for Millennials: A Guide to Ending the Oppression Olympics.* New York: Palgrave Macmillan, 2011.

Hau, Caroline S. "'Patria é intereses': Reflections on the Origins and Changing Meanings of *Ilustrado*." *Philippine Studies* 59, no. 1 (2011): 3–54.

Harris, Cheryl I. "Whiteness as Property." *Harvard Law Review* 106, no. 8 (1993): 1707–91.

Hau, Caroline S., and Benedict Anderson. Introduction to *All the Conspirators,* by Carlos Bulosan, vii–xxvii. Seattle: University of Washington Press, 2005.

Haugen, Einar. "The Stigmata of Bilingualism," *The Ecology of Language: Essays*. Selected and introduced by Anwar S. Dil, 307–24. Stanford, Calif.: Stanford University Press, 1972.

Harvey, David. *The Condition of Postmodernity: An Enquiry into the Origins of Cultural Change*. 1990. Reprint, Cambridge, U.K.: Blackwell Publishers, 1992.

Hayakawa, Samuel I. "The Case for Official English (1985)." In *Language Loyalties: A Source Book on the Official English Controversy*, edited by James Crawford, 94–100. Chicago: The University of Chicago Press, 1992.

———. *Language in Thought and Action*. 2nd ed. New York: Harcourt, Brace and Company, 1949.

Heller, Monica. "Globalization, the New Economy, and the Commodification of Language and Identity." *Journal of Sociolinguistics* 7, no. 4 (2003): 473–92.

Holguin, Fernando Valerio. "*En el tiempo de las mariposas* de Julia Alvarez: Una reinterpretacion de la historia." *Chasqui: revista de literatura latinoamericana* 27, no. 1 (1998): 92–102.

Holt, Thomas C. *The Problem of Race in the Twenty-First Century*. Cambridge, Mass.: Harvard University Press, 2002.

Hong, Grace Kyungwon. "Existentially Surplus: Women of Color Feminism and the New Crisis of Capitalism." *GLQ: A Journal of Lesbian and Gay Studies* 18, no. 1 (2012): 87–106.

Hong, Grace Kyungwon, and Roderick A. Ferguson, eds. *Strange Affinities: The Gender and Sexual Politics of Comparative Racialization*. Durham, N.C.: Duke University Press, 2011.

Hosie, Lady. "A Voice from Korea." *The Saturday Review of Literature*, April 4, 1931, 707.

Huang, Betsy. "Citizen Kwang: Chang-Rae Lee's *Native Speaker* and the Politics of Consent." *Journal of Asian American Studies* 9, no. 3 (2006): 243–69.

Huang, Yunte. "Basic English, Chinglish, and Translocal Dialect." In *English and Ethnicity*, edited by Janina Brutt-Griffler and Catherine Evans Davies, 75–106. New York: Palgrave Macmillan, 2006.

Hwang, David Henry. *Chinglish: A Play*. New York: Theatre Communications Group, 2012.

Jacobson, Matthew Frye. *Roots Too: White Ethnic Revival in Post–Civil Rights America*. Cambridge, Mass.: Harvard University Press, 2006.

Jacques, Ben. "Julia Alvarez: Real Flights of Imagination." *Américas* 53, no. 1 (2001): 22–29.

Jameson, Fredric. *The Political Unconscious: Narrative as a Socially Symbolic Act.* Ithaca, N.Y.: Cornell University Press, 1981.

Jin, Ha. *The Writer as Migrant.* Chicago: The University of Chicago Press, 2008.

———. *A Free Life.* New York: Pantheon Books, 2007.

———. *War Trash.* 2004. Reprint, New York: Vintage International, 2005.

———. *Facing Shadows.* New York: Hanging Loose Press, 1996.

Jin, Wen. *Pluralist Universalism: An Asian Americanist Critique of U.S. and Chinese Multiculturalisms.* Columbus: The Ohio State University Press, 2012.

Joseph, Miranda. *Debt to Society: Accounting for Life under Capitalism.* Minneapolis: University of Minnesota Press, 2014.

Johnson, Benjamin Heber. *Revolution in Texas: How a Forgotten Rebellion and Its Bloody Suppression Turned Mexicans into Americans.* New Haven, Conn.: Yale University Press, 2003.

Jun, Helen H. *Race for Citizenship: Black Orientalism and Asian Uplift from Pre-Emancipation to Neoliberal America.* New York: New York University Press, 2011.

Kallen, Horace M. "Democracy Versus the Melting Pot: A Study of American Nationality." *The Nation.* February 25, 1915, 217–18.

Kang, Younghill. Foreword to *Korea: A History,* by Bong-Youn Choy. Rutland, Vt.: Charles E. Tuttle Company, 1971.

———. "Younghill Kang" in *Twentieth-Century Authors,* edited by S. J. Kunitz, 509. New York: The H. W. Wilson Company, 1955.

———. *East Goes West: The Making of an Oriental Yankee.* 1937. Reprint, New York: Kaya Press, 1997.

———. *The Grass Roof.* New York: C. Scribner's Sons, 1931.

Kim, Claire Jean. "The Racial Triangulation of Asian Americans." *Politics & Society* 27, no. 1 (1999): 105–38.

Kim, Daniel Y. "Do I, Too, Sing America? Vernacular Representations and Chang-Rae Lee's *Native Speaker.*" *Journal of Asian American Studies* 6, no. 3 (2003): 231–60.

———. *Writing Manhood in Black and Yellow: Ralph Ellison, Frank Chin, and the Literary Politics of Identity.* Stanford, Calif.: Stanford University Press, 2001.

Kim, Elaine H. *Asian American Literature: An Introduction to the Writings and Their Social Context.* Philadelphia: Temple University Press, 1984.

———. "Yellow English." *Asian American Review* 2 (1975): 44–63.

Kim, Hyung-Chan, ed. *Asian Americans and the Supreme Court: A Documentary History.* New York: Greenwood Press, 1992.

Kim, Uk-tong. *Younghill Kang: His Life and Literature [Kang Yong-hul: ku ui sam kwa munhak].* Seoul, Korea: Seoul National University Press, 2004.

Kingston, Maxine Hong. *China Men.* 1977. Reprint, New York: Vintage International, 1989.

———. *The Woman Warrior: Memoirs of a Girlhood among Ghosts.* 1976. Reprint, New York: Vintage International, 1989.

Kirn, Walter. "Pleased to Be Here." *New York Times,* November 25, 2007.

Klein, Christina. *Cold War Orientalism: Asia in the Middlebrow Imagination, 1945–1961.* Berkeley: University of California Press, 2003.

Kloss, Heinz. *The American Bilingual Tradition.* Rowley, Mass.: Newbury House Publishers, Inc., 1977.

Knadler, Stephen P. "'Blanca from the Block': Whiteness and the Transnational Latina Body." *Genders* 41 (2005).

———. *The Fugitive Race: Minority Writers Resisting Whiteness.* Jackson: University Press of Mississippi, 2002.

Koshy, Susan. "Morphing Race into Ethnicity: Asian Americans and Critical Transformations of Whiteness." *boundary* 2 28, no. 1 (2001): 153–94.

———. "The Fiction of Asian American Literature." *The Yale Journal of Criticism* 9, no. 2 (1996): 315–46.

Kramer, Paul. *The Blood of Government: Race, Empire, and the United States and the Philippines.* Chapel Hill: University of North Carolina Press, 2006.

Kuo, Karen. *East Is West and West Is East: Gender, Culture, and Interwar Encounters between Asia and America.* Philadelphia: Temple University Press, 2013.

Kymlicka, Will. *Multicultural Citizenship: A Liberal Theory of Minority Rights.* Oxford: Oxford University Press, 1995.

Lambert, Wallace E., and G. Richard Tucker. *Bilingual Education of Children: The St. Lambert Experiment.* Rowley, Mass.: Newbury House Publishers, 1972.

Lawtoo, Nidesh "Dissonant Voices in Richard Rodriguez's *Hunger of Memory* and Luce Irigaray's *The Sex Which Is Not One.*" *Texas Studies in Literature and Language* 48, no. 3 (2006): 220–49.

Lazzarato, Maurizio. *The Making of the Indebted Man: An Essay on the Neoliberal Condition,* trans. Joshua David Jordan. Los Angeles: Semiotext(e), 2012.

———. "Immaterial Labor." In *Radical Thought in Italy: A Potential Politics,* edited by Paulo Virno and Michael Hardt, 133–47. Minneapolis: University of Minnesota Press, 1996.

Lee, Chang-rae. *Native Speaker.* New York: Riverhead Books, 1995.

——. "The Faintest Echo of Our Language." *New England Review* 15, no. 3 (1993): 85–92.

Lee, James Kyung-Jin. *Urban Triage: Race and the Fictions of Multiculturalism.* Minneapolis: University of Minnesota Press, 2004.

——. "Where the Talented Tenth Meets the Model Minority: The Price of Privilege in Wideman's *Philadelphia Fire* and Lee's *Native Speaker.*" *Novel* (2002 Spring/Summer): 231–57.

Lee, Jennifer, and Frank D. Bean. *The Diversity Paradox: Immigration and the Color Line in 21st Century America.* New York: Russell Sage Foundation, 2010.

Lee, Julia H. *Interracial Encounters: Reciprocal Representations in African and Asian American Literatures, 1896–1937.* New York: New York University Press, 2011.

Lee, Rachel C. "Reading Contests and Contesting Reading: Chang-rae Lee's *Native Speaker* and Ethnic New York." *MELUS* 29. 3/4 (2004): 341–52.

Lee, Robert G. *Orientals: Asian Americans in Popular Culture.* Philadelphia: Temple University Press, 1999.

Lee, Sunyoung. "The Unmaking of an Oriental Yankee / Chronology: The Life and Work of Younghill Kang." In *East Goes West: The Making of an Oriental Yankee,* by Younghill Kang, 375–413. New York: Kaya, 1997.

Lee, Yoon Sun. *Modern Minority: Asian American Literature and Everyday Life.* New York: Oxford University Press, 2013.

Leibowitz, Arnold H. *The Bilingual Education Act: A Legislative Analysis.* Rosslyn, Va.: National Clearinghouse for Bilingual Education, 1980.

Lennon, Brian. *In Babel's Shadow: Multilingual Literatures, Monolingual States.* Minneapolis: University of Minnesota Press, 2010.

Leong, Karen J. *The China Mystique: Pearl S. Buck, Anna May Wong, Mayling Soong and the Transformation of American Orientalism.* Berkeley: University of California Press, 2005.

Lewis, Oscar H. *Five Families: Mexican Case Studies in the Culture of Poverty.* New York: Basic Books, 1959.

Lim, Jeehyun. "'I Was Never at War with My Tongue': The Third Language and the Performance of Bilingualism in Richard Rodriguez." *Biography: An Interdisciplinary Quarterly* 33, no. 3 (2010): 518–42.

——. "Cutting the Tongue: Language and the Body in Kingston's *The Woman Warrior.*" *MELUS* 31, no. 3 (2006): 49–65.

Lipsitz, George. *The Possessive Investment in Whiteness: How White People Profit from Identity Politics.* Philadelphia: Temple University Press, 1998.

Lipski, John M. "The Linguistic Situation of Central Americans." In *New*

*Immigrants in the United States: Readings for Second Language Educators,* edited by Sandra Lee McKay and Sau-ling Cynthia Wong, 189–215. Cambridge: Cambridge University Press, 2000.

Liu, Lydia H. *The Freudian Robot: Digital Media and the Future of the Unconscious.* Chicago: The University of Chicago Press, 2011.

Liu, John M. "The Contours of Asian Professional, Technical and Kindred Work Immigration, 1965–1988." *Sociological Perspectives* 35, no. 4 (1992): 673–704.

Lo, Kwai-Cheung. "The Myth of 'Chinese' Literature: Ha Jin and the Globalization of 'National' Literary Writing." *Journal of Modern Literature in Chinese* 6, no. 2 / 7, no. 1 (2005): 63–78.

Lowe, Lisa. *Immigrant Acts: On Asian American Cultural Politics.* Durham, N.C.: Duke University Press, 1996.

Lye, Colleen, "The Afro-Asian Analogy," *PMLA* 123, no. 5 (2008): 1732–36.

Lyons, Bonnie, and Bill Oliver. "Julia Alvarez: 'A Clean Windshield.'" In *Passion and Craft: Conversations with Notable Writers,* 128–44. Urbana: University of Illinois Press, 1998.

Macpherson, Crawford B., ed. *Property: Mainstream and Critical Positions.* Toronto: University of Toronto Press, 1978.

Macpherson, Crawford B. *The Political Theory of Possessive Individualism: Hobbes to Locke.* Oxford: Oxford University Press, 1962.

Madsen, Deborah L. "(Dis)Figuration: The Body as Icon in the Writings of Maxine Hong Kingston." *Yearbook of English Studies* 24 (1994): 237–50.

Maeda, Daryl J. *Chains of Babylon: The Rise of Asian America.* Minneapolis: University of Minnesota Press, 2009.

Mardorossian, Carine M. "From Literature of Exile to Migrant Literature." *Modern Language Studies* 32, no. 2 (2002): 15–33.

Martín-Rodríguez, Manuel M. *Life In Search of Readers: Reading (in) Chicano/a Literature.* Albuquerque: University of New Mexico Press, 2003.

Martínez, Elizabeth Coonrod. "Teaching Spanish Caribbean History through *In the Time of the Butterflies*: The Novel and the Showtime Film." *Journal of Hispanic Higher Education* 5, no. 2 (2006): 107–26.

Marx, Karl. *Economic and Philosophic Manuscripts of 1844.* Edited by Drik J. Struik. Translated by Martin Milligan. 1932. Reprint, Moscow: Progress Publishers, 1964.

Matsuda, Mari J. "Voices of America: Accent, Antidiscrimination Law, and a Jurisprudence for the Last Reconstruction." *The Yale Law Journal* 100, no. 5 (1991): 1329–407.

May, Charles. "Review: Ha Jin's 'A Free Life.'" *SF Gate.* November 14, 2007.

McCallum, Shara. "Reclaiming Julia Alvarez: *In the Time of the Butter-flies.*" *Women's Studies: An Interdisciplinary Journal* 29, no. 1 (2000): 93–117.

McCracken, Ellen. *New Latina Narratives: The Feminine Space of Post-modern Ethnicity.* Tucson: The Universitiy of Arizona Press, 1999.

McGurl, Mark. *The Program Era: Postwar Fiction and the Rise of Creative Writing.* Cambridge, Mass.: Harvard University Press, 2009.

Melamed, Jodi. *Represent and Destroy: Rationalizing Violence in the New Racial Capitalism.* Minneapolis: University of Minnesota Press, 2011.

Milian Arias, Claudia M. "Brown Is the Color of Philosophy: An Interview with Richard Rodriguez." *Nepantla: Views from South* 4, no. 2 (2003): 269–82.

Miller, Joshua L. *Accented America: The Cultural Politics of Multilingual Modernism.* Oxford: Oxford University Press, 2011.

Mirandé, Alfredo. "'En la tierra del ciego, el tuerto es rey' ('In the Land of the Blind, the One-Eyed Person Is King'): Bilingualism as a Disability." *New Mexico Law Review* 75 (1996): 25–105.

Mohr, Nicholasa. "The English Lesson." In *Nueva York* by Nicholasa Mohr, 49–82. 1977. Reprint, Houston, Tex.: Arte Público Press, 1985.

Moran, Rachel F. "Undone by Law: The Uncertain Legacy of *Lau v. Nichols.*" *Berkeley La Raza Law Journal* 16, no. 1 (2005).

Mullen, Bill V. *Afro-Orientalism.* Minneapolis: University of Minnesota Press, 2004.

Nash, Philip T. "Asian Americans and Their Rights for Employment and Education." In *Asian Americans and the Supreme Court: A Documentary History,* edited by Hyung-chan Kim, 897–908. Westport, Conn.: Greenwood Press, 1992.

National Education Association of the United States. "The Invisible Minority: Report of the NEA-Tucson Survey on the Teaching of Spanish to the Spanish-Speaking" Washington DC: National Education Association, 1966. http://www.nea.org/home/46866.htm.

Negrón-Montaner, Frances. "English Only Jamás but Spanish Only Cuidado: Language and Nationalism in Contemporary Puerto Rico." In *Puerto Rican Jam: Rethinking Colonialism and Nationalism,* edited by Frances Negrón-Montaner and Ramón Grosfoguel, 257–85. Minneapolis: University of Minnesota Press 1997.

Nelson, Adam. *The Elusive Ideal: Equal Educational Opportunity and the Federal Role in Boston's Public Schools, 1950–1985.* Chicago: The University of Chicago Press, 2005.

Ngai, Mae M. *The Lucky Ones: One Family and the Extraordinary Invention of Chinese America.* New York: Houghton Mifflin Harcourt, 2010.

———. "History as Law and Life: *Tape v. Hurley* and the Origins of the Chinese American Middle Class." In *Chinese Americans and the Politics of Race and Culture*, edited by Sucheng Chan and Madeline Y. Hsu, 62–90. Philadelphia: Temple University Press, 2008.

———. *Impossible Subjects: Illegal Aliens and the Making of Modern America*. Princeton, N.J.: Princeton University Press, 2004.

Nguyen, Viet Thanh. *Race and Resistance: Literature and Politics in Asian America* Oxford: Oxford University Press, 2002.

Ninh, Erin Khuê. *Ingratitude: The Debt-Bound Daughter in Asian American Literature*. New York: New York University Press, 2011.

Oboler, Suzanne. *Ethnic Labels, Latino Lives: Identity and Politics of (Re) Presentation in the United States*. Minneapolis: University of Minnesota Press 1995.

O'Brien, Eileen. *The Racial Middle: Latinos and Asian Americans Living beyond the Racial Divide*. New York: New York University Press, 2008.

Omi, Michael, and Howard Winant. *Racial Formation in the United States: From the 1960s to the 1990s*. New York: Routledge, 1994.

Ong, Aihwa. *Flexible Citizenship: The Cultural Logics of Transnationality*. Durham, N.C.: Duke University Press, 1999.

Owen, Stephen. "What Is World Poetry?" *New Republic*, November 19, 1990: 28–32.

Paredes, Américo. *George Washington Gómez: A Mexicotexan Novel*. Houston, Tex.: Arte Público Press, 1990.

Parikh, Crystal. *An Ethics of Betrayal: The Politics of Otherness in Emergent U.S. Literatures and Culture*. New York: Fordham University Press, 2009.

Park, You-me and Gayle Wald. "Native Daughters in the Promised Land: Gender, Race, and the Question of Separate Spheres." *American Literature* 70, no. 3 (1998): 607–33.

Pérez-Firmat, Gustavo. *Life on the Hyphen: The Cuban-American Way*. 2nd ed. Austin: University of Texas Press, 2012.

———. *Tongue Ties: Logo-Eroticism in Anglo-Hispanic Literature*. New York: Palgrave Macmillan, 2003.

Pérez-Torres, Rafael. *Mestizaje: Critical Uses of Race in Chicano Culture*. Minneapolis: University of Minnesota Press, 2006.

Petersen, William. "Success Story, Japanese-American Style." *New York Times*, January 9, 1966.

Phillipson, Robert. *Linguistic Imperialism*. Oxford: Oxford University Press, 1992.

Phillipson, Robert, Mar Rannut, and Tove Skutnabb-Kangas, eds. *Linguistic*

*Human Rights: Overcoming Linguistic Discrimination.* New York: Mouton de Gruyter, 1995.

Ponce, Martin J. *Beyond the Nation: Diasporic Filipino Literature and Queer Reading.* New York: New York University Press, 2010.

Prashad, Vijay. *Everybody Was Kung-Fu Fighting: Afro-Asian Connections and the Myth of Cultural Purity.* Boston: Beacon Press, 2002.

Pratt, Mary Louise. "Building a New Public Idea about Language." *Profession* (2003): 110–19.

Quinby, Lee. "The Subject of Memoirs: *The Woman Warrior*'s Technology of Ideographic Selfhood." In *De/Colonizing the Subject: The Politics of Gender in Women's Autobiography,* edited by Sidonie Smith and Julia Watson, 297–320. Minneapolis: University of Minnesota Press, 1992.

Raley, Rita. "On Global English and the Transmutation of Postcolonial Studies into 'Literature in English.'" *Diaspora: A Journal of Transnational Studies* 8, no. 1 (1999): 51–80.

Ravitch, Diane. "Politicization and the Schools: The Case of Bilingual Education." *Proceedings of the American Philosophical Society* 129, no. 2 (1985): 121–28.

———. *The Troubled Crusade: American Education, 1945–1980.* New York: Basic Books, 1983.

Rivera, Tomás. "Richard Rodriguez's *Hunger of Memory* as Humanistic Antithesis." *MELUS* 11, no. 4 (1984): 5–13.

Rodríguez, Cristina M. "Language and Diversity in the Workplace." *Northwestern University School of Law* 100, no. 4 (2006): 1689–773.

———. "Language and Participation." *California Law Review* 94, no. 3 (2006): 687–767.

Rodríguez, Randy A. "Richard Rodriguez Reconsidered: Queering the Sissy (Ethnic) Subject." *Texas Studies in Literature and Language* 40, no. 4 (1998): 396–423.

Rodriguez, Richard. *Brown: The Last Discovery of America.* New York: Penguin, 2002.

———. *Days of Obligation: An Argument with My Mexican Father.* New York: Viking, 1992.

———. "Bilingualism, Con: Outdated and Unrealistic." *New York Times,* November 10, 1985.

———. *Hunger of Memory: The Education of Richard Rodriguez.* New York: Bantam, 1982.

———. "Beyond the Minority Myth." *Change* 10, no. 8 (September, 1978): 28–34.

Saldaña-Portillo, María Josefina. "'Wavering on the Horizon of Social

Being': The Treaty of Guadalupe-Hidalgo and the Legacy of Its Racial Character in Américo Paredes's *George Washington Gómez.*" *Radical History Review* 89 (2004): 135–64.

Saldívar, José David. *Border Matters: Remapping American Cultural Studies.* Berkeley: University of California Press, 1997.

Saldívar, Ramón. *The Borderlands of Culture: Américo Paredes and the Transnational Imaginary.* Durham, N.C.: Duke University Press, 2006.

———. "Ideologies of the Self: Chicano Autobiography." *Diacritics: A Review of Contemporary Criticism* 15, no. 3 (1985): 25–34.

San Juan, E., Jr. *From Exile to Diaspora: Versions of the Filipino Experience in the United States.* Boulder, Colo.: Westview Press, 1998.

Sánchez, Rosaura. "Calculated Musings: Richard Rodriguez's Metaphysics of Difference." In *The Ethnic Canon: Histories, Institutions, and Interventions,* edited by David Palumbo-Liu, 153–73. Minneapolis: University of Minnesota Press, 1995.

———. *Chicano Discourse: Socio-Historic Perspectives* Houston, Tex.: Arte Público Press, 1987.

Schaffer, Kay, and Sidonie Smith. "Conjunctions: Life Narratives in the Field of Human Rights." *Biography: An Interdisciplinary Quarterly* 27, no. 1 (2004): 1–24.

Schildkraut, Deborah J. *Press One for English: Language Policy, Public Opinion, and American Identity.* Princeton, N.J.: Princeton University Press, 2005.

Seliger, Mary A. "Colonialism, Contract and Community in Américo Paredes's *George Washington Gómez* and . . . *And the Earth Did Not Devour Him* by Tomás Rivera." *Latino Studies* 7, no. 4 (2009): 435–56.

Sexton, Jared. *Amalgamation Schemes: Antiblackness and the Critique of Multiracialism.* Minneapolis: University of Minnesota Press, 2008.

Shell, Marc. "Language Wars." *CR: The Centennial Review* 1, no. 2 (2001): 1–17.

———. "Babel in America; or, the Politics of Language Diversity in the United States." *Critical Inquiry* 20, no. 1 (1993): 103–27.

Shih, Shu-mei. "Comparative Racialization: An Introduction." *PMLA* 123, no. 5 (2008): 1347–62.

Sollors, Werner, ed. *Multilingual America: Transnationalism, Ethnicity, and the Languages of American Literature.* New York: New York University Press, 1998.

Sommer, Doris. *Bilingual Aesthetics: A New Sentimental Education.* Durham, N.C.: Duke University Press, 2004.

Sommer, Doris, ed. *Bilingual Games: Some Literary Investigations.* New York: Palgrave Macmillan, 2003.

Song, Min Hyoung, *Strange Future: Pessimism and the 1992 Los Angeles Riots*. Durham, N.C.: Duke University Press, 2005.

Sowell, Thomas. *Race and Culture: A World View*. New York: Basic Books, 1994.

Smith, Sidonie. *A Poetics of Women's Autobiography: Marginality and the Fictions of Self-Representation*. Bloomington: Indiana University Press, 1987.

Steinberg, Stephen. *Race Relations: A Critique*. Stanford, Calif.: Stanford University Press, 2007. Kindle Edition.

———. "Human Capital: A Critique." *The Review of Black Political Economy* 14, no. 1 (1985): 67–74.

———. *The Ethnic Myth: Race, Ethnicity, and Class in America*. 1981. Reprint, Boston: Beacon Press, 2001.

Strange, David. "Thomas Wolfe's Korean Connection," *Thomas Wolfe Review* 18, no. 1 (1994): 36–41.

Suárez, Lucía M. "Julia Alvarez and the Anxiety of Latina Representation." *Meridians: Feminism, Race, Transnationalism* 5, no. 1 (2004): 117–45.

Taylor, Charles. "The Politics of Recognition." In *Multiculturalism: Examining the Politics of Recognition*, edited by Amy Gutmann, 25–74. Princeton, N.J.: Princeton University Press, 1994.

Thomas, Megan C. *Orientalists, Propagandists, and Ilustrados: Filipino Scholarship and the End of Spanish Colonialism*. Minneapolis: University of Minnesota Press, 2012.

Tolentino, Cynthia H. *America's Experts: Race and the Fictions of Sociology*. Minneapolis: University of Minnesota Press, 2009.

Tong, Benjamin R. "On the Confusion of Psychopathology with Culture: Iatrogenesis in the Treatment of Chinese Americans." In *The Iatrogenics Handbook: A Critical Look at Research and Practice in the Helping Professions,* edited by Robert F. Morgan, 355–74. Toronto: IPI Publishing Limited, 1983.

———. "The Ghetto of the Mind." *Amerasia* 1, no. 3 (1971): 1–31.

Torres, Hector A. "'I Don't Think I Exist': Interview with Richard Rodriguez." *MELUS* 28, no. 2 (2003): 165–202.

Troutt, David Dante. "Defining Who We Are in Society." *Los Angeles Times,* January 12, 1997.

Tsu, Jing. *Sound and Script in Chinese Diaspora*. Cambridge, Mass.: Harvard University Press, 2010.

Turner, Fred. *The Democratic Surround: Multimedia and American Liberalism from World War II to the Psychedelic Sixties*. Chicago: The University of Chicago Press, 2013.

Umpierre, Luz Maria. "Unscrambling Allende's 'Dos palabras': The Self, the Immigrant/Writer, and Social Justice." *MELUS* 27, no. 4 (2002): 129–36.

United States Equal Employment Opportunity Commission. "Laws Enforced by EEOC." http://www.eeoc.gov/laws/statutes/index.cfm.

United States Congress. Subcommittee on the Constitution of the Committee on the Judiciary *The English Language Amendment*, 2nd Sess., June 12, 1984.

———. Special Subcommittee on Bilingual Education of the Committee on Labor and Public Welfare, *Bilingual Education, Hearings Part I*, 1st Sess., May 18, 19, 26, 29, 31, 1967.

———. Special Subcommittee on Bilingual Education of the Committee on Labor and Public Welfare *Bilingual Education, Hearings Part II*, 1st Sess., June 24 and July 21 1967.

United States Department of Labor. "The Negro Family: The Case for National Action," Office of Policy Planning and Research. Washington, DC, 1965.

Updike, John. "Nan, American Man." *New Yorker,* December 3, 2007.

Urciuoli, Bonnie. "Skills and Selves in the New Workplace." *American Ethnologist* 35, no. 2 (2008): 211–28.

"U.S. English." http://www.us-english.org/.

Venuti, Lawrence. *The Translator's Invisibility: A History of Translation.* London: Routledge, 2004.

Wald, Alan M. *American Night: The Literary Left in the Era of the Cold War.* Chapel Hill: University of North Carolina Press, 2012.

Wallerstein, Immanuel. *World-Systems Analysis: An Introduction.* Durham, N.C.: Duke University Press, 2004.

Wang, L. Ling-chi. "*Lau v. Nichols*: History of a Struggle for Equal and Quality Education." In *The Asian American Educational Experience,* edited by Don Nakanishi and Tina Nishida, 58–94. New York: Routledge, 1995.

Welles, Elizabeth B. "Foreign Language Enrollments in United States Institutions of Higher Education, Fall 2002." *Profession* (2004): 128–53.

Williams, Raymond. *Marxism and Literature.* 1977. Reprint, Oxford: Oxford University Press, 2009.

Wolfe, Thomas, "A Poetic Odyssey of Korea That Was Crushed." *New York Evening Post*, April 4, 1931.

Wollenberg, Charles. *All Deliberate Speed: Segregation and Exclusion in California Schools, 1855–1975.* Berkeley: University of California Press, 1978.

Wong, Sau-ling Cynthia. "Autobiography as Guided Chinatown Tour?

Maxine Hong Kingston's *The Woman Warrior* and the Chinese American Autobiography Controversy." In *Maxine Hong Kingston's "The Woman Warrior": A Casebook,* edited by Sau-ling Cynthia Wong, 29–53. New York: Oxford University Press, 1999.

———. *Reading Asian American Literature: From Necessity to Extravagance.* Princeton, N.J.: Princeton University Press, 1993.

Wu, Ellen D. *The Color of Success: Asian Americans and the Origins of the Model Minority.* Princeton, N.J.: Princeton University Press, 2014.

Yao, Steven G. *Foreign Accents: Chinese American Verse from Exclusion to Postethnicity.* Oxford: Oxford University Press, 2010.

Yildiz, Yasemin. *Beyond the Mother Tongue: The Postmonolingual Condition.* New York: Fordham University Press, 2012.

Yu, Henry. *Thinking Orientals: Migration, Contact, and Exoticism in Modern America.* New York: Oxford University Press, 2001.

Yoshino, Kenji. *Covering: The Hidden Assault on Our Civil Rights.* New York: Random House, 2006.

———. "Covering." *The Yale Law Journal* 111 (2001): 769–939.

Zentella, Ana Celia. "Puerto Ricans in the United States: Confronting the Linguistic Repercussions of Colonialism." In *New Immigrants in the United States,* edited by Sandara Lee McKay and Sau-ling Cynthia Wong, 137–64. Cambridge: Cambridge University Press, 2000.

Kim, Elaine, 33–34, 37, 218n22, 245n9
Kim, Uk-tong, 217n14, 217n19
Kingston, Maxine Hong, 15, 27–31, 93–
    94, 106–21, 194; *China Men*, 27,
    29; *The Woman Warrior: Memoirs
    of a Girlhood among Ghosts*, 15,
    30–31, 93–94, 106–21
Kirn, Walter, 188
Kloss, Heinz, 74–75
Knadler, Stephen, 218n23
Korea, 37, 58, 59, 145
Korean War, 58
Korzybski, Alfred, 222n14
Kuo, Karen, 44
Kymlicka, Will, 114

La Malinche, 139, 237n64
Lambert, Wallace, 224n47
language: as capital, 8–16; as cultural
    right, 130–31. *See also* Asian
    American literature; bilingualism;
    English; Latino literature
language covering, 31, 122–58; in
    Lee's works, 144–58; in post-civil
    rights jurisprudence, 125–32; in
    Rodriguez's works, 132–44
Language Resources Project, 73, 77
Latino literature: bilingual personhood
    in, 61–90; cultural politics of, 1–32;
    dormant bilingualism in, 132–44;
    multiculturalism in, 95–106. *See
    also specific authors and works*
*Lau v. Nichols* (1974), 24, 71, 223n41
Lazzarato, Maurizio, 13, 14, 212n39
League of Latin American Citizens
    (LULAC), 230n53
Lee, Chang-rae, 31, 124, 144–58; "The
    Faintest Echo of Our Language,"
    144–45, 146; *Native Speaker*, 31,
    124, 144–58
Lee, Rachel, 238n93
Lee, Rose Hum, 217n19
Lee, Sunyoung, 217n13
Lee, Yoon Sun, 40, 219n37
Levi-Strauss, Claude, 239n98
liberalism: and bilingual personhood,
    62, 70; and multiculturalism,
    96; and Orientalism, 43–44, 60;
    racial, 30, 65–70, 222n14. *See also*
    neoliberalism
*Liberating Voices* (Jones), 20
life narratives, 178–79
Lincoln, Abraham, 99
Lipsitz, George, 34
Liu, Lydia H., 222n7
Lo, Kwai-Cheung, 172–73, 242n36
Locke, John, 10–11, 64

Lye, Colleen, 233n5

MacCabe, Colin, 159–60
Macpherson, Crawford, 12, 83
Marx, Karl, 11, 15
May, Charles, 187–88
McCallum, Shara, 176
McCracken, Ellen, 170
McGurl, Mark, 38, 191
Melamed, Jodi, 162–63, 166–67, 168
Melville, Herman, 28; "Bartleby, the
    Scrivener: A Story of Wall Street,"
    28
Mexican Americans, 95–106
Mexico, multiculturalism in, 133–34
Miami Spanish, 5
middle class, 87–88, 106, 121
millennial bilingual writers, 32, 162–
    63, 169–70, 185, 195–96. *See also*
    Alvarez, Julia; Ha Jin
Miller, Joshua, 210n10
Milosz, Czeslaw, 185–86, 243n72
minimum sociality, 40
minority elites, 97–98
mistranslation trope, 187, 194
Misty Poets, 190
model minority concept, 81–82
Modern Language Association, 25
Mohr, Nicholasa, 63, 86; "The English
    Lesson," 63
monolingualism: in Alvarez's works,
    169–85; and multiculturalism, 159–
    97; of national literature, 22; and
    translations of works, 169–85
multiculturalism, 91–121; and bilingual
    personhood, 79–86; in *George
    Washington Gómez*, 95–106; and
    monolingualism, 159–97; and
    neoliberalism, 133–34; politics
    of, 30; and translations of works,
    164–69; in *The Woman Warrior*,
    106–21
Myrdal, Gunnar, 81, 85; *An American
    Dilemma*, 81, 85

National Defense Education Act of
    1958, 79, 226n76
nationalism, 41, 42–43, 98–99
national minorities, 114
necessity, 14–15
Negrón-Muntaner, Frances, 5
Nelson, Adam, 72, 227n102
neoconservatism, 80
neoliberalism: and dormant
    bilingualism, 129, 131, 132–57;
    and *homo oeconomicus*, 13–
    14; in Lee's works, 144–58; and